a taste of the unexpected

a taste of the unexpected

Mark Diacono

photography by Mark Diacono

recipe photography by Laura Hynd
recipe development by Debora Robertson

Quadrille
PUBLISHING

Contents

Foreword

I've been fortunate to live a life where I've been able to pursue my passions, to dream of a different life and to try to make it real. One of the most satisfying aspects of this adventure has been sharing that journey with others – in particular discovering that the desire to live a little closer to nature, and to the source of one's food, is gaining momentum across the country. It is latent in all of us perhaps. To see it rekindled and spark into life-changing activity, both in individuals and whole communities, is a pleasure beyond words.

That's why it's so great to meet the people who come down to River Cottage, to learn about beekeeping or butchery or baking. At the end of their time with us, we know that they're taking their new found passion and knowledge back with them to their own corners of the country, to their own kitchens and families, where it will be be generously shared.

I'm lucky, too, to work around people from whom I learn much every day. Mark Diacono is one of them. Without him, I doubt very much that, alongside the apples and asparagus at River Cottage, we'd be growing almonds and Szechuan peppercorns. But to be honest we didn't get off to the most promising start.

A good few years ago now, Mark wrote to me about collaborating on a book. He was working as an environmental consultant and he wanted to write about eating the view, how the countryside we see is a result of how and what we eat. Fascinating stuff, but I was to tied up with other projects to tke him up on his offer. I was intrigued though, and invited him down to Weymouth for a day's fishing.

I would have loved to talk to Mark during this trip, to get to know him better, and hear his ideas. But he was otherwise engaged. He spent the entire trip throwing up over the side of the boat. Save for a few minutes – as he never misses an opportunity to remind me – when he caught a couple of bass, including the biggest of the day.

But we kept in touch and in 2005, I went to visit him at Otter Farm. It was then 17 acres of former county council farmland where, embracing the possibilities that our changing climate offered, Mark had begun to plant apricots, olives and almonds. I was inspired by what I saw, and Mark got more involved in River Cottage courses and events, eventually becoming our Head Gardener.

We're fortunate to have him, not just because of his passion for growing, but because he is also an inspirational teacher.

He makes growing fun, exciting, thrilling even, but at the heart of what he does, there is a serious, life-changing message. In a time of shifting climate patterns, he maps out what's possible if we embrace the inevitability of change.

Mark approaches growing with hard-won practical knowledge but he isn't hide-bound by tradition. He comes to it with a sense of wonder, with a sense of 'What if?' With Mark, it's not about perfection, but about having a go. I can't emphasise enough how important that spirit of 'just doing it' is to the grow your own movement. It chimes with so many people I have met over the years who have done just that. And it recalls the fantastic feelings I got when I first started growing my own food at River Cottage, almost 15 years ago.

But Mark has a strategy as well as unlimited enthusiasm. Whether you have 10 acres or 10 square metres, Mark believes life is too short to grown unremarkable food. He would rather we grow things that thrill us and delight our palates. It might be a particularly delicious variety of tomato, such as sungold, or an 'unbuyable' potato, such as ratte. Or you might want to fill your plot with exotic kai lan, cardoons and Chilean guava. Mark makes growing your own in to a rather swashbuckling and delicious adventure – where you travel the world and taste its finest fruits in your own back garden.

And there's one other thing that I know about Mark. He is a greedy man. This, for our purposes, is a good thing. It means that all of his experiments take place with one goal in mind: good eating. Is this the best peach / mulberry / artichoke / walnut you've every tasted? Is this going to bring you and your family pleasure as you sit round the table together? If so, then plant, tend, harvest and enjoy…

What you have in front of you is, undoubtedly, a beautiful book. And I think it's not too impertinent to suggest that I hope it gets grubby with muddy fingerprints, and smeared and splattered with butter and beetroot. Because I believe that this is a book that will, if you let it, if you really use it, change how and what you grow, what you cook and how you eat, forever and for the better.

Hugh Fearnley-Whittingstall

Introduction

I wish we'd stop growing potatoes, carrots and onions. I'm sure we'd all be happier. It's as if we were brainwashed by the Department of Miserable into dedicating our time, energy and money to growing what is cheaply and widely available and tastes largely the same whether you buy it or grow it. It's worked perfectly.

I grew exactly the same standard varieties in my first year of growing food. I dedicated evenings and weekends to looking after the brown space between the plants – hoeing off the weeds that took advantage of the invitation to grow, and watering to replace the water that evaporated from the bare ground. And my reward? Sackfuls of perfectly ok food. I'd dedicated much of spring and summer to growing the cheapest, plainest food I eat. Never again.

When we moved to Otter Farm, my own smallholding in Devon, someone gave me the antidote: Jane Grigson's *Fruit Book* and *Vegetable Book*. Two months after moving, and with a large mortgage over our heads, I knew what I didn't want to grow, but the list of plants I wanted to grow was short. It read 'Mulberries'. When my wife – not unreasonably – reminded me of my lack of progress I snuck off to the bath to read about the one future harvest I was sure of. I took Jane Grigson's books for company.

I opened *Fruit Book* somewhere in the middle and hit 'Medlars'. It reminded me of an article I had read about them and I added them to the list. The penny dropped. I kept reading and scribbling.

By the time I'd done the same with vegetables, salads, nuts, spices and herbs I had a wet, uninhibited list of everything I like to eat. I did a little research and knocked out everything grown locally as well as the truly tropical. I had my first wishlist and what a menu it was: quince, mulberries, apricots, medlars, peaches, pecans, Szechuan pepper, mizuna, daylilies, kai lan and Chilean guava amongst them.

I wasn't sure if they'd all succeed here in England and there were certainly some that I'd yet to taste but they had one essential in common: I was looking forward to tasting each and every harvest that might come my way. Otter Farm had begun.

Of course, French onion soup can be fabulous and there's nothing wrong with a jacket potato, but unless you're striving for self-sufficiency, why put the effort into growing those staples when you can grow wonderful alternatives such as oca, yacon and Egyptian walking onions for your larder instead?

Life is too short to grow unremarkable food. It's simply not worth the time or effort and – happily – it's no more tricky to grow the utterly delicious than it is the entirely ordinary.

This book is an invitation to grow and to eat a little more adventurously, in order to go about creating your own unique edible garden. Every food here is remarkable in one way or another.

You may choose to discover the subterranean 'potatoes' that taste of pear and the spicy warmth of the Carolina allspice. You may be one of those that helps us remember the 'forgotten' fruit of the mulberry, quince or medlar. Perhaps you'll gamble on the summer ripening the very finest peaches, apricots and wineberries that money can't buy. And along with some incredible underappreciated herbs and vegetables, you'll find a wealth of leaves and flowers for your salad bowl that are so different to those that are widely available.

And of course, I'm not saying don't grow the perfectly familiar. Potatoes, carrots and onions can be entirely delicious – the first new 'Belle de Fontenay' potatoes, the small, early 'Nantes' carrots and Egyptian walking onions are better than any you'll find in the shops – I'm just encouraging you to actively *choose* to grow everything that makes it into your garden, rather than simply automatically including the usual suspects because you feel you should.

In this book I hope to remind you that yield isn't your primary harvest, flavour is.

Growing your own food should be about inviting new flavours into the kitchen, about eating what's in season at its absolutely finest.

Some of the foods in this book may not seem unexpected to you. Whichever food you care to think of is grown by someone somewhere and in some localities where conditions are ideal this can evolve into a local speciality.

This is a food book, it just happens to start its journey in the garden rather than in the kitchen. It follows every food from plot-to-plate so you know how to grow as well as cook each of them.

Growing is a simply beautiful process. Plants create new material with little more than sunlight, water and a few nutrients from the soil. If we gathered the world's great minds and tasked them with imagining a sustainable way of keeping us fed they couldn't hope to rival this perfect chemistry. A plant is the original solar-energy unit.

And yet, sadly, someone, somewhere decided it wasn't happening quite fast enough. Rather than rely on current energy (sunlight) we began to dig up old sunlight energy – stored in the form of fossil fuels – and use it to create nitrogen fertilisers, our own version of one of the nutrients found in the soil. The vast majority of food grown in the developed world is now grown using these man-made fertilisers.

The story is similar for phosphate, a naturally occurring, essential plant nutrient which we mine and import to fertilise the land. In a few short generations our food has become a slave to our oil and phosphate supply. We've taken that simple, beautiful process and twisted it so that what should simply give us energy now accounts for around 30 per cent of our carbon footprint.

With climate change, oil and phosphate resources reaching their peak and increasingly unreliable water availability, the 21st century promises to radically alter the way we grow our food. A low-carbon diet in which our food production is more energy efficient will result, whether we choose it or it chooses us.

I'm optimistic. If we can wipe off 30 per cent from our carbon footprint simply by eating more sustainable food, reducing what we import, cutting down on packaging and tearing ourselves a little further away from the supermarket, then that doesn't sound like too much of a bitter pill to me. And if that comes about in part by growing some of those foods we otherwise import, so much the better. And what a sweetly virtuous circle, that climate change should allow us the possibility of growing many of the foods we currently import and that we can take advantage of that shift to help arrest its progress.

So, while you may grow some of your own fruit, vegetables and other crops because you want to eat wonderful food, you'll be casting your vote for a new way of feeding ourselves and for the future.

You may also find that life, as well as eating, becomes more pleasurable. While it's great to be able to reach for a vacuum pack of sweet chestnuts ocassionally,

I wouldn't want to be without the slow toasting and peeling in front of the fire that comes with eating fresh sweet chestnuts in winter. For me, that is part of what sweet chestnuts are all about.

Strip away the traditions, customs and palaver involved with food and we are left with fuel; nourish them, value the producers and take time to enjoy the entire process that brings each forkful to our mouths and we have pleasure and the most vibrant, egalitarian culture. And it needn't be at others' expense.

Food is at its finest when it slows down a little, when we give it a chance to be enjoyed for the journey as much as the result.

Growing even a little of what you eat helps you do just that. And once you start, you'll very quickly find that food becomes something that you do rather than simply what you eat, and that life becomes quietly, immeasurably, sweeter.

Choosing
what to Grow

Getting started

Choosing what to grow is really about choosing what you want to eat but this isn't as simple as it may seem.

As with many things, growing is full of received wisdoms and accepted 'truths', most of which tend to limit rather than inspire. Ask anyone who grows their own food or is thinking of starting how they go about their planning and almost all will show you a picture of their plot, split into four equal parts, each assigned to 'potatoes', 'peas and beans', 'brassicas' and 'roots and onions'. Salads and any others that don't fit those groups will be squeezed in where space allows, and any fruit will be grown elsewhere. This isn't a random occurrence; it results from most books urging us to think about plants and plant groups too early on, assuming that we want to grow most of what we eat.

Few of us are able to grow all our own food, yet we are quietly compelled to grow those foods that will reward our efforts with the biggest yield. The first year I tried growing some food, like most people, I followed the books and grew the usual suspects. I wouldn't recommend it. If the sun shines when it should and it rains when you're at work, you may well get exactly what you asked for: a perfectly respectable harvest dominated by maincrop potatoes, onions, carrots and cabbages with a few salads round the edge. Success will taste like the dull end of your weekly shop. If that's what you dream about eating in the bath, then happy days; if not, then this is the book for you.

Whatever form your garden takes it should be a place of happy productivity, somewhere you look forward to spending time and where you can anticipate the delicious produce you hope to harvest from it. Getting there is all down to the questions you ask yourself indoors, before the surface of the earth is broken.

'growing is full of received wisdoms and accepted "truths", most of which tend to limit rather than inspire'

Making a wishlist

Start by making a wishlist of everything you'd like to eat. You may choose to grow almost everything from this book and little else – perfect if you want to buy most of the usual suspects and widen your range. You may plump for much of what you can buy in the shops: fine too. Whatever you choose, make sure that every food on your list is something you'll look forward to eating.

The time you spend drawing up your wishlist will define everything that follows. What goes on that paper sets the framework for what success can be, so spend some time getting that list right.

Ignore plant groups for now. Forget about any limitations such as a lack of space or a temperamental climate that your garden may have. Concentrate instead on what it is you want to eat, the flavours you want to bring into your kitchen, and the tastes that'll lift every meal.

There's no blueprint for the perfect edible garden but, by starting with food rather than plants, you'll begin thinking in a way that most people don't. And it will help you make a garden unlike any other.

You'll need to think imaginatively when making your list and you may need to alter it to take into acount the specifics of your location in order to create your own unique edible garden, but think about the food first, and rationalise it later if you need to.

LET FLAVOUR BE YOUR GUIDE

Make a list of all the foods you love, or love the sound of. Get your cookbooks out, look through shopping lists and let your imagination go, forgetting about any limitations your growing space may have. What you're after is a food list, not a plant list. Don't discount anything early on, create a list based on flavour first – you'll be surprised at what you can find a way of growing. For example, apricots can be grown as dwarf varieties in pots, while growing strawberries in hanging baskets can be a good way of making the most of any available vertical space. Nose around on the internet, sign up to a few online forums, talk to fellow gardeners and allotmenters and, of course, look at the foods in this book.

GROW SOME UNEXPECTED FLAVOURS

This book is dedicated to unexpected flavours and, even if you've eaten more adventurously than most, there are always some new tastes to grow for yourself. You may not find many in the shops and some you may not have realised can be grown in your garden, but every one of the foods in this book is at its best when grown for yourself, and every one is worthy of a space on your wishlist and in your own edible garden.

Don't be put off if you haven't eaten, or even heard of, any of these foods, it is an almost perfect law that the lesser known a fruit or vegetable, the finer it is. In nearly all cases a food won't make it to our kitchens because there is a tricky step along the way that impedes the smooth flow from soil to shelf for the shops. Mulberries stain, quinces can take too long to ripen, salsify has tricky side roots — and all are amongst the very finest food you can eat.

MAKE YOUR GARDEN UNBUYABLE

Look as hard as you like but you're unlikely to find blue honeysuckle, Carolina allspice, yacon and many other wonderful foods for sale. Climate, fragility, supermarket sensibilities or lack of awareness can all keep entirely delicious food from our kitchens.

Even some of our traditional favourites are way past their best by the time their journey ends in our homes. Asparagus, sweetcorn, peas, leafy herbs and almost all the softer tree fruit may look ok, they may taste fine, but they have either lost most of their sugars to the rapid conversion to starch that follows picking or (in the case of peaches, apricots etc.) were picked early and firm for easier transportation before the sugars had a chance to develop properly. The same is true when it comes to texture and aroma. What you see in the shops may look like a peach but they are unrecognisable when compared to one picked straight off the tree, when they're at the height of their unbuyable deliciousness.

These foods are the ones I really urge you to prioritise. Eating them feels beautifully luxurious, and this is exactly what we should each be insisting on from our edible garden — the best that food can be.

5 UNBUYABLES
Mulberries *p.37*
Alpine strawberries *p.68*
Autumn olive *p.71*
Fuchsia *p.81*
Daylilies *p.140*

DON'T GROW FOOD THAT'S CHEAP TO BUY

Dedicating your space (as many do) to maincrop foods like carrots, potatoes, cabbages and onions doesn't make sense to me. All of these are readily available and cheap to buy in the shops, involve a reasonable amount of hard work and, for the most part, are largely indistinguishable from what you find on the shelves. Growing these foods is also the most likely way of turning yourself into one of those unfortunates who revel in advising everyone else that growing your own food is a dreadful commitment to hard labour for limited rewards. Unless what you are growing really is your *favourite* food and you can't possibly manage without it, save yourself the trouble and grow something else instead. Something delicious.

DO GROW FOOD THAT'S EXPENSIVE TO BUY

Expensive foods tend to cost more due to them only being available for a short season, or because they involve some difficulty in growing, harvesting or storing. Asparagus, salad leaves, forced rhubarb, globe artichokes and Szechuan pepper all command a high price in the shops, so if you love them why not grow them? As well as the wonderful flavour, you'll be saving yourself plenty of money. And if you haven't tried them before, what's stopping you?

5 TRANSFORMERS
Carolina allspice *p.98*
Lovage *p.104*
Sweet cicely *p.107*
Szechuan pepper *p.110*
Egyptian walking onion *p.158*

DON'T FORGET TO GROW THE TRANSFORMERS

The transformers are those harvests that are long on flavour and usually short on volume. A little of any transformer goes a long way, transforming otherwise plainer ingredients into sensational meals. It also means that even if you've only got room for a small patch, a single plant or a few pots you will have access to a flavoursome larder that will lift meal after meal.

'Asparagus, salad leaves, forced rhubarb, globe artichokes and Szechuan pepper all command a high price in the shops, so if you love them why not grow them?'

THINK SEASONALLY

It can be tempting to concentrate on the height-of-summer loveliness, ignoring the fruit, greens, buried treasure, salads and nuts from almost all other parts of the year. Be inquisitive. Rocket, salsify, mizuna, coriander and rhubarb are just a handful of the fabulous fresh flavours you can be eating through the leaner months.

5 FOR SPRING
Alpine strawberries *p.68*
Blue honeysuckle *p.74*
Rhubarb *p.88*
Asparagus *p.120*
Sorrel *p.153*

5 FOR SUMMER
Apricots *p.30*
Mulberries *p.37*
Peaches *p.40*
Kai lan *p.128*
Daylilies *p.140*

5 FOR AUTUMN
Pecans *p.58*
Autumn olive *p.71*
Szechuan pepper *p.110*
Borlotti beans *p.124*
Cardoons *p.131*

5 FOR WINTER
Medlars *p.34*
Sweet chestnuts *p.54*
Chilean guava *p.78*
Jerusalem artichokes *p.161*
Yacon *p.170*

BALANCE THE RISK

Wherever you live some plants will be racing cert to thrive, others much more of a punt on the conditions. I can tell you that it's hugely enjoyable planting peaches or pecans in hope which borders on expectation and much less so in the sober light of winter when you're wondering how they're doing out there in the big freeze. With adventure comes uncertainty which is all part of the fun, but do spread your bets with a few less risky crops to ensure you get to pull something from as many of the food groups in the book if you can.

QUICK RETURN

Look at your wishlist and make a note by each crop of when you hope to harvest them. Planting a few fruit or nutty futures is absolutely to be encouraged but most of us need a little reward coming back way nearer to when all the effort of planting and sowing is made. Growing is very much about confidence and momentum so make sure success comes early – get yourself a few perfect salads or some intense microleaves within a few weeks or even days of sowing and you'll taste the difference of what you're doing almost immediately.

GO FOR SOME BREADTH

When your top-of-the-head list starts to slow down, think about the food groups in this book and ask yourself whether there are some from each that take your fancy. If you want only fruit, that's fine, but taking a look at each group won't do any harm and may throw up something you hadn't thought of.

Remember, don't think about what you feel you should grow or what you think you can or can't grow. This list should make you hungry. If you fancy eating nectarines you've grown yourself, write them on the list even if you've only got a few square feet of balcony. You may be pleasantly surprised to discover you can buy dwarf varieties which grow and fruit perfectly happily in a pot.

Turning your wishlist into reality

Having drawn up your wishlist with flavour at the front of your mind, it's time to consider how well it works as a whole. The following considerations will help you to transform your wishlist into your perfect edible garden.

THE VALUE OF DIVERSITY

A diverse environment, whether it's a forest, a veg patch or windowsill, is inherently more resilient to pests and diseases or fluctuating resources and changing conditions. Grow an acre of potatoes and when blight comes knocking you've every chance of being cleaned out. But simply growing more than one food limits the damage, raising the likelihood of harvesting at least something. And the more you increase the diversity of what you grow, the more resilient your garden becomes and the more insured against losses you are.

Extending your wishlist beyond a few foods encourages a harvest that gives you little of lots rather than lots of a little and this is one of the secrets to happy growing and eating. It leads to pleasure in the kitchen. If you've grown a dozen foods you'll have more combinations to play with, and in more reasonable quantities, than if you're faced with a bumper haul of one or two crops.

Similarly, unless you've a very good reason to do otherwise, always grow a few varieties of everything you sow or plant. Some will do better than others in your soil and in your climate, and be differently resistant to pests and diseases. You will almost certainly prefer one variety over the others when it comes to the eating too. Ask ten people for their favourite potato and you're unlikely to find any of them agreeing, even over something so commonplace. So cover yourself by growing a few varieties, happy in the knowledge that you're also partially immunising yourself against the worst that diseases and pests can bring.

CHOOSING YOUR VARIETIES

It's worth taking time over the varieties you choose. Some have characteristics that will suit your garden or climate a little better; disease resistance varies and the flavours of each can be markedly different. I've flagged up the varieties I know to be delicious – there are undoubtedly others, and your taste may be for something sweeter, sharper or of a different shape. Take the time to look for local varieties and go for others if you prefer the sound of them, but do be aware of any characteristics, such as late-flowering, that you might want to retain in the variety you choose.

BE INVENTIVE

Don't discount anything from your wishlist too early. There's often a way of bringing that plant into your garden, however small, shaded or otherwise limited you may feel your space is.

Trees are increasingly available on dwarfing rootstocks that keep the overall height to a minimum; you can train your trees to be lost against a wall, which magnifies the heat they'll receive; you can interplant more inventively; or find varieties that suit where others may be less suitable.

There is always someone somewhere out there with the same problem as you have, and things are always changing. Ten years ago, for example, apricots were difficult to grow in Britain, not (for the most part) because of the length or intensity of the summer, but due to the last frosts taking care of the early apricot blossom. Happily apricot varieties are now available that flower a little later, and with climate change nudging the last frosts back into the year, many Britons now have a racing chance of growing their own perfect apricots.

BE REALISTIC ABOUT YOUR TIME

Almost all plants are easy to look after on their own, it's the combinations that can take you over and leave you flummoxed. There's little fun in feeling like it's all hard work – unless you love the hard work of course. In your first year, I advise you to bite off less than you can chew. It's a recipe for success that will keep you hungry for more the year after. If I gave you a tomato plant to look after you'd probably find the time; if I gave you a two acre field you might find other commitments get the better of you. Your happy medium will be somewhere between the two and, believe me, it's better to find where that is by working up from the tomato than it is working back from the field.

DECIDE WHAT YOU'LL DO WITH YOUR HARVEST BEFORE YOU PICK IT

There is a particular weight of guilt that comes with seeing beautiful food go to waste: it undoes much of the pleasure that goes before. You wouldn't be the first person to be caught out wondering what to do with a bumper harvest, however delicious it may be. Every crop in this book includes ideas and recipes to help you make the most of what you've grown, but this is just the starting point from which you can explore further. Many also work equally well with another starring ingredient – the Japanese wineberry trifle is equally fabulous with mulberries, the Chilean guava muffins are deliciously different with blue honeysuckle, for example.

It's also worth becoming acquainted with the craft of preserving. Jams, curds, leathers, cheeses, chutneys are far more than just handy repositories for a glut. Try the recipes here, they'll give you the core skills to take your harvest into the months when they'd have otherwise perished.

GROW IN SUCCESSION

Usually it's better to have your harvest come at you as you like to eat it – a little at a time. Occasionally a glut is unavoidable – a bumper haul of mulberries that is ready now – but with many plants how you get your harvest is largely down to you. By choosing varieties (of apricot, for example) that ripen in succession you'll have a steady unbroken supply for much of the summer rather than one huge harvest.

For annual plants (those sown, grown and eaten within the year) you have even more influence. Rather than sow all your peas and beans, for example, in one day, sow them in smaller batches every fortnight and they'll mature (and go over the top) in sequence, giving you longer, more consistent picking. You can also sow some in a range of conditions. A handful of seeds sown today outside and another started off undercover will grow and become productive at different rates. Both strategies work well in combination too, helping ensure that you get a drip drip drip of peas over a longer period.

PLUMP FOR PERENNIALS

Perennials are plants that live longer than a year. Most, such as trees, have a yearly cycle that includes a dormant period in temperate areas where they may lose their leaves, but every spring they continue growing. Some perennial plants, such as Jerusalem artichokes, grow from any tubers left over from the previous year, forming an essentially self-refilling seed bank.

Although the typical allotment is largely filled with annual plants, there are many advantages to growing perennials. The investment of care and energy through the vulnerable early stage in the plant's life while it establishes gives you repeated harvests over the years rather than the cycle of sowing and harvesting every year. And with a root system already established, the plant isn't taking time and energy to emerge and get growing in the same way as an annual. Gardens based on perennials tend to be more energy efficient and have a much higher output relative to effort in.

CHOOSE THE EASY WINNERS

Don't be seduced too much by plants that need endless attention. It can be perversely rewarding to have nurtured some troublesome tuber to harvest or hot water-bottled a tender citrus tree through the cold months, but there is little point in searching out such opportunities: nature is quite capable of throwing you plenty of diseases and ailments without you choosing a garden of high maintenance princesses just for the fun of it.

By all means be adventurous, take a gamble on a few crops that might not be certainties to produce where you live, but don't let that stop you enjoying all the delicious easy winners that almost grow themselves. There is almost such a thing as a free lunch, should you choose to look for it.

Planning your space

Whether you have a hundred acres or just a few feet, getting your space right needs a little forethought, so take some time to consider how to turn your wishlist into your perfect edible garden. With a little creative thinking and a mind looking to integrate plants together wherever possible, you'll be surprised at what you can do, even if you have the smallest of spaces to call a garden. Not that a larger space is not necessarily 'better' – it just means there's more to plan and potentially more to look after.

SMALL SPACES AND CONTAINER GARDENS
Almost everyone thinks their space is too small but, with a little invention and research, you'll be able to accommodate the vast majority of edibles even if your floor space is limited. Small spaces tend to limit only the size and number of what you grow and only rarely will you be prevented from growing anything completely.

OPT FOR DWARF VARIETIES
Dwarfing rootstocks restrict the vigour of fruit trees, allowing the cultivation of trees in a smaller space than possible, had they been grown on their own roots. These rootstocks are now available for an increasing range of fruit trees, and many can be trained flat against a wall in either an espalier or fan shape – taking up almost no room while still giving you a healthy haul. The dwarf apricots, peaches and nectarines even allow you to grow your own exotic fruit on a metre-tall tree in a good-sized pot.

INTERPLANT FOR GREATER RETURNS
The smaller your space, the greater the need for invention and imagination. Consider plants such as borlottis, grapevines and tall-growing peas that have a small footprint but climb into the air, and look for ways of growing plants together. Interplanting not only utilises the space efficiently, it can form a self-rewarding system as with the classic 'Three Sisters' technique of interplanting sweetcorn, climbing bean and squash. The sweetcorn provides the scaffold for the bean to climb, which in turn takes nitrogen from the air and releases it into the soil, feeding each plant, while the squash keeps all the roots cool, mulches out the weeds and retains water. You can even create your own 'unexpected' Three Sisters using a dwarf apricot as the scaffold, the climbing borlotti beans to provide the nitrogen and nasturtiums to mulch out, cool and retain water at their feet.

MAXIMISE BOTH FLAVOUR AND HARVEST

You'll probably want your plants to work hard for their rent so consider growing a good number of 'transformers' – the plants that give you the most flavour for the least room – especially the herbs and spices that take to container growing so easily. You may also want to squeeze out an ongoing harvest from your plants, so look to the crops you can harvest using a cut-and-come-again/pick-and-come-again approach. Many leafy greens and salads can be cut an inch or two above the ground and will grow back rapidly to give you repeated harvests. This works well with most lettuces, oriental greens, chard, spinach and sorrel. Peas and beans produce more pods the more you pick, while the kales will keep throwing out new leaves if you pinch them off the stem rather than harvesting the whole plant.

LARGER GARDENS

If you extend this delightful principle of interdependence and mutual benefit across a larger space you arrive at a forest garden – a multi-level garden where you might find most (if not all) of the tiers and interrelationships of a young forest.

The tiers climb from the subterranean roots, tubers and fungi, through the ground-cover plants, the taller herb layer, up through the shrubs to the smaller trees and up to the canopy layer, with climbers taking advantage of each. It requires careful design but, once established, gives you a low input, high output edible garden. You don't have to have every layer – you can do without large canopy trees, leave out climbers, or just pick and choose as you like. The secret is in integrating the plants you use to their mutual benefit, even if this is simply a matter of allowing them the space, light and shade each requires.

One of the advantages of a forest garden is that it eases you into the habits that lie behind any good garden: creating a beautiful, diverse environment, naturally rich and balanced in wildlife, where the planting is designed to suit the particularities of each plant so that the whole flourishes.

If you have the space for a forest garden, do seriously consider planting one. You don't need a huge area. Robert Hart, who pioneered forest gardening in Europe, had a garden of roughly 450m^2 – the equivalent of a couple of allotments. The principles work at the field scale or even for a small garden. Plan for the plants at their full size and plant accordingly – there will be space while the garden establishes, but it will soon develop into an integrated whole. If you want to find out more about creating your own forest gardens, The Directory (see pp.174–87) contains additional sources of information.

Growing
& Eating

TREE FRUIT

The first tree I ever planted was a medlar. My wife had given me an old book about forgotten fruit and I liked the sound of the way they tasted and looked. A deep, date-like flavour from a tree that grows without order: I was charmed.

I was anxious planting that tree but it quietly changed my life. Something as simple as digging a hole felt entirely alien: I kept asking myself if I was doing it right. Wider? Deeper? I dug for a while, put the tree in and backfilled a whole lot, then in with the stake, the rabbit guard wound around the base of the trunk, I leant back on the spade. There it was: a tree, only smaller. Bald of leaves, lacking in colour, it was hard to believe this stick would become a tree. And yet, a few months later, the first leaves arrived and, a few months after that, a handful of fruit. I couldn't quite believe it had 'worked'.

For all the pleasure of the yearly runaround in the veg patch, planting a tree says something a little more enduring. It sets a marker down that says 'I live here and I intend to stay'. It also bridges the divide between you and the countryside. Dig a hole for a tree and your garden, allotment or field will have shifted up a scale to where 'landscape' begins – in a few short years you'll be eating the view. Yet, beautiful as they often are, the real attraction of a fruit tree will be the prospect of a properly huge haul. We're not talking about a handful of this or a bucketful of that – get yourself a tree and after a few years of tempting tasters you'll be into kilos of fine fruit.

Whether this is a blessing or a bind depends on how well you prepare yourself beforehand. Working your way through a barrowload of peaches may not sound like a chore but if you want to enjoy them before they go past their best it pays to have a few top recipes to hand, along with a few techniques for storing, preserving and processing. Jams, jellies, fruit cheeses, chutneys and leathers make fine vehicles for driving the flavour into the months ahead. The recipes in this section will get you busy in the kitchen but they are just the starter for you to continue inquisitively.

Whether you choose to go for something as seemingly commonplace as an apple or more unusual like a medlar or a peach, you'll be able to look forward to fruit that is finer than any you can buy. Your food miles will become food yards, so there's no need to pick delicate tree fruit like peaches and apricots before they are absolutely

perfect, nor do you have to rush the medlars from the tree before the first frosts arrive. For once you'll have fruit as it was meant to be.

The taste, texture and ripening time of your fruit can vary considerably depending on variety and some may suit your climate more than others, so whatever your choice of tree take your time over choosing the variety. Think about what you want to taste, what time of year you want to eat it, and look to complement what you already grow and cook.

A few moments considering where you want to plant your tree is also time well spent. The difference between picking delicious fruit from some of your more marginal choices is often down to taking care of the last few details. A little more shelter from spring winds and/or a slightly sunnier spot can be the little extra your tree needs to pay you back handsomely. Imagine too, that you are planting the adult tree. If it says 'grows to 10m' then picture it that size. If it doesn't fit your space, think again. This is the most common mistake people make when planting a tree, so be careful not to join them.

If space is limited, fear not, there are dwarfing varieties of many fruit trees. Many of the more common fruit such as apples and pears have long been available on dwarfing rootstocks (root systems) and can also be trained into cordons (single trunks growing at an angle), espaliers (with horizontal branches trained out either side from a single main trunk), fans (branches radiating out from the centre) or even stepovers (T-shapes, only 30cm or so tall). These are being added to constantly, with apricots, nectarines and peaches now able to be grown as small trees only 1.3m or so tall. Ideal for pots or smaller gardens, they need no pruning, form an umbrella of foliage and give dozens of fruit every summer.

When your trees start producing fruit you'll lay your hands on increasingly hefty harvests for years to come, but after a couple of years of eating from it something else happens: you'll remember that this isn't just a fruit machine, it's a tree. And as the tree grows you get to enjoy the shade, have something to string the hammock from and even enjoy the loveliness of watching the wildlife and your children take advantage of it. It becomes part of the place all year round, where things happen, people laugh and play, and that's as good a reason as I can imagine for planting anything.

APRICOTS

'One thing I should like to do is to eat a ripe apricot straight from the tree' writes Jane Grigson in her wonderful Fruit Book. *Having had the pleasure last summer I can say there are few treats like it.*

Apricots arrive pleasingly early, well ahead of even the first delicious peaches. In his 16th century *Book of Herbes*, William Turner describes apricots as a 'hasty Peche tree… a great whyle rype before the pech tree', but don't think of apricots as inferior peaches, in any way disappointing next to their larger relatives. While they may be less refreshing and clothes-splatteringly juicy than peaches, apricots more than make up for this with their honeyed richness and aromatic depth.

The fact that apricots don't need endless sun to ripen only adds to their enjoyment. Most varieties are ready to eat by mid-summer, well ahead of most other tree fruit. It also leaves plenty of time in a dull summer, or for those who live in a cool area,

for the late season sun to ripen the fruit. And there's nowhere better to enjoy eating them than out in the open. The first twenty or so that my wife and I picked from our initial harvest didn't even make it out of the leaf-fall zone of the small trees. Three days in a row we sat and ate that day's perfectly ripe, fragrant nuggets one at a time with our heads in the shade and our feet in the sun. It was heaven.

However, while the sun may not stand between you and the apricot's fabulous fruit, the frost may. The critical point is early in spring when late frosts can take the vulnerable early blossom by surprise, and with it your chances of fruit. A sheltered spot helps dodge this early season damage – as does a willingness to drape insulating fleece around the plant when late frosts are expected but choosing the later-flowering varieties is crucial, especially if you're growing apricots at the edge of their normal climatic range. With climate change nudging the date of the last frost back earlier in the year, the blossom of these new varieties should arrive late enough to dodge the cold.

An apricot tree is a bundle of contradictions. They love a fair amount of water to grow strongly but the roots hate to be wet; they need a good cold winter followed by a hot summer to ripen the fruit, and after winter they need the frosts to stop promptly (with no late surprises) before their early flowers emerge. It is this combination which makes them famously particular: they can thrive in one area and fail in the next. Their contradictory nature also means one variety may work remarkably better than another in your area – so it pays to ask others growing locally and to speak to knowledgeable local nurseries.

A home-grown apricot tastes so very different to those you may be used to buying. Apricots spoil quickly away from the tree and so are usually picked early for sale, before they are fully ripe. They can never catch up the ripening time that they miss on the tree so, even if you've enjoyed the ones you've bought, you've not yet had them at their extraordinary best.

VARIETIES
If you're thinking of growing apricots as freestanding trees it is almost essential to choose varieties that flower later. Newer varieties such as 'Flavourcot' and 'Tomcot' come into blossom later than most, helping them avoid the last frosts, and are very productive – 'Flavourcot' usually ripening just after 'Tomcot' finishes.

If you live in an area where you don't have to worry about late frosts or if you have a good sunny, sheltered site and/or are training your tree against a wall, then consider 'Moor Park' – an excellent, reliable favourite. 'Goldcot', 'Isabella', 'Bredase' and 'Alfred' are also hard to beat for flavour, though they need a warm, sheltered spot to thrive.

In hotter areas with milder winters it's best to choose a variety with a 'low chilling hours requirement' (i.e. one that doesn't need so much cold during the winter). 'Early Golden' and 'Katy' have succeeded well in California, but your nursery supplier may well stock other varieties.

New dwarf varieties such as 'Champion' grow to only 3m in height and spread, and will be perfectly happy grown in a large pot (80cm in diameter).

GROWING
Success with apricots is largely down to getting the details right. Choosing the right varieties for your location and giving them the conditions they like are crucial – every small benefit you can give them increases your chance of eating their fine fruit.

Apricots like a well-drained soil, a good sunny spot and shelter from harsh winds. There is a school of thinking that apricots should be ideally planted on a north-facing slope as this stops them from coming into blossom too early in spring, yet still gives the fruit plenty of time to ripen through summer. Apricots need a reasonable amount of water, especially while establishing, so be prepared to water them through dry periods.

EATING

Unless you have a real glut of apricots, forget jam- or preserve-making: leave that to the other fruit. The first few dozen apricots are for eating fresh, selfishly, in stolen moments of genuine luxury under the leaves. There is no shortage of fine ways of enjoying the rest that make it to your kitchen and, if the summer proves just too elusive to ripen your apricots fully, you'll find they take very well to cooking – bringing out most of the rich sweetness they

have when perfectly ripe. Use apricots instead of the peaches in the Peach and Frangipane Tart (see p.41), in place of the quince in the Lamb and Quince Tagine (see p.46) or alternatively, try baking them.

It's rather marvellous that something as simple as baked apricots can taste so sophisticated. Beat together about 80g of softened unsalted butter with 3tbsp light muscovado sugar, then beat in an egg yolk, a pinch of salt and

½ tsp Grand Marnier or Cointreau. Finely chop a small handful of almonds or pecans and beat them in too. Cut 10 or so apricots in half, remove the stones, arrange them cut-side up in a buttered baking dish and stuff each of the cavities with a little of the mixture. Sprinkle on some crushed amaretti biscuits and a little more sugar, then trickle about 4t bsp pudding wine into the bottom of the baking dish. Bake at 190°C/Gas 5 until the apricots are

Apricots can be grown either as freestanding trees (as open-centred bushes or pyramids) or fan trained on a south- or south west-facing wall. Although the latter option gives you the smaller potential harvest, your chances of getting it are improved by the additional warmth radiating from the wall. Allow for a 4m spread and 2.5m in height if fan-training your apricot. Apricots are self-fertile, so growing a single tree is fine, but as the blossoms are usually out a little early for the bees it helps to hand-pollinate the blossom using a soft paint brush.

Apricots are available grafted onto a range of rootstocks – St Julien A, Myrobolan, Mont Clare and Torinel are the most common. Consult with your nursery as your choice will depend on soils, location and whether you are training them or not. When late frosts are predicted cover your tree with fleece to protect the blossom, though remember to take it off in the day to allow pollinating insects to reach the blossom.

Apricots are stone fruit, and as such should be pruned when the sap is rising in warm weather in spring and summer. This keeps the risk of disease (especially silver leaf and bacterial canker) to a minimum. Other than removing dead, diseased or crossing branches, you should prune to suit the shape you want (see p.177). Keep an eye out for small branches growing up from the rootstock – these suckers take nutrients and water from the heart of the tree and should be snipped off close to the trunk. Your tree will grow to 3–5m depending on variety and the shape you decide to prune to.

There is some disagreement about whether to thin out apricots as they grow. With many fruit (such as apple and pears) it can be beneficial to control the amount of fruit your plant produces. In a less than ideal summer, the tree may not have the resources to grow all the fruit to ripeness, so some may fail. To combat this, many people prefer to remove some fruit when marble-sized, leaving at least 8cm between each fruit. Others trust the tree to jettison any that it cannot sustain. The choice is yours.

HARVESTING
Harvesting time varies considerably with site and variety, but you can expect most apricots to mature in mid-summer. Apricots can produce a few dozen fruits in the third year, growing in clusters on wood from the previous years' growth.

As with peaches, you'll need to show a little restraint when it comes to picking: leave them until they develop their sweet aroma and part easily from the tree. This is a tricky balance as apricots can go over quickly – the secret to getting them in their perfect prime is to check daily near the time.

---

tender and the tops bubbling, about 25–30 minutes. Serve hot with ice cream or Greek yoghurt and the juices from the bottom of the dish spooned over the top.

However you choose to use your apricots in the kitchen, do so quickly – apricots deteriorate rapidly after a few days

CHOCOLATE SOUFFLÉS WITH APRICOT SAUCE
This recipe makes more apricot sauce than you'll need to serve with the soufflés, but leftovers are delicious with pancakes, ice cream or Greek yoghurt.

SERVES 6

For the apricot sauce:
300g apricots, pitted and cut into chunks
About 3 tbsp vanilla sugar or caster sugar
Juice of 1 small orange
1 tbsp Grand Marnier or other orange-flavoured liqueur (optional)

For the soufflés:
30g unsalted butter, chilled and cut into small pieces, plus 15g, softened, for greasing
40g caster sugar, plus 2 tbsp for coating
100g good quality dark chocolate, broken into pieces
½ tsp vanilla extract
Pinch of salt
3 egg yolks
4 egg whites
¼ tsp cream of tartar

First, make the apricot sauce. Put the apricots in a pan with the sugar, orange juice and 150ml of water and heat over a medium-low heat, stirring, until the sugar has dissolved. Cover and cook for about 5 minutes until the apricots are completely soft. Purée in a food processor or with a stick blender until completely smooth. Pour in the Grand Marnier if using and taste – add more sugar if you think it needs it, stirring until it dissolves into the purée.

Preheat the oven to 190°C/Gas 5. Butter 6 ramekins or small soufflé dishes with the softened butter and sprinkle with the 2 tbsp sugar to coat, tapping out any excess. Refrigerate until needed.

Place a heatproof bowl over a pan of barely simmering water (the base of the

CHOCOLATE SOUFFLES WITH APRICOT SAUCE

bowl should not touch the water) and melt the rest of the butter and the chocolate pieces together. Take off the heat, stir in the vanilla and salt and leave to cool.

In a bowl, whisk together the egg yolks with the rest of the sugar until very light and thick – when you lift up the whisk, a ribbon trail of batter should remain on the surface. Stir into the cooled chocolate mixture until well combined.

In a scrupulously clean bowl or mixer, beat the egg whites until foamy. Add the cream of tartar and continue beating until they form stiff peaks. Take a quarter of the beaten egg whites and stir into the chocolate until it's thoroughly combined. Gently fold in the remaining egg whites until just incorporated. Divide between the chilled dishes, wiping down any spills and running your thumb around the edge of the dishes to help the soufflés rise. Place them on a baking sheet and bake for 7–8 minutes – the middle should still be a bit wobbly.

While the soufflés are cooking, warm the apricot sauce, thinning it slightly with a little hot water if necessary – you want it to be thick but pourable.

Serve the soufflés immediately with a little of the sauce in a jar or jug on the side; as soon as you've broken into a soufflé with your spoon, pour a little of the sauce into the middle and devour.

MEDLARS

Medlars' characteristic open-endedness and brief window of soft perfection before rotting has seen Shakespeare, Chaucer and many others using them as literary metaphors, especially for rapidly fading beauty. But if a person knows anything about medlars it's usually nothing quite so highbrow – it's that they are widely known as 'dog's arse'.

The French make no bones about it, they call them '*cul-de-chien*', and to the Victorian English they were 'open arse' or 'dog's arse'. Look at them end on and it's hard to describe them better in two words or twenty. Medlars are similar to small apples with leathery, russeted skin, except the end not attached to the branch (the calyx) spreads wide open – it's an arse, simple as that.

As Chaucer alluded, medlars are usually eaten in the short period of transition as their flesh starts to soften and turn brown. They look a little bruised at this stage but this is all to the good. This gentle decay is known as bletting (from the French '*blettir*'

– to make soft) and is something the medlar shares with persimmons. Bletting not only softens the texture, it also boosts the sugars and lessens the sharp tannins, resulting in a much richer, winey flavour – think stewed apple crossed with dates – along with a characteristic granular texture. Their individual flavour made medlars popular throughout Europe for centuries, but in England this declined towards the end of the 19th century as exotic fruit arrived from around the globe in increasing volume. As a result culinary attention drifted away from the less sweet fruit, leaving medlars to cling on in pockets here and there, especially in monasteries, royal gardens and estates.

In more recent times, the fact that they are usually eaten in a soft condition that's hard to accurately predict and makes them difficult to transport results in them proving incompatible with the supermarket supply chain. They're hard to describe as appetising in appearance however interesting they may look, and convincing the wider public to eat something they see as half-rotten isn't an easy sell, so you'll rarely find them for sale. Luckily these considerations don't bother the gourmet gardener.

The medlar is a beautiful and charmingly individual tree. It develops the sheltering droop of an informal umbrella, as if it has hit a glass ceiling as it grows. Its branches dog-leg randomly so no two trees look alike. The twisted, elbowed framework reveals itself after the leaves have fallen in late autumn, decorated by the still-clinging fruit.

The leaves and buds are slow to come in spring, protecting them from frost. The leaves are one of the great pleasures of having a medlar tree, emerging large, long and waxy before turning brittle as they colour to stunning reds, oranges and crimsons into autumn. The flowers are reminiscent of lazy dog roses – large, creamy white, turning pale pink as they fade. They are also loved by bees, which flock to their nectar in early summer. The flowers have a delightful habit of appearing throughout the year, often late into autumn, alongside the ripening fruit.

VARIETIES
Wild medlars, which grow scattered throughout Europe, have thorny branches but, happily, named varieties for cultivation are thornless. There are a few very reliable, trusted varieties of medlar – 'Nottingham' and 'Royal' are the most common – with 'Large Russian' bearing unusually large fruits (6cm rather than the usual 3–4cm across), that make for easier processing. Some believe that small-fruiting varieties are better flavoured, but I find them equally good.

GROWING
Medlars tolerate most soils, but try to avoid planting on chalk or sites that become waterlogged. They enjoy full sun, but will live with a little shade.

EATING

While medlars' unique apple-date flavour fills a wonderful gap in the kitchen and lends itself to all manner of delicious preserves, you should first try the fruit straight up.

Bake a few bletted medlars in a moderate oven for 15 minutes and spoon out the soft pulp (leaving the 5 large seeds) and try it with a little honey and cream, or with blue cheese and a glass of port or Tokaji. A wintery fireside treat if ever there was one.

Medlar pulp is ridiculously versatile, especially if its rich datiness is mixed with a little honey. Whether made into a sauce, added to a pie, filling a cake or incorporated into a crumble, you'll find endless uses for it.

Beautiful and jewel-like, medlar jelly is the prince of all jellies – you really have to make it if you lay your hands on any fruit.

MEDLAR JELLY

Try to use a mixture of bletted and unbletted medlars here – the unbletted fruit has a higher pectin content, so a combination ensures your jelly will set more easily.

MAKES ABOUT 4 x 225G JARS
500g unbletted medlars
500g bletted medlars
Juice of ½ lemon
About 500g granulated sugar
1 vanilla pod

Cut the medlars in half, put them in a large pan and pour in just enough water to cover. Add the lemon juice, bring the water to the boil, lower the temperature and simmer gently for an hour. Don't mash the fruit, as this will make your jelly cloudy.

When the fruit is soft, strain overnight through a jelly bag into a bowl. (If you don't have a jelly bag and stand, try the following instead. Turn a chair onto a table so that the seat is flat on the tabletop. Tie knots into each corner of a large square of muslin, so that it hangs from the legs of the upturned chair and place the bowl between the legs. Pour the fruit into the muslin and, as before, leave to strain into the bowl below. Give it a go, you'll see what I mean.)

Next, put a couple of saucers into the freezer. Measure the juice and pour it into a clean pan (using the discarded pulp to make the chutney on the following page). For each 500ml of juice, add 375g of granulated sugar. Add the vanilla pod, split along its length, and warm gently, stirring, until the sugar has dissolved. Turn up the heat and boil, without stirring, for 5 minutes or so. Test the jelly for the setting point by dribbling a little onto a chilled saucer, leaving it for a minute and then pushing it with your finger – if it wrinkles, it's done. Allow another 5 minutes boiling if the setting point hasn't been reached and test again. Repeat if necessary.

Pour while still warm into sterilised jars and seal. The jelly will keep, sealed, in a cool, dark place for 12 months.

As with most fruit trees, the choice of rootstock is as important as the variety itself. It will control both the vigour and the size of your tree, as well as give you options to suit your soil type. Get a medlar on a quince rootstock and it will thrive in a damp site where most other fruit will struggle.

Medlars make an ideal urban tree, they grow to a height of around 5m or so and are self-fertile, so you will only need to plant one.

Pruning is limited to removing dead, diseased or crossing branches. Be careful if you are trimming your tree for shape – the ends of the branches are the main flowering and fruiting zones, so you may have a reduced harvest to follow.

Medlars are rarely troubled by pests or diseases, are hardy to -20°C, and are extremely long lasting. With a little luck you (and your ancestors) may get 300 years of harvesting from one.

HARVESTING

You have a choice when harvesting medlars. Pick them in mid-autumn when they are still hard and allow them to blet indoors or wait a few weeks and let them fall from the tree semi-bletted and gamble on who wins the race – you or the wildlife.

Whichever you prefer do pick on a dry, bright day to keep any moisture on the fruit to a minimum. I tend to pick half of my crop early, just as the leaves are on their way from the tree, and half later, when the last fruit hang on the bare trees like Christmas decorations. The first half I let just part-blet indoors – this may take a fortnight – as this is the perfect state for making jelly. The second softer harvest I use for just about everything else.

There is some disagreement between those who think it's frost that brings on bletting and others who believe it's just the result of a long season – either way, bletting brings out the best in your medlars.

MEDLAR AND APPLE CHUTNEY

Two preserves from one fruit? Yes, if it's a medlar. Use the pulp leftover from making the jelly to make this spicy chutney.

MAKES ABOUT 5 x 225G JARS
12 cloves
4 tbsp mustard seeds
3 tbsp crushed Szechuan peppercorns
   or black peppercorns
1 tbsp cumin seeds
1 tbsp coriander seeds
2 tsp turmeric
3 tsp mild chilli powder
1 tbsp sunflower oil
1 whole bulb of garlic, peeled and grated
5–7cm piece of fresh ginger, peeled
   and grated
Pulp from the Medlar Jelly (see p.35)
500g dark Muscovado sugar
500ml cider vinegar
2 tbsp salt
2kg Bramley apples, peeled, cored
   and chopped

MEDLAR JELLY

Pound the spices in a pestle and mortar until they are broken up, but not so much that you have a fine powder. Warm the oil in a heavy-bottomed saucepan over a medium-low heat and add the spices. Fry until they start to pop and crackle, then add the garlic and ginger and cook gently for a few minutes, stirring as you go.

Add the medlar pulp and stir until well combined with the spices. Next, add the sugar, vinegar and salt, and lastly the apples, incorporating well.

Cook on a low heat, stirring constantly, until the sugar dissolves, then simmer gently for a couple of hours. The mixture will thicken, so stir occasionally and add a little boiling water if it begins to look dry.

Pour your chutney while still warm into sterilised jars and seal. The chutney will keep, sealed, in a cool, dark place for up to 12 months.

MULBERRIES

My very first plant list just had one entry on it, 'mulberries'. At the time I had only had the pleasure of eating mulberries once – but that once was enough to fix my mind.

Staying with friends, I'd been lucky enough to be around when the last of the fruit was being picked from their single old tree. I wasn't that excited at the prospect – like most people, I assumed that if mulberries were that good they'd be more readily available. I couldn't have been more wrong.

With its long, dark, succulent berries, the mulberry has everything you could want from a fruit. The flavour is unlike any other – somewhere between blackcurrant and raspberry with a touch of sherbet thrown in. Although sweet enough to be a favourite with children, there is a faint tartness to most varieties that lends them a more sophisticated roundness. I took my time over every single one of that first small bowlful. Luckily it was a stormy,

unseasonably windy night. With a log fire roaring it was the perfect weather for the mulberry vodka that followed. Made with the previous year's mulberries, it's a deep purple vodka that tastes as good as it looks and making it has since become a feature on my own calendar every summer, much as making sloe gin is later in autumn.

Mulberries are one of the year's seasonal alarm clocks. Late to awake, they come into leaf only once winter is very much behind. The Elizabethan poet Barnaby Googe wrote 'when soever you see the mulberie begin to spring, you may be sure that winter is at an end'. This patience in waking up means that the mulberry flowers always dodge the frosts, ensuring you get reliable fruit as a result. The

tree itself has a magical, slightly weeping, randomness that makes it perfect as a single tree in a garden. What it lacks in showy flowers, it more than makes up for with its large, heart-shaped leaves: one of the last emperors of Constantinople named the south of Greece 'the Morea' in recognition of its shape. Hats off to him.

Once common, the mulberry probably declined in popularity due to both the fact that the fruit stain as well as the length of time it takes some varieties to produce a first harvest – a decade for many. However, so long as you choose the right variety you can get delicious, peerless berries in as little as three years. And they are worth the wait. Although it probably changes as often as my favourite album, if anyone asks me what my favourite fruit is I'll answer instinctively 'mulberry'. If I had room for just one fruit this would be it. There's simply nothing to touch it.

VARIETIES

There are three main mulberry species: black (*Morus nigra*), red (*Morus rubra*) and white (*Morus alba*). Just to keep us on our toes, the fruit isn't necessarily the colour suggested by its species name.

I will try to keep it simple. Red mulberries are native to North America; their fruit can be delicious but trees are less readily available from nurseries. White mulberries are ok, occasionally wonderful, but are often a little one-dimensionally sweet, without any tartness to shine a light across the sugar. Their fruit can be black, white, red or anywhere in between. Black mulberries always have black fruit and include some of the finest varieties. There are crosses between any of the three, many of which are delicious. If you're confused, you're not alone – don't worry about the botany too much, just go for the best varieties, below.

Apart from flavour, your main consideration is the time a variety takes to produce a harvest. 'Illinois Everbearing' is the best of all worlds, giving you large, slender, almost seedless fruit within about 3 years of planting. They're also particularly hardy (easily down to -30°C) and make a fine choice for colder areas.

'Chelsea' and 'Wellington' are also excellent and widely available varieties. 'Carmen' is the finest tasting of the mulberries with white fruit (confusingly, it's a cross between white and red).

EATING

If (and it's a big 'if') you don't eat all the fruit straight from the tree then mulberries will take perfectly to any blackberry, raspberry or strawberry recipe – they are particularly good used in place of the strawberries in my Spectacular Strawberry Scones (see p.69) or as a substitute for wineberries in a trifle (see p.94). Elizabeth David also suggests trying mulberries in a summer pudding, and if they're recommended by her then that's all fine with me.

Generally speaking though, I like to keep mulberries' unique flavour separate from other fruit – ice cream, sorbets and fools are ideal for showing off these delicate berries at their best.

MULBERRY CLAFOUTIS

The secret to a perfect, light clafoutis that's creamy in the middle and crisp on the top is using as little flour as possible, a light touch when whisking the batter and a blisteringly hot oven. This recipe is also excellent with apricots, peaches and nectarines cut into slices, pieces of roasted rhubarb or mignonette strawberries.

SERVES 6

70g plain flour, plus a little
  more for dusting
¼ tsp salt
340ml whole milk
½ tsp vanilla extract
1 tbsp crème de mûre, cassis or
  Chambord (optional)
2 eggs
40g caster sugar

300g mulberries
15g unsalted butter, chilled and cut into
  small pieces, plus a little more for greasing
1 tbsp icing sugar, for dusting

Preheat the oven to 220°C/Gas 7. Butter a gratin or baking dish (about 28cm x 20cm) and dust it lightly with flour.

Sieve the flour and salt into a bowl and whisk in half the milk, the vanilla and liqueur, if using, until you have a smooth batter. Add the eggs one at a time, whisking briefly after each addition. Whisk in the sugar and remaining milk.

Scatter the mulberries into the gratin dish, pour over the batter and dot with butter. Place the dish on a baking tray and bake until puffed up and golden, about 25 minutes. Remove from the oven, leave to cool slightly and dust with icing sugar just before serving.

Check local nurseries for hardy varieties suited to your area – some are more frost tolerant than others – and try to avoid non-named varieties as they can take a dozen years or more to fruit.

GROWING
Mulberries make an excellent slow-growing, medium-sized, deciduous tree for any garden. Their lazy habit and their large eye-catching leaves are a pleasure in themselves and you get the fabulous fruit to go with it.

Mulberries like a sheltered site in full sun with reasonably fertile soil, although they are tolerant of anything other than extremes of drainage. Mulberries are happy espaliered although I've never seen one trained like this, and it seems a shame to control this most appealing of free-growing habits. They're also self-fertile, so planting a single tree will be fine.

Pruning a mulberry is simple – apart from chopping out any dead or diseased wood, prune for shape only. Although mulberries are prone to a little canker and dieback, this is not usually very significant.

Do watch out for slugs and snails – in summer they can decimate trees very quickly, so you'll need to take whichever measures you feel happiest with (see p.176). Unchecked, they'll strip every last sliver of leaf from the tree, checking its growth and potentially killing it. Birds love the mulberry's fruit, but once established they fruit in such profusion that there'll be plenty left for you too.

Plant a mulberry and you may well get a proper return on your investment – black mulberries can live for hundreds of years.

HARVESTING
The price of the mulberry's succulence is fragility. Mulberry fruit is delicate, giving up its juice easily, and so doesn't travel well. You'll need to pick carefully or lay a sheet on the ground and shake the tree to release the fruit. The sheet sidesteps the need for washing the fruit, which causes them to break up. Leave the grass to grow under the tree in the weeks leading up to harvest time – the cushioning under the sheet will help protect the falling fruit.

The fruit of the mulberry tree is usually ready in the second half of summer, although some varieties ripen gradually across the tree over a period of a few weeks, giving you a steady harvest. Don't rely solely on colour to indicate when you should pick your fruit – mulberries can be anywhere from white to lavender through to black depending on variety – go on taste instead. Some ripe fruit fall, but some can cling to the branch even when perfectly ripe, so pick any stubborn ones with care. Mulberry juice stains purple, so wear clothes to suit.

MULBERRY CLAFOUTIS

PEACHES & NECTARINES

If you are after perfection, plant a peach tree. You may prefer other tastes, sharper or sweeter fruit, but nothing touches your own first-of-the-summer, fresh-from-the-tree peach for complete sensory satisfaction.

Unless you've grown your own or had the fortune of being in an Italian peach orchard in the summer, you have yet to enjoy all that a peach has to offer. While plunging into your own aromatic, perfectly ripe peach is raw food heaven, their shop-bought sisters often disappoint. The reason lies with food miles. Most of our peaches and nectarines come from warmer, distant climates and transportation necessitates picking before full ripeness, creating a flavour gap that is never quite bridged. While a picked peach may get softer and juicier from the moment it leaves the tree, it will not get any sweeter – so every extra second it remains attached is a second dedicated to flavour, and to pleasure.

On top of all that sensory pleasure, peaches and nectarines deliver nutritionally too, being a rich source of protein, almost all essential amino acids, vitamins A, C and E and a whole raft of other beneficials. And if you need any further encouragement to grow your own peaches, bear in mind that no food attracts the sprayer's attention more. Their divine succulence isn't lost on insects and, at the commercial scale, a little shared with the wildlife simply isn't tolerated. The peach tops the list of foods most contaminated with pesticides, with nectarines faring little better. This is serious stuff – even washing the fruit doesn't work, as the chemicals soak through the skin.

Like so much of the fruit we think of as Mediterranean, peaches and their smooth-skinned nectarine relatives originate in China, only extending their fruity fingers into Europe a couple of thousand years ago. Every food finds a spiritual home, and with the peach it is Montreuil, a village to the east of Paris which has become synonymous with the very finest peaches. It was here that the French pioneered espalier training (see p.29), claiming it to be the secret to producing the best peaches. The walled gardens of the village, each up to three acres in size and covering a total of 1500 acres at their peak, were once edged with thousands of trained peach and nectarine trees growing fruit for the Paris market. Almost all of these gardens have since been lost, but we're left with one of the most popular methods of fruit training, some of the finest culinary varieties, and an invitation for us to create a new peach culture of our own.

VARIETIES

Peaches and nectarines are essentially identical, save for a single gene that's recessive in nectarines resulting in smooth skin, and dominant in the fuzzy-skinned peach. Both can have white or yellow flesh that either grips the seed (clingstone) or separates easily (freestone), any permutation of which can be delicious. The odds are, though, that you won't have tasted a fresh clingstone peach – most are snapped up by the canning industry which gets them ripe from the orchard and into cans within 24 hours, resulting in a peach that is often higher in nutritional value than supermarket fresh fruit.

Apart from lack of sun, peach leaf curl is likely to be the largest obstacle to you producing your own mouth-watering peaches and nectarines. A fungus carried in Spring rains infects the plant, blistering the leaves, which can stress the tree into losing most of its foliage, flowers and, with them, the potential for fruit, so choose your variety and the site well. Avoid planting in damp areas and, if you can, give it some protection from the rain.

The choice of variety, as with most edibles, is vital: 'Peregrine' is the peach variety to go for if you have a warm and sheltered site, but for anywhere else try the equally delicious 'Rochester' and 'Redwing' that flower a little later, giving the blossom a better chance of dodging the last frosts, which climate change is also moving back earlier in the year. And don't believe the hype about leaf curl-free trees – it's cobblers. I grew the apparently immune peach 'Avalon Pride' and all 40 trees became riddled with peach leaf curl, so by all means look for varieties with some resistance but keep flavour as your priority.

GROWING

As with all fruit trees, ensure the area around the trunk is clear of grass – the trees dislike competition in the early years so the area should be well mulched – and use a tree guard as rabbits love the young bark. If your tree arrives in a pot, plant to the same depth; if bare rooted, ensure you keep the graft well above soil level. If you're planting a number of trees, then give them 6m spacing in all directions. Once established, chives and garlic are reputed to work well as beneficial companions if grown underneath – possibly helping reduce peach leaf curl.

EATING

Just in case you don't eat all your peaches under the tree, there are a thousand wonderful ways to consume any glut. Firstly, my favourite, the bellini. Invented by Giuseppe Cipriani of the legendary Harry's Bar in Venice, Bellinis are traditionally made only with white peaches but taste equally fine when made with any homegrown nectarines or apricots.

Whichever you choose, remove the stones, swizz in a food processor and push the pulp through a fine-meshed sieve. Add a little sugar to any underripe fruit, and refrigerate. Cipriani would have reached for the prosecco, but then he wasn't lucky enough to have Will Davenport's amazing English organic Limney Sparkling wine at his disposal: mix 1 part purée with 3 parts Limney Sparkling and serve. The taste of summers to come.

If you've been away or misjudged and have peaches or nectarines that are slightly past their best, they will freeze and dry well, and if your summer doesn't bring with it the heat to fully ripen the fruit, don't despair either – poached in wine or grilled, they are still wonderful.

And it's not only the fruit that can be added to your newly expanded larder. Peach flowers are delicious sprinkled over salads and make a refreshing tea (simply add some water, a minute after boiling, to a cup containing 3 or 4 flowers).

PEACH AND FRANGIPANE TART

This recipe works beautifully with nectarines, apricots or plums too. If you can, make your own ground almonds by pulsing whole ones until fine in a food processor. It's worth a little extra effort as the flavour and texture will be so much better.

▶

Peaches and nectarines require a well-drained soil that never becomes waterlogged. The old adage of not planting a £20 tree in a 20p hole holds true: excavate a 1m² hole to a spade's depth greater than the depth of the roots. The important thing is to keep the bottom and sides of the hole forked up and loose – you don't want to create a 'bucket' underground that will hold water and drown the roots. I always stake trees low, driving a 1m stake 60cm underground, and tying the tree near to the top of the 40cm above ground. This anchors the roots yet allows the upper tree to sway with the wind and develop its own strength.

Every advantage you can give your peach or nectarine bumps up your chances of a better harvest. Avoiding frost pockets and exposure to cold easterly winds is vital to allow the flowers a chance to develop. Both peaches and nectarines take to various methods of training (see p.29), and fan training against a sunny wall provides shelter and radiated warmth from the bricks.

Fan training is also the perfect way to accomodate a peach or nectarine tree if you're short of space. Buy a two-year-old fan which has been started off for you, it'll come with instructions for further training. You can go even smaller and choose one of the new dwarf varieties – the peach 'Bonanza' and the nectarine 'Nectarella' are fabulous. These varieties grow happily in large pots to perhaps 1.5m in height and spread, need no pruning and throw out endless succulent fruit.

Peaches and nectarines need to be watered steadily through fruiting – though be careful not to overwater – using a comfrey tea (see p.183) once a fortnight.

Prune peaches and nectarines in late spring, following the guide on page 177.

HARVESTING
Depending on location, variety and aspect, the fruit will be ready for picking in late summer. The period of fruiting is typically around a month, so depending on the number of trees planted, pick every few days using a twisting motion. Treat the fruit like a meringue – don't squeeze it, prod it or knock it. Wait for the smell. Wait some more. Wait for a warm orange glow to take to the skin, and only then should you very carefully cup it in your palm and try a quarter turn. If it doesn't part company with your tree, be happy: the longer it stays on the branch the sweeter it will become. Ripe, your peaches or nectarines will keep in the fridge for up to a week, but for full succulence, allow them to reach room temperature again before eating.

◀
SERVES 6–8
For the pastry:
150g plain flour, plus a little more
   for dusting
50g icing sugar
½ tsp salt
Finely grated zest of ½ small lemon
90g unsalted butter, chilled and cut into
   small pieces, plus a little more for greasing
2 egg yolks (reserve 1 egg white and beat
   with a tablespoon of water to glaze the
   bottom of the tart)
1–2 tbsp iced water

For the frangipane:
120g unsalted butter, softened
120g caster sugar or vanilla sugar
1 egg
1 egg yolk
120g ground almonds

40g plain flour
4–5 ripe peaches, each halved, pitted and
   cut into 6–8 slices

For the glaze:
4 tbsp peach or apricot jam
Juice of ½ lemon

To make the pastry, put the flour, sugar, salt and zest in a food processor and pulse to blend. Add the butter and pulse until the mixture resembles coarse breadcrumbs. Tip in the yolks and pulse a few times until they're well incorporated. Put the mixture in a bowl and, cutting into the mixture with a knife, add just enough water to bring it together into a dough.
   Turn out onto a lightly floured surface and bring the pastry together into a flattened disc. Wrap in cling film and

refrigerate for an hour.
   Butter a 22cm loose-bottomed flan tin and dust with flour, tapping out any excess. On a lightly floured surface or between two sheets of baking parchment, roll out the dough into a circle. Line the flan tin with the pastry, pressing it gently into the sides, leaving any excess to hang over. Place it on a baking sheet and chill for 30 minutes.
   Preheat the oven to 190°C/Gas 5.
   Prick the tart shell all over with a fork, then line with baking parchment or foil and fill with ceramic baking beans, dried pulses or uncooked rice. Bake for 18 minutes; remove the foil or baking parchment and baking beans and brush the base with the egg wash. Return to the oven until the base is cooked and golden, about 8 minutes. Remove from the oven, leave to cool, then

NECTARINE SALSA

trim off any excess pastry with a small, sharp knife. Reduce the oven temperature to 180°C/Gas 4.

Next, make the frangipane. In a mixer, beat together the butter and sugar until light and fluffy. Add the eggs and beat until just combined. Stir in the ground almonds and flour until smooth. Spoon the filling into the cooled tart shell and smooth with a spatula. Arrange the peach slices on top of the frangipane, placing them close together. Bake until the frangipane is puffed up and golden, 25–30 minutes. Remove from the oven and leave to cool.

Make the glaze by warming the jam and lemon juice in a saucepan and then straining through a fine sieve. Brush the glaze generously over the fruit.

Serve cold.

NECTARINE SALSA

This zingy salsa is wonderful with meaty barbecued fish, chicken or lamb. Leave the tomato out if you like, and play with your seasonings until you have exactly the combination you like. A little more mint? More coriander? Less chilli? Spring onions instead of red ones? It's entirely up to you.

SERVES 4–6 AS AN ACCOMPANIMENT
2 nectarines, pitted and cut into
   5mm dice
1 ripe tomato, deseeded and cut into
   5mm dice
½ small red onion, finely diced
Juice of 1 lime
1 small serrano or jalapeño chilli, halved,
   deseeded, membrane removed
   and finely diced

Small bunch of coriander, tough stalks
   removed and roughly chopped
3–4 sprigs of mint, stalks removed
   and chopped
½ tsp caster sugar
Salt and freshly ground black pepper

In a medium-sized bowl, mix together all of the ingredients and season with a good pinch of salt and a few grinds of pepper. Leave for 10 minutes for the flavours to mingle, but serve fairly promptly after that so each ingredient still shines through.

QUINCES

If you think you may have found 'the one' or perhaps would like to bewitch a hesitant someone a little more deeply with your charms, give them a quince tree. Quinces have long been symbols of marriage, fertility and enduring love itself, from the 'apple' in the Garden of Eden to the golden 'apples' of Greek mythology, famously given to Aphrodite, the goddess of love. While peaches are about hot summer and instant pleasure, quinces are a longer, deeper, less transitory satisfaction. The pleasure isn't all at once, it's played out over the year.

Quinces flower safely into spring every year, letting out their gentle daffodil perfume when the frosts are well past. This is no rushing, passing pleasure: the blossom needs a still day and a still person for its scent to be enjoyed. The upright barbershop-striped flowers are as lovely as you'll find on a fruit tree. They open into cupped dog roses, releasing the gentle scent of undiluted spring. Sit beneath the branches on a breezeless day and you'll wonder how you missed it rushing past.

The fruit follow quickly but can seem a little discouraging – they sit there, mostly unchanging for a few summer months until autumn approaches, when they push on quickly to plumpness. If you live somewhere with sufficient heat, the fruit may ripen late on the tree. If not you will, like me, have a little longer to hold on for your pleasure. And yet picking them plump but unripe opens the door to another delight – that of having them in the house. Over the coming days your quinces will ripen gently from green to yellow, filling the room with their sweet, spicy perfume. Store them in a frequently opened drawer, where they will release their perfume gradually as they ripen. If they were inedible, I'd grow them for this alone.

Quince was the third 'forgotten fruit' to make it on to my original wishlist. It is at the opposite end of the spectrum to most of what we look for in fruit – while its plump pear shape is entirely seducing, few people enjoy them raw. Get a quince into the kitchen though and it undergoes one of the great culinary transformations. The hard, astringent fruit, cooked slowly (whole, halved or in slices) with a little sugar and butter, becomes pink, fragrant and sweet; just a slice of which will liven up even the dullest apple pie.

The quince takes its latin name (*Cydonia*) from Cydon in Crete, from where it was once imported to Ancient Greece and into so much of their mythology. The fruit vary in size from small pears to something much, much larger: Jane Grigson saw the largest quinces she'd ever seen in the local market in Cydon, where she was reminded of the marble breasts of Michelangelo's sleeping *Night*. The largest I've seen were at the somewhat less exotic location of the RHS Harvest Show in central London. I was reminded of plump baseballs rather than breasts of marble, which perhaps says more about me than the quinces.

Native to Asia, grown around the Mediterranean for thousands for years and even naturalised here and there, we have royalty to thank for bringing them to England. King Edward I planted the country's first four quinces in the grounds of the Tower of London in the 13th century. They quickly became perfectly common for all but the last hundred or so years, since when our affection for apples and pears and the increasingly widespread availability of sweeter, softer fruits has led to a decline.

Although the trees are widely available from nurseries, you'll rarely find quince fruits for sale. As such they make perfect candidates for growing yourself.

EATING

As botanist John Parkinson wrote 500 years ago, 'there is no fruit growing in this land that is of so many excellent uses as this'. Equally at home in savoury or sweet dishes, gently poached or cooked long for preserves, you'll not be short of ideas for quinces.

Quince flesh turns a beautiful, deep rose pink (which I am reliably informed by those better educated than I, is most accurately described as 'carnelian') when cooked which, in combination with their high pectin content, makes them ideal for jams, jellies and firmer-set preserves including the classic membrillu (cotignac in France)

Whatever you're using them for, once cut or peeled, rub them with lemon juice or pop them into acidulated water to prevent them browning quickly.

If you're new to quinces go for a simple recipe to start – baked quinces. Peel, quarter and core 4 quinces, dropping each one into a bowl of water in which you've squeezed a lemon to prevent them from turning brown. Put 750ml of water into a pan with 200g golden caster sugar. Stir over a low heat until the sugar has dissolved, then add 3 cloves, 1 stick of cinnamon, a strip of orange zest, a split vanilla pod and a cardamom pod, crushed slightly. Simmer for 5 minutes, then whisk in 3 tbsp honey. Place the quinces into an ovenproof dish in a single layer, pour in the syrup and its aromatics and cover tightly with aluminium foil. Bake at 150°C/Gas 2 for 2 hours; remove the foil, turn the quinces, return to the oven and bake for a further hour, or until the fruit are very tender.

Serve with yoghurt for breakfast or with ice cream as a quick pud, or try using the baked quinces in cake or tart recipes as a substitute for other fruit.

VARIETIES

There are numerous varieties of quince (*Cydonia oblonga*) widely available. 'Meeches Prolific' and 'Vranja' are early-ripening heavy croppers, with large fruit of fabulous flavour. They also produce early in life and cross-pollinate each other, giving a bigger crop. There are also few newer varieties available, such as 'Lezcovacz' and 'Krymsk', which are supposed to ripen fully on the tree even in cooler areas such as England in good years.

GROWING

Quince trees are lazy looking, self-fertile, deciduous trees, ideal for the garden. They tend to grow slowly, to around 5m or so tall and a little narrower (those with smaller spaces should consider opting for a

Quince C rootstock which gives a tree with a smaller, 4m spread) and can be grown either with a single trunk or as multi-stemmed bushes. Their branches twist as they grow, forming a loose, almost shaggy mop of long, oval, glossy leaves that are particularly beautiful as they yellow into autumn. Look closer, or better still sit beneath the branches, and you'll notice the leaves are lightly downy underneath, reminiscent of the pale fuzz on the ripening fruit.

Quinces will grow in all but alkaline soils, although a deep, fertile loam is ideal. Their roots are happy with moisture (but not waterlogging), which makes them perfect for sites where other fruit may do less well.

Quinces have lower chilling requirement than apples so often thrive in sunny regions, but they are hardy to around -20°C. Give them a sunny spot and a little shelter and you will tip the balance your way if you live in a cooler climate.

Pruning a quince is simply a matter of cutting out dead or diseased wood, and any crossing stems that are rubbing. Quinces' natural, happy irregularity means they don't take easily to being trained.

Quince leaf blight can be a nuisance – it speckles the leaves and fruit with dark brown dots. Usually damage will be cosmetic only, but bad infections

---

Quinces are also delicious pickled. Pour 800ml cider vinegar into a non-reactive pan and stir in 400g golden caster sugar, 6 black peppercorns, 3 whole cloves, 2 star anise, a thumb-sized piece of ginger, peeled and finely sliced, and a bay leaf. Bring to a simmer, stirring to dissolve the sugar, then add 3 peeled, cored quinces cut into 8 pieces lengthways. Cook for 15 minutes or until the quince are tender, then strain, reserving the pickling liquid. Spoon the quinces while still warm into sterilised jars, pour over the strained liquid and seal.

Pickled quinces will keep for up to a month and make a wonderful accompaniment to sliced ham, cheese or charcuterie.

LAMB AND QUINCE TAGINE

You can certainly use mutton in this tagine if you prefer – it will have a stronger, slightly gamier flavour. Either way, the quince adds a pleasing, melting sweetness to the dish. Moroccans don't brown the meat before adding it to the dish, so this makes for a quick (prep) slow (cook) dish. If quinces are out of season, add some prunes instead to give it that essential dash of sweetness.

SERVES 4

4 lamb or mutton shanks, or 1.2kg boned lamb or mutton shoulder, cut into 3cm cubes
2 medium onions, halved and finely sliced
20g fresh ginger, peeled and finely grated
1½ tbsp tomato purée
2 tbsp fruity extra-virgin olive oil
4 garlic cloves, peeled and finely sliced
1 cinnamon stick
2½ tsp ground cumin
1½ tsp paprika

1 tsp ground coriander
½ tsp freshly ground black pepper
¼ tsp ground cardamom, or 2 cardamom pods, lightly crushed
12 threads of saffron
1 tsp salt
6 tbsp clear honey
Juice of 1 lemon
2 quinces
15g fresh coriander, tough stalks removed and roughly chopped
To serve: Rice or couscous

Put the lamb or mutton into a large pot with the onion and just enough water to cover. Bring to a simmer and skim off any scum that rises to the top. Add the ginger, tomato purée, olive oil, garlic, cinnamon, cumin, paprika, ground coriander, pepper, cardamom, saffron and salt. Give everything a good stir, bring to a very gentle simmer and cook, partially covered, for about 2 ½ hours, or until the meat is very tender.

require you to rake up fallen leaves, destroy any affected fruit and, if your sensibilities allow, consider using a spray of Bordeaux mixture (a fungicide comprised of copper sulphate and hydrated lime) as the leaves emerge.

Quince can also suffer from brown rot – a fungal infection that results in soft brown areas developing on the skins of the fruit and the flesh deteriorating. This is best dealt with by removing any affected fruit and incinerating them immediately to prevent any further infection.

A monthly spray or feed around the roots of your quince tree with comfrey tea (see p.183) from the start of flowering to harvest will give it a welcome nutrient fix throughout the fruiting season.

HARVESTING

Quince fruit swell disconcertingly late in summer, so don't worry if they seem small in mid-summer. The fruits ripen from green to yellow as autumn arrives. Leave them on the tree as long as possible to encourage a fine flavour, but make sure to pick them before the frosts arrive. They should come away with a soft twist – whatever you do don't pull them. If they seem reluctant to give, cut the fruit (including a little stem) from the tree using secateurs. Handle the fruit with care – even rock hard they bruise easily.

Indoors your quinces will ripen over the coming days and weeks, releasing their spectacular smell as they do. They will store for 2–3 months in a cool, dry place, but do keep them separate from other foods as they may take on the quinces' perfume.

While the meat is cooking, bring a pan filled with 700ml water to the boil and stir in 4 tbsp honey and the lemon juice. Peel and quarter the quinces and drop them into the boiling water as you go. Reduce to a bare simmer, cover and poach for 30 minutes, until the quinces are tender. Drain, cool slightly, and core the quince before halving each quarter vertically.

Stir the remaining honey into the tagine and simmer, uncovered, for 10 minutes until you have a rich sauce. Taste, adjust seasoning if necessary, then stir in the quince pieces and half the fresh coriander.

Serve with rice or couscous, with the remaining coriander scattered over the top.

LAMB AND QUINCE TAGINE

NUTS

All of us eat vegetables, most of us eat fruit, yet only some of us eat nuts. Even fewer of us grow them. Perhaps it's our desire for sugar: if we are going to plant a tree let it be fruity; if we are going to have a raw snack let it be sugary sweet. We even ignore the wealth of wild nut harvests, leaving the hazels, chestnuts and the rest to the squirrels and other wildlife that are more than happy to get fat without the competition.

At Christmas, at least in Britain, we relent and let the nuts into our homes — bowls of walnuts, the odd toasted chestnut, perhaps a scattering of Brazil nuts here and there. It's a pity our enjoyment is mostly festive. Almost without exception nuts are hugely nutritious, entirely delicious and sit happily between savoury and sweet. All you have to do is nudge them one way or the other in the kitchen.

Granted, getting to the tasty bit usually comes with a touch of palaver that borders on ceremony. Nuts are proper slow food and are all the more rewarding for it. What lovelier wintery pastime can you have than roasting a few chestnuts over the embers? If you have yet to enjoy this seasonal pleasure, don't be put off by the minor messabout involved — it is precisely this sort of gentle, unhurried task that ensures food remains something we do rather than simply what we eat.

Fruit tempt us with their sugar (and we're all too happy to be seduced), but without a similar sweet covering nuts have a harder time in attracting us. There are no great shows of colour nor clouds of fragrance to draw you in, no green-to-red transformation to tell you when to get picking. Nuts call for a sharper eye. Some come with a fleshy, often leathery casing that tends to stay green until splitting to release the seed. Others lose their leaves when the nuts are perfect or rely on the taste test. One thing's for sure, if you see the wildlife helping themselves, it's time you did too.

Nut trees tend to like the warmth and typically grow larger than most fruit trees, which can put them beyond some gardens. There are smaller varieties of some nuts available but if you have room for one or two larger trees in your garden why not make them deliciously productive nut trees? You'll get less trouble for your harvest than with fruit as nuts are less attractive to most animals, and pruning is minimal — usually just a case of establishing the shape and removing dead and diseased wood.

If space, climate or inclination prevents you from growing your own then I hope that, if nothing else, the following pages raise your interest in eating more nuts. Even if you can't grow them, you can always find better sources of them. A little asking around locally, for example, should find you a supplier of those otherwise unbuyable treats, the green walnuts and green almonds. I hope you'll be tempted to nose around for local wild sweet chestnuts or perhaps try to persuade someone with a larger garden or field to invest a little in the future by planting a pecan or two.

If you are going to plant a nut tree there are a few very simple ways of increasing your chances of success. A sunny site is nearly always best and every extra degree of shelter from harsh winds and late spring frosts you can provide will be repaid at harvest time. Nuts like a deep, well drained soil — many throw a long tap root into the ground — so don't be tempted to plant them in a shallow soil. They'll probably live, they may even flower and produce a few nuts, but they won't thrive.

Spend some time considering the tree itself. Many varieties aren't self-fertile so you may need to plant two or more varieties. Flowering should at least partially coincide for cross-pollination to occur — I've recommended some good varieties in the following pages, but it's also worth speaking to your local nurseries for other good, compatible varieties for your location.

You'll also have a choice to make about whether to buy grafted trees or grow seedlings. Grafted trees have a rootstock joined to the main trunk of the nut variety you want to grow — they tend to grow faster, more reliably and produce more quickly than nut trees grown from seed. Because the main part of the above-ground tree comes directly from a parent tree, you can be certain it will be of that variety; seedlings, growing from seeds that are a result of pollen from two parents, can be fabulous, disappointing or anywhere in between, but you won't know until they produce nuts many years into the future. Unless money is a real issue and time isn't, there's no choice — go for grafted trees. They may cost more to buy but you'll get a livelier tree, you'll know the variety you bought will be the variety you taste, and you'll have nuts perhaps a decade before you might with seedlings. You'll also make the extra money you spent back in one harvest.

ALMONDS

This morning I made a happy deal with a bee-keeping neighbour. He's moving a couple of his hives here in early spring when the almonds should be in blossom and in return I'll give him a leg of pork in the autumn from one of the pigs grazing near the orchard. For me, these few weeks when the flowers emerge are critical. Depending on the weather there may be few bees around and so these new arrivals can make all the difference in improving the pollination rates and ensuring a bumper harvest.

It feels like a good piece of old-fashioned barter but without thinking I've replicated, on a very different scale, something happening a few thousand miles away in the USA, where almonds are the country's largest horticultural export.

California produces three quarters of the world's almonds and, as on my small farm, most trees flower early, at a time when there are precious few wild pollinators around. The entire harvest rests on the simple act of bees taking pollen from the blossom of one tree and dropping it in the blossom of another. The bee is everything.

Millions of hives containing billions of bees arrive in the state in February to take part in what is the largest managed migration on the planet. This solves the pollination problem in the short term but such mass movements leave the door open to a more rapid spread of new diseases amongst the bees. In recent decades bee populations have declined rapidly due to a whole range of diseases, most recently Colony Collapse Disorder, with half of the USA population of bees is thought to have been lost since 1980.

This scale of growing is a long way from when the Franciscan monks first brought almonds to California in their ones and twos a few centuries ago and has led to an almost complete reversal of the grower–bee relationship. Where small scale almond farmers used to supplement their income by keeping a few bees that took advantage of the blossom to make honey, now they rely on importing bees for their main harvest.

Almonds are native to the east of the Mediterranean, where they make for something of a wild lottery. There are two types of almond tree, one producing sweet almonds (their blossom is usually white), the other bitter (usually with pink flowers). The nuts can therefore be deliciously sweet or unpleasantly bitter depending on the species and any natural crossing that may have occurred between the two. The sweetest almonds have long been selected for domestication, with the best finding new homes along the Mediterranean shores of northern Africa and southern Europe, and in recent decades in other parts of the world as new almond varieties and rising temperatures increase the chances of commercial success.

The Romans and Ancient Greeks believed that bitter almonds prevented you from getting drunk, although this may just have been achieved by preventing you from being alive. Bitter almond varieties (*Prunus*

amara) owe their harsh flavour to hydrogen cyanide which is poisonous, so if you're trying the nuts from an uncertain variety it would be wise to go for an exploratory nibble at first. Bitter almonds are grown commercially in some areas but the harvest goes predominantly towards making oil for the cosmetics and medical industries.

VARIETIES

'Mandaline' and 'Ferragnes' are two of the newer almond varieties that tend to flower a little later than many, giving the flowers a better chance of beating the last frosts in cooler areas. They also have compatible flowering periods and so make for an excellent combination when grown together.

Almonds have recently been hybridised with peaches to produce deep-rooting, early-producing varieties such as 'Ingrid' and 'Robijn'. Their nuts taste like 'regular' almonds and their blossom is a little more hardy – ideal for trying in cooler areas such as England, where the frosts may linger later.

'Marcona' is a Spanish variety and well worth searching for if you live in a warm climate. Sweeter and with a more delicate texture than many varieties,

EATING

Like most nuts, almonds are excellent raw, however, a little toasting suits them very well and draws out their natural sweetness. Almonds are equally happy in savoury dishes as sweet, and just about every culture has added its stamp to the almond recipe book – marzipan, tagines, amaretti, frangipani, all manner of cakes, romesco sauce, pasanda curries and a simple, salty tapas are just some of the many ways in which they can be used.

As with chestnuts, almonds make an excellent carbohydrate-free, gluten-free flour which is perfect for diabetics as well as coeliacs and other wheat allergy sufferers. This flour is also a key ingredient in many of my favourite cakes (chocolate and orange, and carrot and almond in particular) giving them both a fudgy texture and a gentle almond fragrance.

Almonds also make a wonderful, allergy-friendly alternative to peanut butter that's delicious spread on toast or with crisp slices of apple as a healthy breakfast or snack. Make your own by toasting a couple of handfuls of almonds on a tray in a 180°C/Gas 4 oven for 5 minutes, then blitz the still-warm nuts in a food processor until creamy. Scrape the sides down with a spatula one or twice, continue to blitz and keep the faith – it will soon transform itself into a creamy butter.

Almond butter is delicious eaten as it is, but try adding a sprinkling of sea salt and a tablespoon of clear honey at the end to make it into an especially flavoursome treat.

The Egyptian spice mixture dukkah is a wonderful dip to enjoy with drinks before dinner – take a piece of bread, dunk it into olive oil before dipping

it into the dukkah. You can also mix your dukkah with some grated lemon zest and finely chopped mint, basil or parsley leaves and sprinkle it over fish before roasting.

To make your own dukkah batch, warm 4 tbsp coriander seeds and 2 tsp cumin seeds in a dry frying pan over a medium heat until they just begin to release their fragrance. Tip them into a mortar and return the pan to the heat. Add 5 tbsp sesame seeds and warm until toasted before adding to the coriander and cumin. Next, warm a handful of blanched almonds or hazelnuts and stir in the pan until golden and toasted. Pour these into the mortar too and, with the pestle, pound with 1 tsp flaky sea salt, a few grinds of black pepper and a good pinch of chilli flakes until you have a coarse, well combined mixture.

'Marcona' makes for a smaller tree than most and is therefore perfect for those with a smaller space. So, too is 'All In One' – a self-fertile dwarf variety which grows to around 3m.

GROWING

While almonds may survive drought and tolerate poor soils, these are not the perfect conditions for them to thrive. If you grow an almond in a well drained yet moisture-retentive soil, of reasonably neutral pH, you'll end up eating many more nuts. A sunny spot is vital for good fruiting. Almonds are fairly cold hardy, down to around -15°C.

Even a summer in a relatively cool climate such as England is usually plenty long enough to ripen the nuts, but often the damage is done months earlier. Almonds have a fairly low chilling hours requirement (the cumulative time spent below a critical temperature in winter), and so tend to come into flower early, often before the risk of late frosts has past, leaving the flowers vulnerable. Susceptibility to late frosts is the main limitation to getting an almond harvest in cooler areas, so choice of site and variety is crucial.

Early-flowering plants like almonds can also find themselves blossoming in a period where there is a shortage of pollinating insects. Combat this by using a soft paintbrush to transfer pollen between flowers. Alternatively you could try, like me, to persuade a bee-keeping neighbour to transfer their hive to your growing space, or look into keeping your own bees to boost your chances of a good crop. Spacing varies with variety, rootstock and your soil type, so speak to your supplier, but allowing 6m or so between trees is a reasonable guide.

Leaf curl can be a problem. Some varieties (including the peach hybrids) are more resistant to this leaf-blistering disease than others. Any protection that you can give your tree from spring rains (which encourage the disease) will be a big help. Growing your tree in a large pot and keeping it indoors until late spring is an excellent way of enuring you minimise the risk of the disease. Slugs and snails love the leaves on young almond trees, so do protect against them (see p.176) in the early years.

Almonds are self-fertile so growing a single tree is fine, although if you grow two or more varieties you're

CHICKEN MOLE

This is loosely inspired by the sexy mole in Laura Esquivel's book Like Water for Chocolate. *While mole is traditionally made with turkey I think it's just as good using chicken instead.*

SERVES 6
2cm cinnamon stick
¼ tsp whole cloves
¼ tsp fennel seeds
10 threads of saffron
2 dried chilli peppers (ancho, chipotle, chilhuacle negro or a combination if you can)
70g sesame seeds
4 tbsp groundnut oil
85g whole almonds
70g good-quality dark chocolate, coarsely chopped
600ml chicken stock
1.5kg chicken pieces, on the bone
Salt and freshly ground black pepper
1 medium onion, halved and finely sliced
5 garlic cloves, finely sliced
To serve: Rice

Preheat the oven to 180°C/Gas 4.

In a dry frying pan over a medium-low heat, dry fry the cinnamon, cloves, fennel, saffron and chillies for a couple of minutes until they release their aromas. Remove to a plate then soak the chillies in some boiling water for 20 minutes until softened; drain, reserving the liquid. Purée all these ingredients in a blender or food processor, adding enough of the chilli soaking liquid to form a coarse paste.

Toast the sesame seeds in a dry frying pan until they crackle and pop, a couple of minutes. Remove from the pan, then add 1 tsp oil and gently sauté the almonds until they begin to take on a little colour. Add the almonds and sesame seeds to the blender with the spice mixture and 50g of the chocolate and purée until smooth. Add 300ml chicken stock and pulse to blend.

Warm the rest of the oil in a large casserole dish over a medium-high heat. Season the chicken and brown on all sides; you may have to do this in batches. Remove the chicken from the dish, pour off some of the excess fat and sauté the onion over a low heat until softened; add the garlic and cook

for a minute. Pour in the remaining stock and stir to deglaze the dish. Add the spicy sauce, stirring to combine, then return the chicken to the pan, turning it over well in the sauce. Cook, covered, in the oven for 1 hour until the chicken is tender. Stir in the remaining chocolate and serve with rice.

ALMOND TUILES

Scattering some toasted almonds over the top of these tuiles will make for a more substantial biscuit, though they should still be light as air and melt in your mouth. Serve with ice cream or sorbet, or simply enjoy them with a cup of tea.

MAKES ABOUT 24 TUILES
55g ground almonds
25g plain flour
Pinch of salt
2 egg whites
120g golden caster sugar
65g unsalted butter, melted and cooled
20g flaked almonds (optional)

Preheat the oven to 180°C/Gas 4. In a bowl, whisk together the almonds, flour and salt.

likely to get larger harvests. Whether you're planting one tree or two hundred, don't grow almonds near peach trees: they can cross-pollinate, leading to bitter-tasting nuts, which should not be eaten.

Pruning should be kept to a minimum. Just nip out dead, diseased or crossing branches in summer and avoid pruning in winter in damp areas as this will encourage fungal diseases and canker.

HARVESTING

Strictly speaking, the almond isn't a nut, it's a drupe made up of a fleshy, greenish hull, a hard, pitted shell within, and the 'almond' inside that. Almonds resemble small peaches in appearance until fairly late in the season.

Growing your own almonds gives you the chance to try a rare delicacy, 'green' almonds – picked early and whole before the shell forms. They're soft and giving at this stage and in the odd places you can find them (try the Paris markets in late spring) they'll be much in demand. They don't have that classic almond flavour – it's much more like pea pods – but once you wipe all thoughts of 'almond' from your

expectant tastebuds they're well worth investigating. You can eat them whole very early in the season, or a little later, when it's best to split and remove the shell to get at what looks like an ivory broad bean within. Try them dipped in a little salt to balance out any lingering sourness.

Almonds may reach their full size months before harvesting, so judging the time for picking needs a little care. As maturity approaches, the suture (the ridge around the fleshy hull) splits. Harvest time is usually around six weeks from this point. The split will widen gradually, exposing the shell within. Hold off until the stalk attaching the nut to the tree starts to degrade. When this weakens to the point that the nuts fall when the tree is shaken, it's harvest time. Lay a blanket or similar on the ground to catch the nuts as this helps keep them dry as well as preventing you losing any in the grass.

Nuts at the centre of the tree may ripen a little later than the rest – come back for these in a few days. Don't be tempted to pick these almonds at the same time as the others – until they're ready to fall, they won't be ripe.

In a medium-sized bowl, whisk the egg whites to loosen them a bit, then add the sugar and whisk until frothy. Fold in the almond flour mixture and then the butter until smooth. Leave the batter to rest for a couple of minutes while you toast the almonds, if you're using them. Warm a frying pan over a medium heat and add the flaked almonds, stirring them until they begin to turn golden. Remove from the pan.

Line two baking trays with baking parchment. Place teaspoons of batter onto the tray about 4cm apart and smooth them into an oval with the back of the spoon. Scatter over the flaked almonds if using.

Bake for 6–7 minutes until just beginning to turn golden around the edges. Cool on the tray for a minute, then transfer to a cooling rack with a thin palette knife. If you want to make curled tuiles, cover a rolling pin with cling film and lay the still-warm tuiles on it, leaving them for a couple of minutes so that they hold their shape. If the ones still on the tray begin to harden before you curl them, return to the oven for a minute to soften up again.

Tuiles will keep for a couple of days in an airtight container.

ALMOND TUILES

SWEET CHESTNUTS

Sweet chestnuts are everything a peach is not and I love them for it. A just-picked peach is about blissful, summertime moments alone: there is simply nothing better than eating one in the shade of the tree that grew it. Sweet chestnuts are a longer pleasure, giving sustenance and enjoyment over weeks and months, often through the colder, leaner times.

They also take some beating for culinary adaptability. Get them into your kitchen and you're a short step away from delicious soups and stews, staples such as breads, porridge and polenta, not to mention entirely decadent desserts like marron glacé and chocolate chestnut cake.

Easy to grow and easy to store, sweet chestnuts are a healthy source of energy that has kept communities going through hard times. The autumn-ripening nuts are rich in carbohydrates, contain two essential types of vitamin B, have a protein content similar to eggs and milk and, in contrast to most nuts, are low in fats but high in the fatty acids which help to prevent heart disease. This is life-giving food that's often acquired an affectionate name that attests to its sustaining role – 'tree cereal' in France, and 'the bread tree' in Tuscany.

Sweet chestnuts have also suffered to a degree from this association with being the food of poverty. For the most part that has now faded away: there are only so many marrons glacé one can eat before any association with hardship takes a back seat.

While far from rare in many parts of the world, sweet chestnuts are surprisingly localised in the foodscape, but where they are grown in number they often become a core part of local life. As with most precious harvests, seasonal ceremony and invention have woven their way into proceedings. Less widespread than the grape harvest and perhaps less romantic than the olive picking, the autumnal sweet chestnut harvest is still every bit the celebratory centre of community life and is a magical time, with the arrival of the first frosts, the trees bare, the ground carpeted in leaves and nuts and mists hanging in the air.

Away from the mechanical collection and dehusking of industrial production, the sweet chestnut harvest is proper hard work. The nuts and leaves desert the tree together when the kernels are ready, signalling the start of the backbreaking picking and sorting of the sweet chestnuts from their leafy blanket. Not only that, their spiky husks needed splitting off to get at the nuts inside – usually best done by rolling the sole of your boot over them.

Harvested sweet chestnuts will last for many weeks if kept cold, but drying retains their goodness and flavour for months and even years. Drying huts are common on farms with larger harvests to deal with; most are simple buildings with two rooms separated by a slatted floor. At ground level a slow fire burns gently, drying the chestnuts spread on the floor above. Prunings from the trees, husks and the shells from last years harvest act as the fuel. Nothing is wasted. It can take a fortnight to gently drive the water from the sweet chestnuts, after which they are threshed to remove the shells and the bitter thin skin, and sorted to weed out the rotten and low-quality nuts. Many of those remaining are ground into a soft, sweet, characterful flour that has just a hint of bitterness. It is naturally very high in carbohydrate yet gluten-free and is used to make breads, cakes, polenta and any number of local staples.

With a nutrient profile similar to rice and wheat but without the water requirement and chemical inputs usually associated with both, sweet chestnuts offer a sustainable, adaptable carbohydrate for the future – and with new varieties starting to yield within three or four years (rather than a dozen or more for older varieties) you don't have to be too patient to get it.

VARIETIES

Sweet chestnuts (*Castanea sativa*) are also known as European chestnuts, or Spanish chestnuts in the United States. They have a few close edible relatives (the Chinese, Japanese and American Chestnuts) but should not be confused with the unrelated, and inedible, horse chestnut.

Originating in southern and eastern Europe, sweet chestnuts have a peculiar history of colonisation throughout the rest of Europe, where they appear to have been grown either enthusiastically or hardly at all. Similarly, while there are pockets of local cultivation elsewhere around the world, expansive production is limited. This may be due to the lengthy wait for trees to become productive. Fortunately new varieties sidestep much of this wait.

'Bouche de Betizac' and 'Marigoule' are two of the newer French varieties that are doing well in England, so if you fancy trying sweet chestnuts and are in a slightly marginal area these may be your best bet. There are many other new varieties around the world – 'Pilonga' in Spain, for example – all of which may be best suited to your location. Check with your local tree nursery supplier for details.

Sweet chestnut varieties are rarely self-fertile so you will need at least two varieties if there are none in

EATING

Sweet chestnuts are a ridiculously versatile ingredient. They are wonderful in soups, stews, burgers, when cooked with game and stronger meats, in stuffings, as marron glacé, made into a fabulously different jam or sweet sauce, puréed with brown sugar and vanilla into chestnut cream, or when combined with chocolate to make the finest chocolate cake there is.

Do try them – as Nat King Cole suggests – roasted on an open fire. Knick the pointed end of the shell with a knife to prevent them exploding, then spread a handful on a shovel or similar to roast in the fire. It works best when the flames aren't too fierce – ideally over embers. For the less romantic amongst you, spread a few handfuls on a baking tray in the oven for 25 minutes at 200°C/Gas 6.

Whichever way you choose, turn the chestnuts until they are charred all over – this usually takes around 12 minutes. When they're cool enough to handle, peel them and munch on their sweet, floury, earthy centre. An accompanying glass of good bitter won't go amiss.

To prepare chestnuts for anything other than simply eating raw, make a knick in each and either roast or boil

nearby hedges and orchards. Even those varieties that are self-fertile, such as 'Marigoule', are more productive with a partner.

You can grow sweet chestnuts from seed but results are variable and the time to harvest is very much extended. Grafted trees of these new varieties are more expensive than most fruit trees but, having tasted the nuts, I can tell you that paying a little extra now for earlier, better sweet chestnuts is money well spent.

GROWING

Sweet chestnuts are typically long-lived and fast-growing, reaching a height of around 12m in 20 years, although they can grow to twice that in time if not kept smaller. There are no dwarf varieties of sweet chestnut that I am aware of, making this a tree suitable for the larger garden only.

If you choose one of the newer varieties you'll find sweet chestnuts grow quickly and start producing within four years or so. Look for a well-shaped tree with a good, even spread of branches. If you are buying younger trees you'll only need to prune for the first couple of years to develop an open goblet shape. After that just prune to remove dead or crossing branches.

Sweet chestnuts favour a well drained, loamy soil and, though they will tolerate a little deviation from the ideal, avoid waterlogged or chalky soils. If planting more than one tree, plant each at least 8m from its neighbour. Sweet chestnuts like good sun to fruit to full potential, however the new varieties produce reliably well in cooler climates, if with marginally smaller kernels.

Although there are a few pests that can trouble commercial sweet chestnut production these tend to be less common with individual or small groups of trees. On the upside, the three main fungal attacks you may suffer from are untreatable, so you can at least relax safe in the knowledge that there's little you can do about them. Chestnut weevil and chestnut codling moth can both eat away at the kernels unnoticed – you can use pheromone traps or sticky traps to control these pests, however extensive damage is rare.

HARVESTING

The last few weeks before harvest are crucial to the quality of your sweet chestnuts. The kernels can put on half of their growth during this time, so do water your trees if you're experiencing a dry period. Fast

---

them for a few minutes. How you cook sweet chestnuts affects their flavour and texture considerably. Boil them and the water content increases while the calorific value slides a little, whereas roasting drives water off, with the sugars and energy value nudging up by around a quarter. Take a handful at a time out of the water/off the roasting tray – they are easiest to peel when just hot enough to handle. Peel them with the aid of a short, firm-bladed knife and take care to remove the skin that comes away easily from the kernel – even a little will carry it's bitterness into the recipe.

Chestnuts add complexity and richness to many savoury dishes. Of course, there's the Christmas classic of steamed Brussels sprouts sautéed

with pancetta and chestnuts, but they're delicious added to braised red cabbage too. Or use them in an earthy, autumnal pasta sauce. Sauté some mushrooms in butter until browned, add some peeled, cooked sweet chestnuts and a clove or two of finely sliced garlic and cook for a further couple of minutes. Tip in a generous slug of double cream, simmer for a couple of minutes and throw in some finely chopped sage before tossing with hot pasta.

CHESTNUT, PRUNE AND ARMAGNAC STUFFING

Chestnuts and armagnac-laden prunes combine beautifully in this rich and flavoursome stuffing, which works equally well for either goose, turkey or duck.

SERVES 6–8 AS AN ACCOMPANIMENT
160g d'Agen prunes, pitted and coarsely
   chopped
100ml Armagnac
15g unsalted butter, plus a little more
   for greasing
1 medium onion, finely diced
1 stick of celery, finely diced
500g coarsely minced pork
200g peeled cooked chestnuts,
   roughly chopped
1 small eating apple, Cox's or similar,
   peeled, cored and finely diced
75g fresh breadcrumbs
1 egg, lightly beaten
Finely grated zest of 1 lemon
2 tbsp finely chopped parsley
1 tsp fresh thyme leaves,
   finely chopped
¼ tsp freshly grated nutmeg
2 tsp flaky sea salt
½ tsp freshly ground black pepper

growth during these weeks can lead to splitting of the outer coat – the kernels should be fine, but you'll need to check your harvest over and use any split ones quickly.

As the leaves fall, so too do the sweet chestnuts. You'll need to be ready to harvest immediately as the squirrels and other hungry wildlife will be happy to relieve you of the burden of picking them up if you don't. They also deteriorate quickly on damp ground. This year I used a Nut Wizard (a sort of cylinder of wires attached to the end of a broom handle) for the first time and harvesting got a whole lot easier. One pass over the ground under a sweet chestnut tree is all you need to be convinced – the gentle pressure on the ground forces the wires apart just enough to allow the nuts through. As you release the pressure, the wires close, trapping the nuts inside. Beautifully, astonishingly simple and pleasingly low-tech.

Sweet chestnuts typically fall over the course of one or two weeks, so you'll need to go out and gather every other day to get them in good condition. Unless it's particularly windy, a stick comes in handy to move aside leaves in your search for the sweet chestnuts. If the husk hasn't split, you can run the sole of your shoe over them to split it – gloves can be handy in extracting the chestnuts inside. It may only take the first small harvest to convince you of the worth of investing in a Nut Wizard.

Chestnuts are living seeds at harvest time so their water content is high (around 50 per cent), making them more perishable than most nuts. Commercially this is tackled either by keeping them at a low temperature with high humidity or by drying them for flour. Domestically this isn't necessarily practical. Instead, allow them to air dry for one to two days in the sun or indoors at room temperature. This not only reduces the moisture content of the kernel, it also encourages the starches to start to turn to sugars. A sweeter flavour and a crunchy soft texture results. Any sweet chestnuts that show signs of shrinking away from the shell and dullness to their coat are unlikely to keep for long – eat these first. Store the rest in paper bags in the fridge, where they'll keep for a few weeks.

Sweet chestnuts also freeze very well. Add them to a large pan of boiling water, bringing it back to the boil for five minutes. Drain and plunge them into cold water for four minutes. Peel them immediately and, when cold, freeze them in bagged batches to suit your needs. They should keep for a year. Defrost them by microwaving on high for 15 seconds or allowing them to reach room temperature slowly.

Net bags (I reuse the ones onions are sold in) are ideal if you want to keep some sweet chestnuts out for roasting a few weeks after harvesting, these will keep the air circulating round the nuts and stop them from spoiling.

Put the prunes in a bowl with the Armagnac. Leave to soak overnight, or for at least 4 hours.

Warm the butter in a frying pan over a medium-low heat. Add the onion and sauté, stirring, until soft and translucent, about 15 minutes. Add the celery and sauté for a further 5 minutes. Remove from the heat and cool.

In a large bowl, combine the drained prunes, cooled onion and celery, minced pork, chestnuts, apple, breadcrumbs, egg, zest, parsley, thyme, nutmeg, salt and pepper. Use your hands to combine them lightly but thoroughly. Break off a walnut-sized piece and fry until cooked through. Taste and adjust seasoning if necessary.

Stuff into the neck end of a goose, turkey or duck (remember to allow for the weight of the stuffing in your cooking time), or spoon into a buttered ovenproof dish, approximately 28 x 20cm, and bake in an oven preheated to 180°C/Gas 4 for 45–50 minutes until cooked through.

CHESTNUT, PRUNE AND ARMAGNAC STUFFING

PECANS

Pecans are for the patient. Plant one and you'll be out there every month with the tape measure checking on its skyward progress, and for a year or two you may well be disappointed. Pecans are unconcerned about offering you any encouragement. They spend their first years growing downwards, thrusting a tap root into the ground and lateral roots to its side. In the third year everything starts to change – branches extend and multiply as the trunk thickens. If you've chosen a variety carefully you are still a year, perhaps two, away from getting your hands on these fine nuts, but at last there's a little hope.

Despite the length of time they take to produce, pecans are definitely worth the wait and the gamble. And if you don't want to take my word for it, why not follow the example of two American presidents instead?

In the late 18th century, Thomas Jefferson planted pecans at his famous Monticello garden and gave a few to George Washington to plant at his home in Mount Vernon, Virginia. Wild pecans were the only native nut tree growing in North America and, being so delicious, nutritious and easy to shell, they quickly became part of Native American diets in southern North America and Mexico. Washington and Jefferson planted theirs at a time when pecans were beginning to be appreciated more widely and considered as a potentially economically valuable crop – within a few short years they were being exported to the West Indies.

By the end of the 19th century nurserymen in the southern states had started the serious business of grafting and propagating pecans which led to improved varieties and greater reliability. A boom in pecan growing followed and the USA now produces over three quarters of the world's pecans, with Israel, Australia, Mexico, China and Argentina chipping in most of the rest.

Almost all of the American crop is grown in the conditions that suit the wild form best – in the sun and fertile alluvial soils of the southern states. Slowly though, new varieties are spreading the range of the pecan further afield.

Pecans fall into eastern, western or northern types depending on their characteristics. The northern varieties are particularly interesting as they have a considerably lower requirement for summer sun, greater frost resistance and ripen their nuts before the first frosts hit. As well as creeping northwards through the USA, some newer cultivars are being grown in Canada with considerable success, opening the door for production in much of Europe.

These northern pecans typically have a deeper, stronger flavour, thinner shell and creamier texture than other varieties. Until these newer varieties were developed, pecans' critical requirement for summer heat hours was way beyond areas like the southern half of England, but this, combined with their hardiness (down to around -25°C) makes them a gamble – albeit a balanced one – for countries with cooler climates.

The fact that the tree itself is so elegantly beautiful means that even if your gamble doesn't immediately pay off, you and your ancestors have 300 years to enjoy it as a shading ornamental tree while you keep fingers crossed that next year will bring a hotter summer and the nuts that you are after.

VARIETIES
Pecan trees (Carya illinoinensis) are native to the southern states of North America. If your climate is similar, then most varieties of pecan should grow perfectly merrily. Check with tree nursery suppliers to identify the particular cultivars most suited to your location.

EATING

Like many nuts, pecans are high in protein and unsaturated, healthy fats, but they also come packed with more antioxidants (which are thought to help fight Alzheimer's, Parkinson's, cancer and coronary heart disease) than any other nut.

They are delicious fresh but are equally wonderful cooked, where their rich, butteriness works well in cakes, biscuits, ice cream as well as the classic American favourite, pecan pie.

Pecans can be used straight from the freezer if they're to be cooked, although it can be easier to defrost them first if you intend to crush or grind them up.

A delicious yet simple way to use them is as a tasty crust for pan-roasted fish made by pulsing a handful of pecans with half a dozen leaves of tarragon, a dozen or so leaves of basil, some flaky sea salt and freshly ground black pepper in a food processor a couple of times. Beat the coarse mixture into 40g or so of softened butter and spread on the fish's skin before putting it in the oven. This works well with chicken breasts or thighs too.

The sweetness of pecans goes beautifully with purple sprouting broccoli. Just blanch a batch of broccoli in lots of boiling, salted water for 2 or 3 minutes. While it's cooking, sauté some bacon in a pan until almost crisp, toss in some pecans and the drained broccoli and fry for a couple of minutes for all of the flavours to blend, then serve immediately.

If you are hoping to grow pecans in less sunny areas, Northern pecans are your best bet. Opt for a grafted tree. This will produce nuts more quickly and the variety (and the nuts) will come true to its parent. Seedlings, on the other hand, can be anything from spectacular to miserable – something that you will only find out when you harvest (which can take some time). Pecans are self-fertile, so growing just one is perfectly fine.

'Carlson 3', 'Lucas', 'Mullahy' and 'Campbell NC-4' are early-producing varieties of northern pecan, all of which grow well in the most northerly limits of traditional commercial pecan-producing areas and should therefore be suitable for growing in cooler areas such as England.

GROWING

Pecans are native to river valleys and so prefer a deep, moist, yet well drained soil to drive their roots down into. They love sun to produce nuts and ripen their wood, so be sure to give them the sunniest, most sheltered spot you can.

Pecans are very low-maintenance trees, but you do need to give them what they need in the first four years or so. They spend this time working away where you can't see them: underground. Water your pecan trees through dry periods and keep

the ground around the trunk free from competing vegetation during this period. Once the taproot is established, pecans can grow relatively vigorously – up to 60cm a year.

With the correct growing conditions, pecans can get pretty large – 30m is possible in time, although they take a while to get there. A height of 5m at 10 years old is normal and you can always keep them pruned to this smaller size if you are short of space.

Pecans bear male and female flowers in late spring. The males are pendulous tinsel catkins that grow in threes, while the females are altogether less striking, pointing upwards in small groups.

The nuts (more accurately, drupes) that follow are ovalish, around 5cm long and 3cm wide, forming in clusters, each with a rough husk that starts green and turns brown, splitting at maturity to release the thin-shelled nut within.

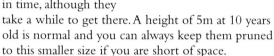

PECAN PIE

With its light, flaky crust and luscious, intensely flavoured filling that teams creamy toasted pecans with whisky, orange zest and cinnamon, this pie is reason alone to grow your own pecans. Serve with whipped cream and a smile.

SERVES 8

For the cream cheese crust:
240g plain flour, plus a little more
　for dusting
½ tsp salt
¼ tsp baking powder
110g unsalted butter, chilled and cut into
　small pieces, plus a little more
　　for greasing
110g cream cheese, chilled and cut
　into small pieces
2 tbsp cold water
1 tsp cider vinegar
1 egg, for the egg wash

For the filling:
250g pecan halves
75g unsalted butter
185g light muscovado sugar
210g golden syrup
1 tbsp whisky or Grand Marnier
1 tsp grated orange zest
1 tsp vanilla extract
½ tsp salt
¼ tsp ground cinnamon
3 eggs

To make the pastry, sieve together the flour, salt and baking powder in a bowl. Add the butter and cream cheese and rub it into the flour with your fingertips until it resembles coarse crumbs, with a few pea-size pieces of butter and cream cheese remaining in the flour. Alternatively, pulse in a food processor until coarsely combined. Pour the water and vinegar together in a jug and slowly trickle it into the dough, mixing with

a knife or pulsing in a food processor as you go, until it just holds together. Turn it out onto a lightly floured surface and press together gently into a round disc. Wrap in cling film and refrigerate for at least 45 minutes. You can make it the day before to this point if you prefer.

　Butter a 22cm loose-bottomed tart tin and dust with flour. On a lightly floured surface, roll out the pastry into a 30cm round. Line the tart tin with the pastry, folding over the excess pastry and crimping into a neat crust which extends 1cm above the top of the tin. Refrigerate for 30 minutes. Preheat the oven to 180°C/Gas 4.

　Prick the pastry base several times with a fork. Line the pastry shell with foil or baking parchment and fill with ceramic baking beans, rice or dried pulses. Place on a baking sheet and bake for 14 minutes. Take the tart shell out of the oven, remove the foil and beans, brush with an egg beaten with a

If you strike it lucky and your trees give you pecans, don't be alarmed if your nutty bonanza is a little less spectacular the following year – it is perfectly common for pecans to follow heavy harvests with one or two lesser ones.

Pecans rarely suffer from pests and diseases. Pecan scab can be a nuisance, but is usually nothing more.

HARVESTING

If the summers have been kind to you and you've chosen the right variety, you may get pecans from the fourth year after planting. The harvesting time for pecans varies considerably with variety, climate and the quality of summer – anywhere through autumn and half way into winter.

As soon as the pecan's husk starts to split, you can get harvesting. Most people use a long stick or shake the branches to get the nuts to fall from the tree. Mowing and/or laying a blanket beneath the tree

before you do so makes the work of collecting them all much easier.

Although you can wait for the pecans to fall themselves, bear in mind that every nut which falls edges nearer the squirrels' and birds' stomachs than yours, so try to shake the majority free when they're almost ready to fall for themselves.

Drying improves everything that is good about pecans – the taste, texture, smell, appearance – plus it helps to prevent them going rancid. To dry, lay them out on sheets of paper in a cold, dry place. After two weeks try one – if they snap when you bend them, they're ready to eat or store. Pecans take on strong smells so ensure that at any stage of drying or storage they are not in close contact with any.

If you store your pecans in paper bags in the fridge they should last a minimum of six months, and will keep for at least twice that if stored in the freezer.

tablespoon of water and return to the oven for 8–10 minutes until the case is cooked through and dried out.

To make the filling, place the pecans on a baking sheet and toast at 180°C/Gas 4 until just fragrant, about 5 minutes. Remove from the oven and cool on the tray; reserve 20 for decorating the pie then chop the remaining ones quite finely.

Melt the butter in a saucepan over a medium-low heat. Add the sugar and stir for 3 minutes. Remove from the heat, whisk in the golden syrup, whisky or Grand Marnier, orange zest, vanilla, salt and cinnamon. When cool, beat in the eggs and chopped pecans.

Pour the filling into the pie crust; arrange the whole pecan halves over the top. Return to the oven and bake for 40–50 minutes until the filling has set but still wobbles slightly when you shake the tin. If the nuts and crust look like they are browning too quickly, cover loosely with foil and continue baking.

PECAN PIE

WALNUTS

For most of us the festive season is the start and end of our relationship with walnuts. It's a shame – good as they can be, these dried walnuts are incomparable with your own, homegrown fresh walnuts. And if you grow your own tree you'll have three chances of a crop.

The walnuts most of us buy are picked in autumn and dried for sale. The drying process gives them a long shelf life (try a bag of Christmas 'special' nuts at Easter and you'll see what I mean – it'll still be perfectly fine) but it does rob them of some of their texture and subtlety.

And yet walnuts don't have to be dried. Straight from the tree, stripped of their green husk, fresh walnuts (also known as wet walnuts) are firm but giving, with a smooth creaminess that's another world from their dried cousins. Their flavour is richer, oilier, and more intense, and the slight tannic edge sets the whole creamy sweetness off a treat. Cracked and eaten,

in salads, without much adulteration, fresh walnuts are the real deal. If you like dried walnuts, you'll love them, and you won't want to wait until Christmas to tuck in.

The term 'wet walnuts' is used purely to distinguish fresh walnuts from dried. They're not 'wet' as such, but the kernel inside the shell is juicy and fresh. Walnuts are also so rarely available to buy in this state that it effectively makes them another of those grow-them-if-you-want-to-try-them feasts. Their bright intensity declines in the weeks following harvest, so you'll want to eat them as near to when they left the tree as you possibly can.

Wet walnuts are delightfully easy to deal with. Peel off the thick green skin and put the point of a knife into the cleft where the shell halves join and twist. Two creamy halves of fresh nut await the corner of the blade to winkle them out. This method works pretty well on dried walnuts too, although nutcrackers are part of the whole pleasant palaver for some.

If you grow your own walnuts, you'll also get the chance to taste an altogether rarer treat – green walnuts. In early summer you can pick some of the walnuts before they approach maturity either to pickle them or to make a fabulous version of Nocino, the Italian green walnut liqueur. I've christened my version 'DiacoNocino', replacing the rocket fuel spirit traditionally used with vodka in the interests of opening (rather than removing) the chuckle valve. In the Italian region of Emilio-Romagna, it's traditional for families to interpret the core Nocino recipe as they like, so I feel in keeping with the spirit of the spirit. There's an annual contest (alas for women only) to compete for the accolade of Nocino of the Year. It's traditional to use an odd number of walnuts, for reasons that appear to have been lost in time. I have no intention of stirring up the wrath of the Nocino ladies.

VARIETIES
Choosing the correct variety is important with walnuts (*Juglans regia*). 'Broadview' and 'Franquette' are two excellent, reliable, early-yielding cultivars that give you nuts within three to four years rather than the dozen or so that the old, ungrafted varieties will leave you waiting.

I haven't grown it, but 'No. 16' is supposed to be late-leafing and more happily self-fertile than many.

'Rita' is a good choice for a smaller space, but it will still grow to 8m or so in time if not kept smaller with a little pruning.

GROWING
Walnuts are easy to grow, require minimal pruning and will fruit reliably as long as you plant the best cultivars. Hardiness varies enormously with variety: late-leafing, late-flowering varieties are essential for reliable cropping in areas like Britain, whereas many of the cultivars available in Californian varieties can get away with being much less so. You may be offered budded or seedling walnuts – go for a grafted variety if you can as these are typically more resistant to frosts and crop much earlier in life.

Walnuts thrive in a temperate climate with cold winters, so much of the world's production is centred in Europe, USA and China. They prefer a moist but well drained soil, good shelter and a site that's not prone to late frosts – young leaves and flowers are damaged by -2°C or below. If your soil is sandy or heavy, speak to your nursery supplier – there are rootstocks available in some areas that will allow you to grow walnuts in these soils.

Walnuts need a little room to grow. Most of the new varieties grow to 6m or so in a decade, and will keep going to three or four times that if they're not pruned back.

EATING

Wet walnuts have all the qualities of the very finest walnuts you can buy, but it a more satisfying balance. They have resistance to the bite rather than crunch, with a creamier intensity that lends itself to all manner of cheeses, in salads, dressings or in sauces. Process a handful of walnuts, a couple of cloves of garlic, olive oil, a slice or 2 of crustless white bread soaked in milk, lemon juice, Parmesan and a good fistful of parsley for a fabulously creamy take on the classic pesto.

If you're eating wet walnuts uncooked, use them as fresh as possible – all that bright intensity declines in the weeks following harvest though they remain perfectly tasty and fine for cooking with. Discard any dark walnuts – they won't be sweet, they may be rancid and they will ruin anything they are in.

Pickling green walnuts is a pleasure reserved for the person who grows them and, as with most recipes, the messabout reads worse than it is.

Prick the walnuts with a fork. Make a brine of 100g of salt to 1 litre of water. Bring the brine and walnuts to the boil, take them off the heat and leave the walnuts to stand in the brine for a day. Drain the brine and lay the nuts out on a tray in a dry, airy place. They'll turn black in two or three days. To make the pickling liquid, for every 2kg of green walnuts add 500g unrefined brown sugar, 1 teaspoon each of black peppercorns, grated ginger, allspice, cloves, and ½ teaspoon of cinnamon

Many walnut cultivars are self-fertile but often the male catkins and female flowers don't appear at the same time, so almost all do better when planted with a compatible partner for pollination.

Maintenance is limited to watering in the first couple of years in dry patches, and pruning in autumn to remove any unwanted branches.

With walnuts, as with most nuts, the squirrel is your nemesis. You'll know if they're about and if they are you have only two choices: humane traps (which in Britain means then killing any trapped), or getting used to some or all of your harvest being shared. You may also lose a few to weevils and other boring creatures but there's little you can do to prevent this, so it is best to accept a little being affected.

Although I've not noticed its effects, juglone is secreted by the roots and washed from fallen leaves. This chemical can inhibit other plants such as apples and Ericaceae, so avoid planting them adjacently.

HARVESTING
Harvest time for green walnuts is a punt: test a few golf ball-sized walnuts as early summer moves into midsummer (the first few days of July in Britain; traditionally the night of 24–25 June in Italy). Jab a knitting needle into the end – if the shell has started to form you'll soon hit it perhaps half a centimetre in. Leave these to grow on. The remainder can be used for pickling or for making DiacoNocino (see below).

Harvesting mid-summer green walnuts may well improve rather than deplete your later crop of wet walnuts. Go for the easy-to-reach lower-growing walnuts early and the tree will have more energy for maturing the main crop nuts to follow.

As the main harvest approaches and the walnuts mature, the husks split to release the nut inside. This is usually in early autumn. Jump into action as soon as you see this start, as pests will step in if you don't. Shake or tap the branches (onto a blanket below if you fancy) and remove the husks the same day if you can as this lowers the threat of fungal diseases.

Removing the fleshy outer husk reveals the walnut's hard shell. This can be broken with a nutcracker, opened with a knife using a twisting motion in the suture, or cracked as pairs squeezed together in your hand. Inside you'll find two nutty halves of a mini-brain. The outer casing is full of tannins which can stain cloth, wood, your hands, whatever – so it's worth wearing gloves for the harvest and dehusking.

Walnuts need to be kept dry and are best refrigerated to store – they can turn rancid very rapidly in warm conditions. To dry your crop (which will extend their shelf-life to at least 6 months, perhaps double that) simply wash the husked walnuts and arrange them in a single layer on a smooth, flat surface somewhere shady but with good air circulation. Leave to dry for 3 or 4 days (or a few days longer if the weather is damp) stirring the nuts up daily to ensure they dry evenly.

(or Carolina allspice) to a litre of malt vinegar. Bring this to the boil, add the nuts and simmer for 15 minutes. Remove from the heat, allow to cool and lift the walnuts out with a slotted spoon into Kilner jars or similar, and cover with the pickling liquid. Now all you have to do is wait until Christmas (and, of course, beyond) to enjoy them with the very finest bit of Stilton you can find.

To make my delicious DiacoNocino liqueur, wash, dry and quarter 29 green walnuts. Mix 1 litre of vodka with 500g unrefined sugar in a large bowl until the sugar dissolves,

then add 20cm or so of cinnamon stick, 12 cloves, ½ vanilla pod (split lengthways) and the zest of a lemon (strips or grated). Fill a large jar with the walnut quarters and cover with your spicy booze. Put it on your desk or by your favourite chair so that you remember to turn it once a day for two months. Let it rest for a further month, and then decant the liquid into another clean bottle and leave to sit until Christmas.

This dark, sweet-bitter, syrupy liqueur is best served stone cold at the end of a meal as a digestif, or over (or indeed in) ice cream.

FESANJAN
This celebrated sweet-sour Persian dish is equally delicious made with duck, pheasant or lamb. It's even better the next day, so it's a great dish to make if you're cooking for a crowd and want to get ahead.

SERVES 4–6
230g shelled walnuts
10g unsalted butter
70ml groundnut oil
2 onions, halved and finely sliced
3 garlic cloves, crushed
½ tsp ground cinnamon
¼ tsp freshly grated nutmeg
170ml pomegranate molasses
650ml chicken stock
2 tbsp caster sugar

FESANJAN

12 threads of saffron
1½ tsp sea salt
2 tsp freshly ground black pepper
1 x 2kg chicken, jointed or about 1.5kg
  chicken pieces, legs, thighs, breasts, skin on
Juice of 2 small limes
Small handful of coriander leaves
Salt and freshly ground black pepper
To serve: Rice, toasted walnuts, roughly
  chopped, the seeds of a small
  pomegranate and a few coriander leaves

In a food processor, pulse the walnuts into
a fine powder, almost a paste. In a large,
heavy-bottomed frying pan over a medium
heat, toast the walnut powder, stirring
constantly, until it is a rich chocolate brown
– be careful not to burn it. When toasted, tip

the powder into a bowl to stop it cooking
any further.

In a medium-sized saucepan, warm
the butter and half of the oil and over a
medium-low heat and sweat the onion until
soft and translucent, about 15 minutes. Add
the garlic, cinnamon and nutmeg and sauté
for a couple of minutes. Add the walnut
powder, pomegranate molasses, 500ml of
the stock, sugar, saffron, salt and pepper.
Bring to a bare simmer and cook, partially
covered, for 30 minutes.

In a frying pan, warm the rest of the oil
over a medium-high heat and brown the
chicken pieces in batches until golden,
removing cooked ones to a large casserole as
you go. Pour off most of the fat and deglaze

the pan with the remaining stock. Add the
pan juices and walnut sauce to the chicken,
bring to a simmer, cover and cook very
gently for 50 minutes to an hour, adding a
little boiling water if it begins to look dry.
Alternatively, cook in an oven preheated to
170°C/Gas 3 for an hour. Add the lime juice
and coriander, taste and adjust seasoning if
necessary. Serve with rice, with some toasted
walnuts, pomegranate seeds and coriander
leaves scattered over the top.

SOFT FRUIT

No matter how small your space may be, with shrubs, scramblers, creepers, clumpers, canes and vines to choose from, everyone can grow a little soft fruit.

Strawberries and raspberries make for many people's first choice, and ubiquitous as they may be, if you get the best varieties you'll not be disappointed. Soft fruit usually has a short window of perfection so even if you grow something you can find in the shops, you'll taste the difference in your own simply because you'll be eating it at the top of its game.

But I hope to persuade you to stray from the well-worn path and try some fruits that you'll simply not find in the shops. Chilean guava, blue honeysuckle and the others in this section are almost too good to be true. Alpine strawberries will leave you wondering why so few people try them when the seed is so widely available and they are so easy to grow.

It is, however, worth bearing in mind that, whatever fruity delight you choose to grow and eat, you'll be falling into a seductive trap created by the tree, which behind the wrapping of those sweet baubles is busy doing the real work – growing seeds. The delicious coating is being prepared simply to allow you and any other ravenous animal to disperse them for it. We eat the fruit, discard the seed and with a little luck it falls on fertile ground. The fruit has served its purpose and the plant has succeeded in its aim: to reproduce itself. So tasty is this fruity bribe that we rarely (if ever) realise or care that it is happening. Or perhaps we're happy to believe that because we put the tree there that everything it does thenceforth is entirely for our benefit as a result of our skill.

Seed isn't the only way to grow new plants for yourself – hardwood cuttings (see pp. 93–4) work really well for many of the soft fruit, including Japanese wineberries, blue honeysuckle, autumn olive and Chilean guava, as does layering. There are a number of layering methods, the simplest of which involves selecting young flexible shoots that can easily be bent down to touch the ground. About 30cm from the tip make a 3cm cut along the stem that runs through a leaf bud. Brush hormone rooting compound to the wound, create a trench 10cm deep and secure the wounded section in the trench with a wire staple or similar, and backfill. Tie the growing tip to a short piece of cane to ensure it is growing upwards and water. Within a year roots should develop, at which point you can sever the new plant from the parent and plant it where you please.

Sometimes with soft fruit it's worth jumping in part way along the road to ripeness and harvesting a few that are a little sharp or sour, especially if you're making preserves. Autumn olive ripens to a lovely sweetness but get it just before it does and the sharp edge makes the autumn olive jam deliciously different to a batch made a week or two later. Gooseberries and rhubarb, for example, are all about that sourness. As with lemons, once you embrace their sharp character you'll find endless opportunities to use them – a sauce made of either and served with oily fish, for example, makes the most of both.

With a reasonable summer you can be in for a bumper harvest of soft fruit from even a few plants in pots. Most make for good raw grazing, but it's good to have a few good recipes up your sleeve too. You'll find most soft fruit recipes delightfully adaptable, including those in this section, so try adjusting them to whatever you have plenty of as you like. The Japanese wineberry trifle and vinegar recipes, for example, will work brilliantly with most other berries – mulberries, strawberries and raspberries in particular.

And if you do have a glut, bear in mind that most soft fruit freezes well if you do it properly. Spread your berries or currants out on a tray and freeze them first to stop them sticking together, before tipping them into freezer bags in quantities to suit your needs.

The jam, chutney, leather and jelly recipes included within this book work equally well for many of the other berries, currants and other soft fruit. Get familiar with the principles of preserving and its core recipes – it's the perfect way to stretch those flavours from the heat of the harvest over the rest of the year. Once you're comfortable with the processes you'll find your preserves are far more than a handy dumping ground for excessive harvests – preserving is a craft, albeit one that can be picked up and developed easily enough. The key is to work carefully and to make small batches to begin with. You may have to play about with a few of them when using fruit that is new to you but don't let that make you hesitate. You may be the first person to make blue honeysuckle vodka or fuchsia trifle, so getting it spot on may need a couple of tries. However, even a trifle that needs a little tweaking is still a trifle, and whose day isn't better for getting stuck into one of those?

ALPINE STRAWBERRIES

Alpine strawberries may well be my favourite of all strawberries. These fingernail-sized berries are full of that familiar sweet strawberry flavour but have an almondy, vanilla undertone absent in their larger cousins. And although I love the fine firmness of summer strawberries, alpines seduce you with their tendency to dissolve on the tongue. You hardly feel them, they're so soft. Perfectly ripe, a handful feels like clouds of strawberry condensing on your tongue.

Though their plants and the fruit may be smaller than the standard varieties, there's definitely no compromise in flavour when it comes to alpine strawberries. If anything their flavour and aroma are even more intense.

Alpine strawberries fill their place in the garden more pleasingly than regular strawberries. Rather than spreading low and wide with the aid of runners, alpines grow in a soft, lazy bush of pale green foliage that turns to classically autumnal shades of red, gold and orange as the cold approaches. Their loveliness belies their hardiness – these are tough little perennial plants that have no difficulty with the cold and need very little encouragement to get growing as the soil starts to warm.

The alpine strawberries produce their sweet, juicy berries to a different timetable than that of the regular strawberry. Instead of the familiar baskets of fruit, within a few short summer weeks, you'll be picking alpine fruit anytime from when the last frost thaws through the warm months until the cold returns. They'll even give you fruit in their first summer if you sow seeds early enough.

Growing from seed also makes them a cheap as well as delicious alternative to common strawberries. A single packet of seed will give you at least two hundred plants to line your vegetable beds, edge your paths or squeeze into any space around your garden.

VARIETIES
'Mignonette' is the finest of all the alpine strawberries. So fine are they that I almost named this section 'Mignonette strawberries' after them. 'Mignonette' is an improved cultivar of 'Renee de Valee' – an old heirloom variety – and bears fruit that are larger, sweeter and more deeply flavoured than other alpines.

There are yellow-fruited varieties such as 'Yellow Wonder' which have an excellent flavour and are taken in even fewer numbers by the birds due to their colour.

Although most alpine strawberries will grow reasonably well in partial shade, 'Alexandria' seems most happy out of full sun.

GROWING
Alpine strawberries are easily grown from seed. Start them off undercover in modules as early as late winter, planting them out when the seedlings are large enough to handle. Alpine strawberries are tolerant of most soil types and are by no means as particular as regular strawberries, but a little compost or well-rotted manure dug into a well-drained spot before planting will ensure that you get them performing at their best.

Plant alpine strawberries 30cm apart and water them during the first few weeks and thereafter only in dry periods. Mulching around the base also helps to

EATING

Alpine strawberries are used (especially in France) for decorating pastries and cakes, which showcases their miniature loveliness perfectly, and they're equally fine dropped into a glass of champagne. Simple usually works better with alpine strawberries: although you can use them in preserves, puddings and any number of berry recipes I find if you mix alpines in with other berries you can lose much of their fabulous individuality.

SPECTACULAR STRAWBERRY SCONES
These are a delicious treat for tea time but are glamorous enough to serve as a pudding.

MAKES 8
For the scones:
150g plain flour
1½ tsp baking powder
¼ tsp bicarbonate of soda
¼ tsp salt
1 tbsp caster sugar
1 tsp finely grated lemon zest
65g unsalted butter, chilled and cut into
 1cm cubes
160ml buttermilk
1 tbsp single cream or milk

For the strawberries:
300g alpine strawberries, rinsed and stalks
 removed
25g caster sugar
200ml double cream, lightly whipped,

or 200g clotted cream
Icing sugar for dusting (optional)

Preheat the oven to 200°C/Gas 6.
 Sieve together the flour, baking powder, bicarbonate of soda and salt into a large mixing bowl. Stir in the sugar and lemon zest. Toss in the butter and work lightly with your fingertips until it resembles coarse breadcrumbs, though it's good to have a few pea-size pieces of butter still in the dough as this will give you a flakier result. Pour in the buttermilk and stir lightly to combine with a fork or knife.
 Turn the sticky dough out onto a well floured surface, knead very gently to bring together, then roll or pat out the dough until

▶

retain water, suppress weed growth and will ensure the roots stay cool in hot weather.

Alpine strawberries are rarely, if ever, troubled by any pests or diseases and usually get away strongly, throwing up leafy growth quickly followed by flowers. Their first flush of fruit will start appearing in just a few months. As with most fruit, a fortnightly feed with comfrey tea (see p.183) from flowering through fruiting will boost the quantity and quality of your harvest.

The plants will be at their best for three years or so. After that they're still delicious, but are more prone to disease and become less productive as they age. It's therefore best to sow new seeds every three years.

Alpine strawberries grow happily in containers and in hanging baskets, or even on a window sill where you can nip off the fruit as they ripen.

HARVESTING

Alpine strawberries have a very long picking season – from late spring through deep into autumn. They keep coming, so check plants frequently for ripe berries. Apart from not wanting to miss out on any, picking encourages the plant to keep producing more fruit.

Perfectly ripe berries can be fragile so only wash them if you need to. Do so by popping them into a bowl of cold water and gently swishing them around – allowing any soil that may have gathered on the berry to sink to the bottom. Remove your berries from the water and pat dry with kitchen paper.

◄

it's about 1.5cm thick. Cut into 6cm rounds (use a wine glass if you don't have a cutter; both should be dipped in flour first), gently rerolling the dough scraps and cutting them out too. Lift onto a baking sheet with a spatula and brush the tops with cream or milk. Bake for 12 minutes, until golden. Cool slightly before filling, but they're best served warm.

While the scones are cooking, toss the strawberries with the caster sugar and leave to macerate for 5 minutes. Purée about a quarter of them in a blender then mix them with the whole strawberries.

To assemble the scones, first slice them in half. Put the bottom biscuit on a plate, add a dollop of whipped or clotted cream and a good spoonful of the strawberry mixture, top with the other half of the scone and dust with icing sugar if using. Serve immediately.

SPECTACULAR STRAWBERRY SCONES

AUTUMN OLIVE

This beautiful deciduous shrub is native to the wooded hills of Japan and China, where its fruits make the finest fruit leather and (along with medlars) the best jam you'll ever taste.

I have a special affection for plants that give you more than their obvious gift. With Jerusalem artichokes you have beautiful sunflowers, a seasonal windbreak, and all the pollinating insects that come with it well before you get to their fabulous tubers in the winter. I'd grow them for the tubers alone, but I love them that little bit extra for their unnecessary, showy generosity. Autumn olive is the fruity equivalent, although it's much more modest about its kindness.

Along with many of its genus (*Elaeagnus*), autumn olive berries are a fine source of vitamins A, C and E, and essential fatty acids, but it's their lycopene content that may be most important. The countless small fruit owe their purple-pink colour to lycopene,

a photochemical that appears to reduce the risk of heart disease and many cancers – prostate cancer in particular. Autumn olive fruit are stacked full of it, containing 15 times the levels found in tomatoes.

As well as nourishing you, autumn olive will quietly go about nursing the rest of your garden too. It forms a symbiotic relationship with particular soil bacteria that form nodules in the plant's roots, giving it the ability to take nitrogen from the air and make it available to itself as food. Autumn olive produces more of this essential nutrient than it needs which makes it an excellent companion plant – any nitrogen it doesn't use enriches the soil and nurtures neighbouring plants. It also improves the structure of the soil by breaking up the ground with its vigorous root system, enriching it through root turnover (the continual process of roots dying, decaying and being replaced), with the fallen leaves adding to the organic matter in the soil below and nearby.

Autumn olive was introduced to North America around 200 years ago where its self-sufficiency and unfussy requirements allow it to thrive, becoming invasive in places where there is little competition or management. In some areas it is treated as a weed with programmes for removal. This, however, is really much more a result of inappropriate planting and lack of management than anything inherently dominating about autumn olive, so don't allow it to cloud your mind.

Countless small, juicy berries appear on the autumn olive in mid-summer, turning livid red-pink as they ripen. Look closely and you'll see their light-catching silver speckle. If you try them before they're fully ripe they'll be quite sharply astringent – even when they've reached a good deep colour they like another week or two to become sweeter inside, so don't rush into harvesting too soon. Fully ripe, the tannin levels will have fallen and the sugars increased: the fruit are deliciously sweet, but even a little shy of perfection they can be sharp. Tasting is the only way

to tell. Do try a few a little early though – when the sweetness has some acid against it they make for a weirdly addictive treat as well as being full of character for cooking.

Autumn olive will give you plenty of pleasure even before you pick the fruit. The long, olive-like foliage appears early in spring – the leaves are green on the upperside but look underneath and it seems as though someone has been to work with the silver spray paint. They catch the light beautifully.

The pale yellow flowers that follow in early summer are small (around 1cm across), growing in clusters anywhere along the length of the branches. Their beautiful fragrance is strangely elusive: you can bend to smell them and get nothing, then be enveloped in a cloud of their perfume as you walk way.

VARIETIES
Autumn olive (also known as Japanese silverberry) is widely and cheaply available from many nurseries specialising in hedging. If you're planning a hedge or long stretch of more than a few plants, it may well be worth buying the majority as unnamed varieties from these suppliers and infilling with a few named varieties for better pollination and fruit.

EATING

Autumn olive's sweet-sharp flavour is particularly suited to preserves – autumn olive jam and fruit leather (see p.82) are as good as any.

Each fruit is usually a little smaller than 1cm across and contains a single chewy edible seed, which some prefer to sieve out when making jams and other preserves but I really can't be bothered – you don't really notice it.

AUTUMN OLIVE GIN

This makes a delicious, ruby-hued alternative to sloe gin. Traditionally, sloes are picked after the first frost or pricked with a pin to encourage the maceration process, and autumn olives benefit from a helping hand too. All that pricking is a bit tedious and the same effect can be achieved by putting the fruit in the freezer for a couple of hours before getting started with the recipe.

MAKES 2 x 700ML BOTTLES
400g autumn olives
1 x 700ml bottle of gin
1 x 700ml (sterilised) bottle
400g caster sugar
2 5cm x 2cm strips of orange zest, from a washed, unwaxed orange
2 sticks of cinnamon
4 cloves

Freeze the autumn olives for a couple of hours. Pour the gin into a large jug. Divide the autumn olives between the gin bottle and the additional sterilised bottle. Add 200g sugar, 1 strip of zest, 1 cinnamon stick and 2 cloves into each bottle, then pour in the gin to fill the bottle. Screw the lids on firmly and give the bottles a good shake.
  Store in a cool, dark place for 8–10 weeks, shaking every day for the first week, and then from time to time to prevent the sugar settling at the bottom. Strain the liquid

through a fine sieve and pour into clean bottles. Ideally, leave for at least 6 months in a cool, dark place before drinking.

AUTUMN OLIVE JAM

Autumn olives are tart little suckers. Keep tasting and testing until their puckering sourness is tempered by a little sweetness. Once they arrive at this point it's time to harvest your berries and transform them into this delightful jam.

MAKES 4 x 340G JARS
1kg ripe autumn olives
About 700g jam sugar with pectin
2 tbsp lemon juice

Put a couple of saucers in the freezer for testing the jam later. Boil your jars and lids or put them though the dishwasher to sterilise them, then put the jars in a low oven to keep warm.

'Brilliant Rose', 'Big Red', 'Newgate' and 'Jewel' are all excellent, high-yielding, delicious varieties that will boost the fruit on the other plants.

GROWING

Not troubled by any pests or diseases, autumn olive is a hardy little thing. I planted two hedges of it 18 months ago, one into mulch mat (to minimise grass competition) and another straight into the grass (I had run out of mulch mat). There has since been scarcely any difference in their progress. This is due, at least in part, to autumn olive's ability to fix its own nitrogen, which gives it the chance to thrive in reasonably infertile locations, and makes it perfectly tolerant of even nutrient-deprived soils.

One thing an autumn olive needs is sun. Give it sea winds, drought or even the odd dip to as low as -40°C and it won't complain too much, but shade (or a chalky soil for that matter) will not bring out its best.

You can grow autumn olive from seed but it can take an age to germinate, and although cuttings apparently take reasonably successfully, both will leave you a long way from a harvest. I would therefore encourage you to just buy young plants – they will fruit a little in their first year, then very enthusiastically thereafter.

You can plant autumn olive plants as lone specimens – they will grow to around 3m tall and wide unless you trim them back – or plant a number of them slightly closer together to grow into a very hardy, beautiful hedge with the bonus of fantastic fruit. Providing it is pruned back ocassionally, Autumn olive can also be grown in containers (80cm).

HARVESTING

As their name suggests, autumn olive fruit ripen through autumn. They are occasionally ready earlier in warm climates but don't be too impatient to start picking. Let the sweetness develop fully after the colour has turned or you'll be rewarded with an eye-watering astringency. Regular taste-testing is the only way to tell – they should be sweet but with a lovely acidic edge.

The fruit are perhaps 7–8mm across, a particularly rich pink-purple with a grey speckle to them that's quite unlike anything else. Their happiness in falling from the plant with only slight encouragement makes picking a perfectly easy task. If you're picking a good haul quickly, a useful method is to pull the fruit from the bush through (and into) a carrier bag with your hand.

Autumn olive fruit keep for about two weeks at room temperature.

Rinse the autumn olives well and put them in a large, non-reactive pan with 250ml of water. Bring to the boil and simmer for 20–30 minutes until the berries are soft. Pass them through a food mill/mouli to remove the seeds, then push the pulp through a fine-meshed nylon sieve.

Weigh the pulp (from this amount of autumn olives, you should get about 1.25 litres of strained fruit pulp) and put it into a large, non-reactive pan with an equal amount of jam sugar and the lemon juice. Stir over a low heat until the sugar has dissolved then bring to a rolling boil. Boil hard for 5 minutes and test to see if it has reached its setting point. Do this by dropping a teaspoon of jam onto a chilled saucer, waiting a minute then pushing it with your finger. If it wrinkles, it's ready. Stir it to disperse any scum then pour it into the warm jars and seal. It will keep for up to a year in a cool, dark, dry place.

AUTUMN OLIVE JAM

BLUE HONEYSUCKLE

Along with Alpine strawberries, blue honeysuckle are often the first fruit of the year at Otter Farm. Their presence means I get to eat summer pudding weeks ahead of when I might otherwise and for that I owe a huge 'thank you' to a few men and women in Russia half a century ago.

Blue honeysuckle fruit have been eaten for many years in their native Siberia and in Japan and China where they are widely grown. Where wild specimens occur they can be reasonably common and often form an important part of the forager's diet, but they are famously variable in taste – being either completely delicious or entirely disappointing. Thankfully, breeding programmes in the 1950s took the best of the best and removed the blue honeysuckle's less desirable traits (such as bitterness), leaving us with the many excellent varieties available today. Thank you, plantsmen and women of Russia.

With a heritage in Siberia it's no surprise that blue honeysuckle can handle the cold, being hardy to around -50°C. More importantly, the open flowers can survive down to around -7°C. This is important for two reasons: not only can you get incredible fruit onto your table in all but the coldest situations; a late cold snap is unlikely to kill off the flowers and with it your chance of a crop.

This hardy early flowering allows the fruit to develop similarly early – often in very early summer, before the first strawberries. It's cause for excitement here, at least partly as it was the first homegrown fruit my daughter ate. Not yet two years old, she tried one and then devoured the whole day's pickings one at a time. She called them 'purple apples' (I think all fruit was a version of 'apple' at the time) and the name kind of stuck.

Blue honeysuckle is not a climber in the way that other honeysuckles can be. Instead it forms a substantial bush up to a couple of metres high and wide. The oval leaves are very similar to climbing honeysuckles, growing in opposite pairs, around 7cm long, bluey-green and usually slightly waxy but there the similarity with its inedible relative ends.

They have small, usually pale yellow flowers that appear in spring. They're not by any means showy, but they are particularly beautiful and well worth the trouble of stooping for a closer look. They appear very early in the season and form a welcome stop off for the earliest bees.

In early to late summer (depending on the variety), the flowers develop into fabulous sweet fruits similar to elongated blueberries – they share that deep matt blue and the skin even has the characteristic dusty white bloom. The flavour is quite unique – predominantly of blackcurrant with a little blueberry and a hint of honey, often with a little sourness to perfectly balance the sweetness. But don't let that description guide you too much, the flavour is very much its own and varies depending on variety. Some have hints of blackberries, raspberries, even rhubarb.

Even by horticultural standards the blue honeysuckle goes by a vast array of other names. Sweetberry honeysuckle, honeyberry, swamp fly honeysuckle and haskap are among the more common ones. Having so many names smacks of trying to find a way to sell something that's not particularly convincing, but it may be partly due to repeated attempts at trying to establish a position in the marketplace that distinguishes blue honeysuckles from blueberries. Parallel breeding programmes in different countries have also thrown up a few new names. Whatever it's called where you live, buy one – blue honeysuckle

is easy to grow, has an edge on blueberries with its ability to tolerate a wide range of pH and soil types, but more importantly it produces its uniquely delicious purple fruit at a time when there's often little else around.

VARIETIES
I've yet to taste a variety that is anything other than excellent, and all have retained those fabulous advantages of hardiness and early productivity.

There are new varieties being added to the catalogues all the time, so keep an eye out for the best. The ones I've found grow best here at Otter Farm are 'Blue Belle', 'Kamchatka', 'Blue Velvet' and 'Berry Blue'.

'Blue Belle' is delicious and very productive, yet doesn't get beyond 1.5m in height or spread and can be grown in a 60cm container, making it ideal if you are looking for a smaller variety.

'Kamchatka' is equally delicious and flowers and fruits a little later than most other varieties, so you get a longer cropping period if you grow this in conjunction with an earlier variety. It apparently originates from the Kamchatka Peninsula in north Siberia which is particularly cold, so this one is likely to be particularly hardy.

'Blue Velvet' looks a little different to many blue honeysuckles, having slightly furry leaves and larger fruit. It too is a great choice for very cold areas as it seems to be especially hardy.

'Berry Blue' is almost identical to 'Blue Belle' but much larger – growing to almost 3m wide and high.

As blue honeysuckle isn't self-fertile, plant at least two varieties to ensure good pollination and fruitset.

GROWING
Blue honeysuckles are not only remarkable in flavour, they blow away the alternatives (such as blueberries) by being so easy to care for and versatile in where they grow.

Wild specimens can be found in wetland, boggy areas with heavy soils and even on thin soils, low in nutrients, although neither are ideal conditions for the new varieties. Blue honeysuckle will tolerate all but extreme pH, soil types and some shade, but give it a good, moist well drained soil, on the sunny side of partial shade and you'll be rewarded with an abundance of fruit from a very happy bush.

It is possible to grow blue honeysuckle from seed although I've not done so. It's much more reliable however to create new plants by layering (see p.67) or taking cuttings instead.

They make remarkably trouble-free additions to your garden: they don't sucker and have very few pests and diseases. Birds can make for the berries, though I have yet to experience this. Netting is a useful protection if they go for yours.

When planting out, allow your blue honeysuckle 2m growing room; a little less if you want to create a honeysuckle hedge.

Blue honeysuckle needs no formative pruning, just the occasional thinning out of any dead, damaged or overcrowded areas. Never remove more than a quarter of the plant as this can knock back its vigour. Do any pruning towards the end of winter or very early spring, and do it with care – the branches are quite brittle.

Water your blue honeysuckle during dry periods for the first couple of years. Once established they are very drought-tolerant.

HARVESTING

Blue honeysuckles come into fruit early in their life and early in the growing season which gets you a quick return on your investment and means you are eating fresh fruit before most other people.

Once established, blue honeysuckles grow healthily and quickly and often produce in the year following planting. In a few years you should be enjoying a couple of kilos of fruit per bush. Depending on variety, fruit can be picked from late spring/early summer right through the season.

Although blue honeysuckle fruit are small (1cm or so long) the berries are produced in clusters which make them easy to harvest – they also separate very easily from the plant so you can pick quite a haul surprisingly quickly.

The berries should be a deep purple/blue before you pick them. If in doubt, pinch a couple off and bite them in half – a sour taste or a hint of green will mean that you should wait a little longer if you want to catch them at their best.

If your variety has large, plump berries you will find they can stay on the bush for a good few weeks before they start to drop, so you needn't be in too much of a hurry to pick them all.

EATING

Blue honeysuckle is one of those delights that it is hard to make it across the threshold from garden to house with. They're the peas of the fruit world: best enjoyed as al fresco sweets. If you don't eat them all like that, freeze some (on a tray to keep them separate, then tip them into a bag) – when you pop them still-frozen into your mouth they dissolve into cool pools of flavour.

They are excellent cooked in all manner of ways – anything you would do with blueberries, you can do with blue honeysuckle – they make excellent jam, pies and are a great

alternative in the Chilean Guava Muffin recipe (see p.80).

The seeds are tiny (like kiwi seeds) and the skin thin – both happily disintegrate, making blue honeysuckles perfect for ice cream, granitas and all manner of incredibly coloured cream-based puds.

Edible honeysuckle is also delicious folded into thick, American-style breakfast pancakes. Stir together 1tsp orange zest with 2 tbsp caster sugar. Whisk the zesty sugar together in a bowl with 150g plain flour, 1 tsp baking powder, ½ tsp bicarbonate of soda and a good pinch of salt. In a jug,

whisk together 240ml buttermilk, an egg and 3 tbsp cooled, melted butter. Pour the liquid into the dry ingredients, stirring as you go to make a slightly lumpy batter. Fold in 160g edible honeysuckle. Warm the barest trickle of groundnut oil in a heavy frying pan over a medium heat and add the batter in small ladlefuls – you can probably do 2 pancakes at a time. Once bubbles appear all over the surface, flip the pancakes over and cook through, about 2 minutes. This batter makes enough for 8–10 pancakes; serve with a drizzle of maple syrup or runny honey and Greek yoghurt.

BLUE HONEYSUCKLE PANCAKES

LEMON HONEYSUCKLE BARS

A tender shortbready base and tangy lemon topping studded with blue honeysuckle berries make these sweet treats a real winner. While they are delicious simply served with a cup of tea or coffee, they are certainly special enough to be served as a dessert in their own right, should you wish.

MAKES 12 BARS

For the shortbread base:
250g unsalted butter, at room temperature, cut into small pieces, plus a little more for greasing
270g plain flour
85g icing sugar
Pinch of salt
1 tsp finely grated lemon zest

For the filling:
6 eggs
300g golden caster sugar
200ml fresh lemon juice, about 4 lemons
45g cornflour, sieved
2 tbsp finely grated lemon zest
130g blue honeysuckle berries
Icing sugar for dusting

Preheat the oven to 180°C/Gas 4. Lightly butter the sides of a non-stick brownie tin, approximately 20cm x 20cm x 4cm.

To make the base, pulse together the flour, icing sugar and salt in a food processor, or sieve them together into a bowl. Add the butter and lemon zest and pulse or work with your fingertips until it resembles coarse, sticky crumbs. Press it into the bottom of the brownie tin and bake until lightly golden, about 25–30 minutes. Cool for 5–10 minutes in the tin (you want it cooled slightly but still warm). Leave the oven on.

To make the filling, beat together the eggs, sugar, lemon juice, cornflour and lemon zest until smooth and well blended. Scatter the blue honeysuckle berries over the shortbread base then pour over the lemon topping. Bake for about 30–35 minutes, until set. Cool completely in the tin then cut into squares. Dust with icing sugar just before serving.

CHILEAN GUAVA

The smell of this delicious fruit gets you keen first, filling your nose with clouds of fragrant strawberry as you pass, tempting you to pick them before they're ready – but let them ripen into mid-autumn, perhaps a little later, and you'll get Chilean guava at its unbelievable best.

Don't expect a cricket ball-sized tropical guava from this rather lovely shrub – you'll get handfuls of cranberry-sized, deep red berries instead. And you won't be disappointed – the flavour lives up to the promise of its scent: kiwi, strawberry and something a little spicier, slightly sherbety, almost like bubblegum. It's entirely unique and very addictive.

Chilean guava (*Myrtus ugni*) grows as a small evergreen shrub, a metre across and, unpruned, can reach a similar height. As with its cousin Myrtle, the leaves are small, waxy and deep green with occasional seasonal flushes of red-purple.

With sun on your side, you'll have pale pink and white bell-shaped flowers hanging in profusion from late spring. Slowly through the summer the flowers turn to fruit that ripen into dark berries in autumn and into winter.

As its name suggests, Chilean guava is native to Chile and neighbouring countries. In South America it is found wild in mountainous, temperate forest clearings, is cultivated commercially, as well as being grown ornamentally and even as an edible hedge in urban areas. I don't know about you, but it sounds infinitely preferable to privet to me.

Chilean guava is not widely grown in Europe. Queen Victoria tried her best to promote it in the 19th century – she had her favourite fruit sent by train to London from the mild climate of Cornwall where it was grown for her table. I can understand why she thought it was worth the trouble – it really is fabulous eaten either raw or cooked.

Chilean guava is, however, beginning to find new homes away from its natural habitat. In Australia and New Zealand it is grown and sold as Tazziberry and is becoming popular as a speciality fruit.

VARIETIES
Chilean guava is almost always sold as a generic variety – although there is a variegated form, 'Flambeau', which is equally delicious and slightly hardier than the unvariegated type.

GROWING
Depending on your location, Chilean guava can be a bit of a gamble. It is hardy down to -10°C or thereabouts and will need a sunny, sheltered spot to induce the plant to fruit but the most trouble it'll give you is in digging a small hole in which to plant it. It really is low-maintenance.

To stack the odds in your favour, plant your Chilean Guava in a moist, well drained soil in full sun, sheltered from cold drying winds. It will tolerate a little drought once established, but any water you can give it in dry periods will benefit it. It also grows very happily in pots.

Chilean guava is self-fertile so can be grown individually, or planted in number to form a low hedge. No pruning is needed, although it is as happy to be shaped as it is left untamed.

Late frost may knock new growth back a little, but the plant will usually recover very well. If you live in a colder region, I'd be tempted to keep your plants undercover, at least through the colder months.

Chilean guava can be grown from seed, but as with most slow-growing evergreens it'll be a long time until you get to enjoy their fruit, so I'd suggest starting off with plants. If you know anyone with a plant or you want to expand numbers of your own, they do grow very easily from cuttings or by layering (see p.67).

As their scent is intoxicating it's worth finding a home for your Chilean guava somewhere that you spend plenty of time – by the backdoor or a seat in the garden, perhaps.

HARVESTING
Chilean guavas start to fruit at quite a small size, just a few berries at first, but in profusion as they develop. The berries are a real late season treat – ripening slowly, usually early in winter. As the deepening of colour is slightly ahead of the development of full flavour inside the berries, the trick is in leaving them attached just that little longer than you feel comfortable with. Try a few before you pick the rest to be sure they are ready.

EATING

Chilean guava berries are, like mulberries, the fruit equivalent of fresh peas – it's hard to get beyond just popping them in as sweets, and for the first year or 2 when the harvest is modest there's simply nothing better to eat fresh in the garden in winter.

As the bushes grow and the harvest increases, so do the uses to which you can put your expanding harvest. Chilean guava make a fabulous alternative to cranberries and blueberries, bringing their own perfume and flavour to any recipe that uses

them. And do try the Autumn Olive Gin recipe (see p.72) with Chilean guava – it's sweeter but equally wonderful.

The berries are also particularly fine in preserves. Try making a delicious and colourful jam, as well as the jelly that was Queen Victoria's favourite, but my favourite way of eating them is by making murta con membrillo, a very popular Chilean pudding made by simmering together quince and the little berries. To make your own, begin by pouring about 1.4 litres of water into a pan with 150g caster sugar,

75g clear honey and 3tbsp lemon juice. Bring to a simmer as you prepare the fruit. Quarter, peel and core about 4 quinces, tipping them into the water as each one is ready to stop them from browning. Simmer for at least an hour until the quince start to feel tender when pierced with a knife (this may take up to 2 hours, depending on the quince). Add a couple of handfuls of Chilean guava and simmer for a further 20 minutes. Try it with Greek yoghurt or spooned over ice cream or a slab of Madeira cake.

CHILEAN GUAVA MUFFINS

CHILEAN GUAVA MUFFINS

This is an excellent, basic muffin recipe which you can adapt as you like. The muffins are great made with edible honeysuckle, mignonette strawberries or wineberries instead of Chilean guava, and are also good with a small handful of chopped pecans thrown into the mix too. If you don't have any buttermilk, you can get the same effect by adding a teaspoon of lemon juice or cider vinegar to 100ml whole milk about 15 minutes before you whisk it together with the rest of the ingredients.

MAKES 12 MUFFINS
250g plain flour
2 tsp baking powder
Good pinch of salt
½ tsp bicarbonate of soda
115g unsalted butter, melted
 and cooled
115g golden caster sugar
2 eggs, lightly beaten
100ml buttermilk (shake the carton before
 measuring)
Grated zest and juice of 1 lemon
130g Chilean guava

Preheat the oven to 190°C/Gas 5.
 Line a 12-hole muffin tin with paper cases.
 Sieve the flour, baking powder, salt and bicarbonate of soda together into a bowl.
 In a separate bowl, whisk together the melted butter, sugar, eggs, buttermilk, lemon zest and juice. Lightly fold the flour mixture into the wet ingredients with a spatula, then fold in the Chilean guava; be careful not to overmix. Divide the mixture between the cases and bake for 16–18 minutes, until a toothpick inserted into the middle of the muffins comes out clean. Cool on a wire rack.

FUCHSIA

I have never been a great fan of fuchsias to look at. They remind me of the gardens of the retirement homes I walked past on my way to school and I loathe their gaudy red/purple flowers. It took me a long time to allow the possibility of growing one, it really did, but I kept finding the odd reference to them being delicious if you could lay your hands on the right varieties. So buy one I did.

Fuchsia magellanica is the one that's best to eat. They come as named varieties, some better than others, but most are easy to grow, producing the flowers so many seem to love, and even though cold weather batters down the top growth, they bounce back happily in spring. The single image that makes me think more fondly of them is that the flowers are so coloured to attract hummingbirds in their native South America to carry out pollination.

Get up close to the flowers and I have to admit that, with their four long, slender sepals and four shorter petals, they are quite a creation, but as soon as I step back and see them scattered over the plant I want to walk away and come back only when they've turned to fruit. And yet, once this has happened, I find I can't tear myself away from the plants. For me, this is one of the greatest of garden transformations, the way that these terrible flowers somehow magic themselves into such lusciously different fruit. Mini-batons, up to 6cm long, develop from the flowers, typically turning from green though reds to a deep purple. They may not be huge, but their flavour is so very special, with suggestions of kiwi, plum and sweet grapes, as well as a gentle edge of pepper that comes along near the end. It's similar to Szechuan pepper in the way that the flavours unravel almost one at a time.

As with many fruit, letting fuchsias get to full ripeness can be tricky – keep taste-testing every day or two. When you finally get one at the top of its game, every morning staring at this plant's visual awfulness will soften in the memory. And every moment looking at it next year will be a little less of a torture, as each flower that hangs there offending will be another fruit swinging the balance back a few short weeks later.

VARIETIES

Fuchsia flowers vary in colour with variety – many have the classic bright red sepals and the purple petals, colours that attract hummingbirds to pollinate them, though some are white, purple, orange or blue. Don't be led too much by colour though – flavour is very much the preserve of a few of the best named varieties.

'Globosa' is low-growing, to around 1m at most, flowers heavily and the fruit it produces are outstanding. Like most, the plant itself is hardy but the top growth dies back in cold below -10°C or so. 'Gracilis' is similarly delicious, but grows taller (up to 2m).

'Riccartonii' and 'Vielebacheis' are the choices for colder areas as their top growth is hardy down to -15°C, the fruit is abundant and as good as any, although be aware that 'Riccartonii' can reach 3m in the right situation.

GROWING

For me, the hardest part of growing fuchsias is looking at them. At least they don't demand much from you as they grow. Native to forest clearings and woodland edges, they prefer a well drained soil in sheltered, partial shade. They'll tolerate fairly heavy soils as long as they're not waterlogged, and are perfectly content in maritime conditions so they make a good choice if you live by the coast.

The top growth and new growth in spring is frost-tender so don't be alarmed at some dieback, but do avoid planting in frost pockets to protect the spring growth from too much damage.

New growth in late spring is usually vigorous, followed by flowers in mid-summer. In the absence of hummingbirds, bees are their likeliest pollinator. The resulting fruit can't come soon enough as far as I'm concerned – for most varieties this is in late summer.

My fuchsias have never suffered trouble from pests or diseases of any kind.

You can grow fuchsias from seed, in pots in spring, moving them to larger pots when they are easy to handle. Keep them undercover in a greenhouse or on a windowsill for their first year before planting out after the last frosts. They also do well grown from cuttings if you know someone with a plant or want to expand your numbers. As with seedlings, give them their first year undercover.

HARVESTING

The sausage-shaped fruit are usually ready towards the end of summer – try one or two every day or two at this time in order to get them at their best.

EATING

Fuchsia batons can vary a little in taste with variety, but most have plum, kiwi, grape and even blackcurrant undertones in there somewhere, along with a characteristic soft hint of pepper. They are perfect when made into sorbets, ice creams, or when used in other desserts where their intensity and unique flavour can shine without any fear of being lost.

Candied fuchsia flowers can add a very pretty finishing touch to a variety of cakes and puddings. To prepare, cut a handful of fuchsia blossoms, keeping the stalks as long as you can. Rinse them gently before drying carefully on kitchen paper. Beat an egg white in a small bowl until foamy and use a small paintbrush to paint the flower thoroughly with the egg white. (Don't be tempted to cut corners and dip the flower into the egg white as you will get it too wet). Sprinkle the flower with caster sugar, using a teaspoon to scatter it into every crevice. Give it a shake to get rid of any excess. Place on a sheet of baking parchment to dry and harden, then snip off the stem. The candied flowers will keep for weeks if stored in an airtight jar.

FUCHSIA FRUIT LEATHER

Use this recipe as a template for all kinds of fruit leathers – it works really well with strawberries, apricots and nectarines too. All it entails is making a thick, gloopy purée of fruit and sugar and then drying it out very slowly in the oven until you have a pliable leather as clear and vivid as a stained glass window.

MAKES 2 SHEETS
A little groundnut oil for greasing the tins
500g fuchsia berries
500g cooking apples, peeled, cored and
    chopped
Juice of 1 lemon
130g honey

FUCHSIA FRUIT LEATHER

Preheat the oven to 70°C/Gas ¼.
Line 2 baking sheets of about 24cm x 30cm with foil or several layers of clingfilm and lightly oil with groundnut oil.

Put the fuchsia berries, apples and lemon juice into a pan. Cook gently, partially covered at first, until soft and pulpy, about 20 minutes. Rub through a sieve or mouli into a bowl. You should have about 700g smooth fruit purée. Add the honey and mix well.

Divide between your baking sheets, shaking the tins and smoothing with a spatula so that the purée reaches right up to the edges. Place in the oven and cook for 6–10 hours. Once cooked, your fruit leather should be a little tacky but no longer sticky and should peel easily off the cling film or foil. Leave to cool completely, then roll up the leather in greaseproof paper or cling film and store in an airtight container in a cool place. Use within two months. Alternatively, you can freeze it, well sealed, for up to a year.

GOJIBERRIES

Gojiberries sound too good to be true. As with most 'superfoods', they blazed onto the shelves and into the papers with a flurry and a fluster about their life-enhancing loveliness. I don't usually pay too much attention to such talk – if you look long and hard you'll find most foods at some time in their culinary history have been known either as a superfood or as an aphrodisiac – with gojiberries, though, there may be a little more to the claims.

For a start, unlike so many other of these overnight superfood sensations, gojiberries have been hard at work for centuries. In their native China, gojiberries are known as red diamonds, sacred berries celebrated for their life-giving properties. The first emperor supposedly ate them daily to keep himself healthy and the legendary Li Qing Yuen apparently lived to be over 250 years old, outliving countless wives and children, largely thanks to his daily diet of gojiberries and ginseng.

The bark and the berries from the bush have long been valued in Chinese medicine as much as cuisine, where their ability to boost the immune system, improve circulation, sharpen eyesight, brighten the complexion, counter the effects of aging, care for the liver and raise the sperm count have contributed to its super-status in the region. Gojiberries are also known as the 'happy berry' on account of their supposedly calming qualities. There's even a two week festival in China celebrating all things gojiberry, and I'm a sucker for a food festival.

Whether gojis contain everything you need to become a happy, mellow double-centurion is debatable, but what we do know for sure is that these small (1–2cm) berries are impressive natural multivitamin pills, containing vitamins B1, B2 and B6, polysaccharides, amino acids, fatty acids (required for healthy brain and nervous system functioning), endless essential minerals and the second highest vitamin C levels of any food (Camu-Camu berries being top of the list, pub-quiz fans). They also have higher levels of antioxidants than any other food.

Antioxidants are thought to fight the effects of aging and a range of cancers and others diseases so perhaps there's something to the legend of Li Qing Yuen.

Gojiberries have a slightly unusual growing habit. They're a deciduous woody perennial plant that grows to 2 or 3m tall, but they rarely grow particularly upright. They lollop, as if they haven't the oomph to hold themselves up straight. It's part of their charm, but you can encourage a little extra vigour by pruning them fairly harshly in winter or growing them as a lazy hedge where they take some support from each other. The foliage is rather lovely, silvery-green, slightly floppy, like a less regal olive.

You may feel, on first growing this remarkable plant, that you've seen gojiberry flowers somewhere before. Gojiberries belong to the Solanaceae family along with tomatoes, aubergines and potatoes and their small purple or white flowers very much replicate the latter through early and mid-summer. The berries follow, appearing anywhere from mid-summer through well into autumn, although this can extend both ways depending on local conditions.

The orange-red berries, looking like modest, slightly old-fashioned earrings, are gently ovate and turn redder as they ripen fully. Each arm of the bush carries dozens, hanging beneath the arc of its lazy bend. Their flavour can be a little peculiar. Get them too early and they'll be sharp yet one dimensional, developing a mild but fuller flavour as they ripen. I've never known ripe berries to be anything other than delicious, but the flavour itself seems to vary

EATING

Sweet, tart and tangy, gojiberries can be used in sweet and savoury dishes. Gojiberries are usually sold dried rather than fresh, and growing your own allows you to have either in your kitchen. They're delicious either way, but differently so. Dried they are much nearer the flavour and texture of raisins than when fresh.

Add them fresh to fruit salads, cobblers, crumbles and pies or use dried ones instead of raisins in biscuits or as an unusual addition to mincemeat.

Gojiberries are also great in chutneys and jellies, make a delectable sauce to accompany duck and a handful of them will enliven any curry, pilaff or tagine.

If you have a juicer, gojiberries make a reviving breakfast juice, if not, whizz them up into a great smoothie with blueberries, orange juice and a couple of tablespoons of Greek yoghurt.

In China, the young shoots are also cooked as a vegetable, so you might like to add them to your stir fries too – I can't personally vouch for their

loveliness or otherwise, however, as I've yet to try them. Goji leaves are also edible but I've not tried these either – they look reasonably unappetising and I've not wanted to impact on the amount of fruit I get.

GOJI GRANOLA
What follows here is more of a blueprint than a recipe, and can be happily played about with. Feel free to substitute walnuts for pecans, dried mango for apple slices, or figs for apricots – use what you have and what you love.

▶

with soil, sun and (who knows) someone upstairs having a little random fun at gardeners' expense. Most often they resemble cranberries, sometimes with cherry to varying degrees, and frequently with a gentle liquorice edge to them. You'll have to grow one or two plants to see exactly how yours turn out – not all mine taste the same even though they grow within feet of each other.

The only way to tell if they're ready is to let them deepen their red colour and try a few. If you like them, pick the rest that are the same colour. Inside are many tiny, largely unnoticeable, seeds that you can munch happily through.

Gojiberries' extensive root systems and tolerance of maritime exposure makes them ideal for holding sandy soils against erosion or as productive hedges in coastal areas. They were introduced to Britain

around 300 years ago by the Duke of Argyll (they are still known as the Duke of Argyll's tea tree in some areas) but failed to make much impression on the fruit culture of the time. You can still find them growing wild in hedges here and there, mostly close to the Suffolk coast. (Obviously the Duke didn't eat enough of them himself, or he'd be here to see them still growing.)

VARIETIES
Gojiberries are sold as wolfberries in some countries, but I'm not aware of them being sold as named varieties – just the generic 'gojiberry'.

GROWING
Gojiberry bushes are as easy and unfussy as soft fruit gets. They'll tolerate anything but waterlogged soils, they fruit reasonably in a little shade and are happy with maritime exposure but give them a fertile, well drained soil with a reasonable amount of sun and rain and they'll thrive.

You can grow gojiberries from seed but you'll need an optimist's heart. They germinate encouragingly but die given the slightest opportunity, usually when only a few centimetres tall. They hate being transplanted so what seedlings do survive will be severely depleted in number. They need to be in the warm for their first year, so grow them undercover in individual pots, taking your favoured precaution

◄

MAKES ABOUT 1KG
360g jumbo oats
90g flaked almonds
150g pecans, coarsely chopped
200ml maple syrup or an equal mixture of
   maple syrup and clear honey
50ml rapeseed or groundnut oil
1 tsp flaky sea salt
½ tsp cinnamon
¼ tsp freshly grated nutmeg
100g dried gojiberries
100g dried apricots, roughly chopped
60g dried apple slices, roughly chopped

Preheat the oven to 170°C/Gas 3. In a large bowl, stir together the oats, flaked almonds and pecans. In a small pan, warm the maple syrup and oil and whisk with the salt, cinnamon and nutmeg until smooth. Pour over the oat mixture and stir until everything is coated. Line a large baking tray, about 45cm x 30cm, with baking parchment and

tip the oat mixture onto it, spreading it out evenly. Bake, stirring occasionally, until it is a nice, even golden brown, about 20 minutes. Cool and stir in the gojiberries, apricots and apple slices. Sealed in an airtight jar, this will keep for up to a month.

GOJI GRANOLA BARS
Once you've made your granola, you can transform it into these granola bars for days when you need to breakfast on the go(ji).

MAKES 12
100g unsalted butter, plus more for greasing
50ml rapeseed oil
50g light Muscovado sugar
130g clear honey
½ tsp vanilla extract
220g porridge oats
130g Goji Granola (see left)
Finely grated zest of 1 small orange
¼ tsp flaky sea salt

Preheat the oven to 180°C/Gas 4. Butter a 22cm x 22cm brownie tin.

In a small pan over a low heat, warm the butter, oil, sugar and honey until blended then boil for 3 minutes without stirring. Remove from the heat and place the pan in a sink filled with about 10cm of cold water to cool for 5 minutes; stir in the vanilla extract.

Mix the oats and granola together with the zest and salt in a bowl. Make a well in the centre and pour in the hot liquid. Use a spatula and then your hands to mix together the ingredients until lightly combined, but well coated. Tip it into the brownie tin and gently pat down the mixture. Bake for 20 minutes until golden.

Leave to cool slightly in the tin for 10–15 minutes, then run a metal spatula around the outside of the tin and cut into slabs. Use a spatula to remove your granola bars carefully from the tin, and leave to cool completely on a wire rack.

for slugs and snails (see p.176). After three months or so they should start growing more quickly and healthily. Plant the survivors out in early summer, snipping out the tips if you want bushier growth.

You are likely to have to wait for another year for fruit, which combined with the low hit-rate of the seeds makes young plants a very attractive option. These are inexpensive and should pay you back by giving you a crop in the first summer after planting. Plant your young gojiberry into the ground or a large pot as soon as it arrives and water well. If you are planting a number of gojiberries, leave a metre between plants, or half as much if you intend to grow them as a hedge.

Once the plants are a year old they are remarkably resilient adaptable bushes, -15°C is easily tolerated, as are periods of drought and high temperatures.

Pruning is best carried out towards the end of winter. They can take quite a snipping although whether you need to prune very much depends on how you fancy growing them. Let them roam about and they'll grow to 3m or more, or prune them back to form a denser bush.

Gojiberry plants can produce suckers (shoots from the base of the plant) which are its way of expanding its territory. If this is a nuisance to you just separate them off from the main plant and replant them elsewhere or pot them up for friends.

Gojiberry plants are successional by nature – flowering occurs through late spring, summer and into autumn with fruit ready a few months after the flowers appear. You'll find flowers, unripe and ripe fruit developing right until the frosts shut the plant down for the cold months.

HARVESTING
Gojiberries can be delightfully productive. Two years from sowing, or later that year if you planted pot plants, you'll start harvesting gojiberries and by year three you should be happily pulling a kilo or so of fruit from each plant.

The fruit aren't ready all at once – rather they ripen in random batches – so you usually get a slow, steady harvest through summer into autumn.

A little care is needed when picking gojiberries. If you pick them before they are fully ripe they'll separate easily from the bush but may be a little shy of perfect sweetness and fullness of flavour. Pick them fully ripe and you may find they react to the slightest pressure by turning black as they oxidise. It doesn't always happen for some peculiar reason, but it's worth shaking the branch a little as the berries may well drop easily for you to gather undamaged.

GOJI GRANOLA BARS

RHUBARB

There is a small patch of English countryside, a few square miles between Wakefield, Morley and Rothwell, which has a reputation for growing the finest rhubarb in the world. The process of growing that was developed here in what has become known as the 'Rhubarb Triangle' can be mimicked on a domestic scale to produce the sweetest, most succulent early stalks.

This spot in Yorkshire is made for rhubarb: it sits in a frost pocket in the shadow of the Pennine hills which provides the essential autumn and winter cold; the soils and rainfall are ideal; the waste wool from the local wool industry provides the nitrogen-rich fertiliser; and the ashes and soot from nearby industries make a perfect conditioner for the soil. A rhubarb industry has been established here since the 19th century, and counted more than 200 commercial producers at its peak.

The crop that is produced here was once so popular that special 'Rhubarb Trains' used to take the precious harvest to London's Covent Garden Market,

from where it was distributed. The race to produce the season's first stalks (and thereby get the highest prices) was keenly contested and saw purpose-built sheds spring up in which rhubarb was grown in such a way as to encourage very early growth.

The method for growing this early or 'forced' rhubarb is simple, if labour intensive. Rhubarb plants are grown outside for two years to allow a strong crown to develop. In subsequent winters the plants are exposed to the frost which induces hibernation and encourages the starches stored in the crown to convert to glucose. The plants are then lifted and taken by hand into the forcing sheds, which are kept warm and dark – the heat triggers the plants hormones into action, and the darkness encourages them to feed on the glucose in their roots. Growth is so rapid that you can hear the stalks creak and pop as they develop over the coming weeks.

Forced stalks are a distinctive, vibrant pale pink with curled mustard-yellow leaves that makes them instantly recognisable from those grown outside, but it is the taste and texture that counts: it is so much sweeter and more tender than outdoor rhubarb.

The harvest is a steady one and the conditions have to be preserved throughout, so the stalks are harvested by candlelight right up to the start of spring, when outdoor rhubarb becomes available. The process has remained pretty much unchanged in the intervening decades.

To produce something so distinctively special and tightly seasonal as forced rhubarb requires expertise built up over generations, along with infrastructure and investment to foster the best growing conditions. The vast majority of income is secured within a very short window of the year. It is a precarious existence at the best of times, and increasingly so as climate change moves the temperatures at the base of the Triangle close to the threshold where the specific period of winter cold that rhubarb needs (its chilling hours requirement) is hard to achieve. If the threshold is crossed the consequences are about more than just food, they are about families, communities and cultures growing up, around and within the business of producing an artisan product every bit as worthy of our celebration as champagne or Parma ham. I buy it whenever I

can – supporting a threatened speciality and those that produce it – but I also grow some of my own and I hope you will too

VARIETIES
There are many varieties of rhubarb available, but few to rival 'Timperley Early', 'Victoria' and 'Glaskins Perpetual' for flavour and reliability.

'Timperley Early' lives up to its name, producing before most other varieties, but it does have a fairly high chilling requirement and so is particularly suited to colder areas.

GROWING
You can mimic the sheds of the Rhubarb Triangle and hurry the natural growing process along with a bucket, large pot or a terracotta rhubarb forcer. Placed over the crown in late winter, it excludes the light and raises the temperature enough to stimulate early growth. Fresh manure heaped around the bucket or forcer speeds this up further with its added warmth as it ferments. Paler, sweeter growth results, a good month or so ahead of your unforced rhubarb, and if you get this to the kitchen as fast as you can you'll be in for the finest rhubarb there is. There is a price for this rarely buyable treat though – you can't pick more from that plant until the following year. After harvesting, remove the pot.

If you're one of those unfortunates with a reputation for plants dying on you, or happen to be a less-than-confident beginner, this is the plant for you. You can be a neglectful, even abusive, carer of rhubarb. It really is quite hard to kill off. I kept a few in pots for

EATING

Rhubarb can be either sweet and mild with a little sharpness if grown by forcing or the more familiar sour, deliciously biting sticks widely available throughout summer. Both are fabulous and take differently to the same treatments. Try either in the kulfi on the following page or roasted and you'll see what I mean.

Roasting rhubarb is simple but if you get the details right it is elevated into a truly fine pud. Preheat the oven to

200°C/Gas 6. Trim the ends off 500g rhubarb and cut into 5cm pieces. Put the rhubarb in a roasting tin, toss with 65g caster sugar and the finely grated zest of a small orange. Arrange in a single layer, trickle over the juice from the orange, cover with foil and roast for 15 minutes. Remove the foil, give everything a good stir and return to the oven for a further 5–10 minutes until tender and the juices are syrupy. Serve with Greek yoghurt for breakfast, ice

cream or pancakes for pudding, or use it puréed as the base for sorbets, ice creams or granitas.

And don't pass up the chance for making rhubarb sauce to go with oily fish, goose, duck and pork – its sharpness makes it a perfect companion. Just chop the rhubarb into 3cm sections and slowly cook 500g of rhubarb with half its weight of caster sugar and half a bottle of white wine until softened.

years, always meaning to plant them out but getting sidetracked by new arrivals. These poor plants were munched and pooed on by rabbits and tipped out of their pots by the little devils, but they survived. I finally felt guilty enough to plant them and have had delicious stalks ever since.

Tough though they are, give rhubarb a little love and it will respond with interest. Rhubarb will tolerate most soils, a little shade and some exposure to wind but, give it full sun, a neutral soil and a little shelter from the wintery winds, and you'll get larger, healthier yields.

You can grow rhubarb from seed or small plants. Rhubarb plants are normally sold as year-old 'crowns' that have been divided from their parent plant – ensuring their variety will be retained. While growing from seed is considerably cheaper, it will be a year longer to that first harvest and plants cannot be guaranteed to come true to variety when grown from seed – in effect you are spinning a coin now that will land in three years' time.

The best time to plant rhubarb is as autumn turns into winter. Prepare your bed a few weeks before planting, digging to 50cm or so, incorporating organic matter (such as your own compost) and removing all weeds. Bear in mind that rhubarb will usually grow happily for ten years or so, therefore any time spent preparing now will pay off for quite some time.

Dig a hole a little wider than the plant, and to a depth that allows the top of the plant to be 2–3cm below the soil surface. Backfill around the plant, easing soil into and around the roots to ensure no air pockets. Water in thoroughly.

If you know someone with rhubarb plants that are more than five years old or if you want to make more plants of your own, you can divide mature crowns into new plants. As well as giving you new plants, it is also a great way of ensuring that the plants retain vigour. This is best undertaken in the cold of winter when the foliage has died away, so mark your plants with a cane by late summer so that you can locate them easily when the time comes to divide them.

Use a large fork to lift and lever at what may be a large crown until it is free from the soil – some root damage is almost inevitable but rarely critical. Carefully line up a spade down the top of the crown – you are aiming to make two or three incisions that will create fairly equal thirds, each with at least one light-coloured bud on it (most crowns will have many even if they aren't obvious to the eye). Use your foot to exert pressure – careful brutality is the order of the day. Plant these new crowns as above.

Ongoing care is minimal. Mulching each year with compost or well rotted manure around (but not on top of) the plant will really pay dividends with

RHUBARB GRANITA

SERVES 8

800g rhubarb, trimmed and cut into 5cm pieces
250g caster sugar
Juice and zest of 1 small orange
1 vanilla pod, split lengthways
2 tbsp white rum

Put the rhubarb pieces into a pan with the sugar, orange juice and zest and the split vanilla pod. Add water to just below the level of the rhubarb. Warm over a low heat, stirring from time to time, until the sugar dissolves. Simmer gently until the rhubarb is very soft and falling apart. Remove the vanilla pod, scrape out the seeds with a small, sharp knife and mix them back in with the rhubarb.

Blitz the mixture in a food processor until very smooth, or press through a fine-meshed plastic sieve. Stir in the rum. Pour into a plastic container or metal tray, cover and freeze for at least 6 hours, or overnight.

About 15 minutes before you want to serve the granita, put it in the fridge to soften up a little. Scrape up the granita with a fork into a mass of pretty, pink crystals and serve in glasses.

RHUBARB KULFI

Kulfi, the sweet treat that ends many an Indian meal, is simplicity itself to make, and a great alternative to ice cream if you don't have an ice cream maker as it doesn't require any churning. The cardamom and rhubarb take the edge off its intense sweetness and give it an extra depth of flavour.

SERVES 6

250ml evaporated milk
250ml condensed milk
250ml double cream
4 cardamom pods, crushed slightly
1.5cm piece of fresh ginger, peeled and finely sliced
150g roasted rhubarb (see p.89), strained

Pour the evaporated milk, condensed milk and cream into a pan and whisk together until well combined; add the cardamom pods and ginger. Bring to a bare simmer over a low heat and stir for 5 minutes. Remove from the heat and leave to cool and infuse for at least 2 hours. Strain the mixture into a bowl; discard the ginger and cardamom.

Blitz the rhubarb in a food processor or with a stick blender, or pass it through a fine-meshed plastic sieve, to make a very fine pulp. Whisk the rhubarb into the infused cream until very well combined and ladle into dariole moulds or ramekin dishes. Freeze for at least 4 hours or overnight.

To make the kulfi easier to unmould, briefly dip each mould into a bowl of very hot water before turning out into a bowl.

rhubarb, helping to retain water, suppress weeds as well as gently feed the plant as it grows. Cut off any flowerheads which may appear in early spring – these seriously deplete energy away from the heart of the plant and may affect your harvests for a few years if left in place.

Rhubarb suffers very few troubles – crown rot (where the top of the plant rots) is the only possibility, but there is no remedy: if it happens, dig the plant up and incinerate it.

You can grow rhubarb in a large pot, but it needs a good nutrient bank to thrive, so you'll need to keep refreshing the compost and watering with liquid feed (see p.183) to keep the plant happy.

HARVESTING

Rhubarb requires a little patience. Think of your plant as an edible savings account: a little investment in the plant now will pay off for years to come. Do not pull any stems during the first year (assuming you've grown from crowns) as the plant will suffer.

Let it develop and establish a healthy root system. In year two pull only a few stems, at most two per plant at any one visit, always leaving a minimum of six good stems.

In year three and beyond you can make repeat visits, taking up to four of the largest stems with opened leaves at a time, always leaving at least four behind.

It's better to pull than cut the stalks – grab a stem low, pulling and twisting at the same time. Tear the leaves off and compost them: they are poisonous.

The main harvest period is from mid-spring to the height of the summer, though forcing your rhubarb will enable you to speed things up a little as well as giving you sweeter, succulent stalks that are rarely available in the shops (and expensive when they are).

RHUBARB KULFI

JAPANESE WINEBERRY

I can't quite remember how I came by my Japanese wineberry. I get a little confused by berries I haven't eaten before – there are so many of them and I tend not to remember which is which until I know their taste. I think a neighbour gave me a Juneberry but maybe it was the wineberry. Regardless, I'm either grateful to her or pleased with the moment of inquisitiveness that got me ordering one.

In truth, some of the lesser-known berries are actually just mediocre crosses thrown onto the market to clean up for a year or two until everyone realises that good old raspberries are so much better. Japanese wineberries are a case apart. A scrambling shrub, it produces large trusses of unbelievably sweet, deep-crimson berries, with an unusual grape-raspberry flavour. Once eaten the berries very much stick in the mind, but by the time mine fruited I'd forgotten whether it was me or someone else I should be thanking.

As with its close relation the raspberry, wineberries pretty much grow themselves. Their reddish canes can be allowed to ramble informally as a lazy, non-spiky blackberry might with multiple stems rising 2m or so from the base, or (if order is your thing) trained against a fence or espalier. They'll also ramble happily through trees and shrubs if you give them the opportunity. They'll fruit equally well either way, so grow them as you like.

Japanese wineberry is native to northern China, Korea and Japan and not related to, or to be confused with, the tree that goes by the same name in New Zealand. The former was introduced to Europe and North America as an ornamental but mostly for breeding hybrids with raspberries, but it is not, as many believe, a cross itself.

It's about as beautiful as a berry plant gets – the small, pale pink flowers shower the plant in early summer, the fruit are a treat to see ripen almost overnight

from radioactive orange to juicy crimson, while the canes have an arching lollop about them that's beautifully revealed in leafless winter when the sun catches their soft, fuzzy, plum-red bristles.

Although the fruits resemble deep-coloured raspberries, the gentle winey flavour sets them apart. They have one other bonus over most berries: the berries remain protected from birds, maggots and disease by a papery calyx which parts its sepals only when the fruit is ready to eat in mid summer. The timing is perfect: bridging the gap between summer and autumn raspberries, so there's no need to stop eating summer pudding.

VARIETIES
Japanese wineberries are almost always sold as a generic rather than a named variety.

GROWING
Growing Japanese wineberries couldn't be easier. They are self-fertile so one plant is fine. Their natural preference is for woodland shade and moist, reasonably drained soil to grow in, so they are as at home in a shady spot as a sunny one. They are resilient, robust plants but if you choose a sheltered spot in a good soil, they'll fruit prolifically.

Do be aware that Japanese wineberries are very capable of invading nearby space if given too much encouragement. They grow rapidly and, like blackberries, can become invasive as they have in some areas of North America.

If you know someone with a plant or you want to have more than one yourself, take advantage of their natural tendency to colonise new territory. Japanese wineberries root so readily that all you need do is encourage the tip of a cane into the ground to be sure of it rooting. Once established, you can snip free this newly rooted part to form a separate plant.

If you're looking for a tidier method, you can take hardwood cuttings during the dormant season between leaf fall and budburst (they work best at either end of this period). Select healthy shoots that have grown that year and snip off the soft growth towards the tip. Aim for 20–30cm long sections, cut just above a bud at the top (a sloping cut allows water to run off and reminds you which way is 'up') and cut straight at the base just below a bud.

Dip the base in hormone-rooting powder – this encourages root formation and helps to protect against rotting – and gently ease them into deep pots filled with a 50/50 mix of compost and coarse grit. Keep the pots in a greenhouse or on a windowsill for a little protection and don't allow them to dry out.

Don't expect overnight miracles: although this is a pretty reliable method of producing new plants, the cuttings take time to harden over the cuts and develop roots at the base. Let them grow on through the following year before potting on until they reach the required size. This method works well for many similar fruit, deciduous shrubs and climbers.

While you can grow plants from seed, it's not widely available. It pays therefore to start with a plant – that way you get them when they're past the vulnerable stage when pests nibble away their new growth, and you'll also be that much nearer the delicious fruit.

Japanese wineberry is a perennial plant that produces canes that grow one year and fruit the next. A new stem can easily grow over 2m in its first year, but it won't branch or produce flowers. The following year, the stem doesn't grow any taller but throws out side shoots with small leaves. Flowers follow in late spring or early summer on the ends of the side shoots, which in turn form the fruits. Although called 'wineberry', the botanists tell us that this fruit is not really a berry, rather a fruit made up of numerous drupelets, but you know it's a berry and I know it's a berry.

You can prune out the canes that have fruited (the old crusty calyxes should give it away) but leave pruning until late winter so you can enjoy the illuminated fuzzy canes in the cold season sunshine.

Wineberries should be susceptible to the same diseases as those that trouble its close relatives, but in practice they seems largely immune. The plants are hardy down to -18°C or so, and even though they may be damaged by lower temperatures they usually bounce back well.

HARVESTING
Wineberry fruit ripen gradually across the plant, so you get a couple of weeks of gentle picking in the middle of summer. The canes have prickles like a raspberry, but not aggressive thorns like a blackberry, so picking is easy. You'll also find you have little competition (other than your family) for the fruit, as birds and insects find it difficult to get at the fruits through the calyxes.

EATING

Japanese wineberries will take to just about any of your favourite berry recipes. The aromatic fruits are delicious for classic desserts such as trifle, summer pud and Eton mess, are equally fine made into jams or jellies and make a great substitute for the fuchsia batons in the Fuchsia Fruit Leather (see p.82).

WINEBERRY VINEGAR
Wineberries make a seductively sweet and tangy vinegar, perfect for trickling over salads, goat's cheese, even ice cream. Ensure you gather the ripened fruit on a dry day. This recipe works very well with mulberries too.

MAKES ABOUT 900ML
1kg wineberries
600ml cider or white wine vinegar
Granulated sugar (see method for quantity)

Put the wineberries into a large bowl and crush them lightly with the back of a wooden spoon. Pour over the vinegar, cover and leave to macerate for a week, stirring from time to time. Strain through a piece of muslin suspended over a bowl (see p.35) or through a scalded jelly bag, squeezing out as much juice as possible. Measure the juice and transfer to a pan. Add 200–350g granulated sugar per 500ml juice, depending on how sweet you would like the finished result to be. Heat gently, stirring until the sugar has dissolved and then bring to the boil. Boil for 10 minutes, removing any scum that rises to the top, and pour into hot, sterilised bottles or jars and seal.

WINEBERRY TRIFLE
If you're looking for a fabulously decadent way to end a meal, then this is it.

SERVES 8
4 egg yolks
100g golden caster sugar
2 tbsp cornflour, sieved
300ml whole milk
1 vanilla pod, split lengthways
400g wineberries
3 tbsp icing sugar

WINEBERRY TRIFLE

250g mascarpone, at room temperature
250ml double cream
1 batch muffins, made as Chilean Guava Muffins (see p.80) substituting wineberries for Chilean guava in the batter or 1 small sponge cake
3 tbsp Chambord or any other berry liqueur or sweet sherry
100g white chocolate

First, make the custard. Put the egg yolks, caster sugar, cornflour and 3 tbsp of the milk into a bowl and whisk until well combined. Put the rest of the milk into a pan, scrape the seeds from the vanilla pod and stir them into the milk along with the pod. Over a low heat, bring to the boil. Discard the pod.

(Though you can wash it, dry it and reuse it, or pop it into a jar of caster sugar to make vanilla sugar.) Pour the hot milk slowly onto the egg mixture, whisking as you go, then pour the mixture into a clean pan. Cook over a medium heat, stirring constantly, for about 6 minutes until thick and smooth (it will continue to thicken as it cools so don't let it go too far). Pour into a bowl and cover the top with a circle of dampened greaseproof paper to stop a skin from forming.

Tip half of the wineberries into a bowl with 1 tbsp of icing sugar and crush lightly with the back of a wooden spoon.

In a bowl beat the mascarpone, cream and remaining icing sugar until well combined and smooth.

Take 4 or 5 of the muffins (save the rest for later, or freeze them for up to 2 months) or the sponge cake and cut into thick horizontal slices. Use them to line the base of a large glass bowl and arrange them around the sides of the bowl too. Sprinkle over the booze and leave to soak in for 10 minutes. Gently mix together the crushed and whole wineberries (reserving a small handful for decoration) and spoon over the muffins or cake. Pour over the cooled custard then spoon on the mascarpone cream. Scatter the remaining wineberries over the top. Use a vegetable peeler to make nice big curls of white chocolate and scatter them over the top too.

Chill slightly before serving.

HERBS & SPICES

Nothing illustrates the rewards of prioritising flavour over yield as well as those catalysts of the kitchen, the herbs and spices. Short on volume and long on flavour, they have the ability to transform the plainest of ingredients and will work their way into everything you cook. If you grow nothing else in this book, I urge you to try growing something from this section – you'll appreciate the difference it makes to what you eat straight away.

Most of us love parsley, rosemary, basil and thyme with very good reason. I'll never live in a garden without them. The following selection takes you sideways from those fine regulars, offering you a few deliciously different flavours to widen the palate you cook with. Do by all means grow these more usual herbs and spices – the selection here should be seen as tastes to investigate and add to those you already love rather than acting as instead-ofs. Start digging around away from the usual suspects and this group of edibles will throw up surprising new pleasures. Exploring them is quietly addictive, as I hope you'll find.

Perhaps more than any other group of foods, herbs and spices are as much about the experience as the flavour. Leaves, bark, flowers and berries can all carry intense flavour and, if you want to enjoy the smells before you pick, or even take a nibble, you have to stop. You have to rub, pinch or crush some part or other, or bend into the flower to take its scent in. If you grow Carolina allspice you'll have one heady fragrance from the flowers and another from the bark and leaves, while Szechuan pepper takes this a step further, introducing you to a whole new feeling, one on the edge of taste and touch.

As well as providing you with a feast of flavours, most herbs and spices do so with the minimum of fuss, calling on you only occasionally for a little watering or pruning, but very little else. The woody, perennial herbs such as thyme, rosemary, bay, oregano and sage are particularly low-maintenance, usually giving you pickings for years and seeming to almost thrive on neglect. Annuals, by their nature, are sown each year, and tend to be leafier and less hardy, although more productive, than their woody cousins. They usually grow quickly and can have a tendency to bolt (run to flower) which can toughen the leaves and taint the flavour. Growing leafy annual herbs in partial shade and watering them through periods of

drought will greatly reduce the likelihood of bolting, as will taking regular harvests that stop the plant becoming too tall and leggy.

Herbs and spices grow perfectly happily in pots and other containers. Many have low nutrient requirements, so as long as you keep them topped up with a yearly dressing of compost and the occasional liquid feed they should provide well. This allows you to move your plants around as you wish and enables you to bring in any that are a little tender, such as lemongrass, during the colder months. A little cold-season protection can also extend the picking time, making many of the herbs good year-round harvests.

If you're really short of space many herbs can be kept in small pots, or even in seed trays on your windowsill. Many, such as coriander, dill and basil, are also fabulous grown as microleaves (see p. 144). This is the way I grow almost all of my coriander now, as I get the best from its flavour and remove the risk of bolting.

However you choose to grow herbs and spices, do so as near as you can to the kitchen – as most are best used fresh, straight from the plant, when they're full of flavour. Once separated from the plant, leafy herbs in particular have a short lifespan, although there are ways you can preserve the flavours for use when the plant is less productive. Hanging herbs upside down in a breezy spot allows them to dry well, however the flavour can be erratic when rehydrated. I prefer to freeze leaves in water or olive oil ice cubes, which keeps the flavours truer to their fresh state.

Most recipes that include herbs and spices reflect their generosity in making other harvests taste better, they're usually the 'director', leading the main ingredients off in different ways, however this isn't always the case. In recipes such as pesto, mayonnaise and blends such as Five Spice Powder, herbs get their own starring role – they are there as the driving flavour, not just the accompaniment.

The recipes contained within this section are a mix of the two – in some the herbs and spices stand at the front and shout, in others they sit back and quietly compliment. Whichever you choose, do have confidence to play with them a little and make them your own. The Mizuna Pesto works beautifully for many other salad leaves and leafier herbs, the Five Spice Powder is as good on rice pudding as it is on roast goose, and any salad you chose to make will benefit from the lift a few small pinches of herbs brings.

CAROLINA ALLSPICE

It can be all too easy to focus on the main summer and autumn harvests and miss the various smaller pleasures in the months leading up to the main event. By planting Szechuan pepper and Carolina allspice on the path down to the vineyard here at Otter Farm I have ensured this never happens.

Now a walk to the vines is always halted by rubbing the leaves of either. Only after they were planted and I found myself stopping every day to enjoy them did I appreciate how much punctuating the day in this way enriched it. Not since I gave up smoking many years ago did I have such a ready excuse to pause. It seems to slow the days down, stopping them running away quite so rapidly.

The Carolina allspice plant is something of a perfume stand. The rusted strawberry-coloured flowers, the waxy green foliage and the bark all carry their own incredible spicy scent. Take a moment to rub your fingers across the leaves to release their camphor perfume or rub the stems to collect the cinnamon aroma – it's an invisible harvest that you can enjoy throughout the year. The mid-spring days when the flowers burst and the scent clouds the air are up there with the first asparagus poking through the soil for anticipation relieved.

The fresh perfume is a little tricky to match exactly, varying between individual bushes and with the intensity of the sun, but it can be anywhere from the clean freshness of a perfectly ripe early apple like 'Beauty of Bath' to the heavier, sweet perfume of strawberries, pineapple and some of the same spicy cinnamon of the bark. The flowers – around 5cm across – keep coming through spring and into summer and, while not obviously showy, they really are worth a closer look.

You may even find a use for their fragrance. In the south-east USA, where Carolina allspice originates, the plant was known (and still is in places) as the bubby bush – a slightly politer version of 'booby bush' – referring to the way in which women traditionally crushed the flowers and placed them in their bosom as a perfume. Warmth releases their scent, so if the idea of a spicy bosom leaves you cold (or you don't possess the necessary frontage) try growing Carolina allspice in a sunny spot near your door or windows to catch the aroma when it flowers instead.

With all that fragrant pleasure through the year, it's easy to forget that what you're after for the kitchen is the bark. Dried, it gives a tremendously aromatic spice – if you like cinnamon, you'll like Carolina allspice – and you can use it in exactly the same ways. Peeled from the wood, the bark is immediately flavoursome but gentle drying in the sun or on a low heat intensifies its perfume and spiciness.

A word of warning: unlike some other allspice plants, Carolina allspice contains calycanthine which is poisonous in large quantities. In warmer areas (very rarely in England) the flowers turn into oval-shaped fruit. These are very beautiful, but are poisonous to cattle, sheep and humans. Eat only the bark.

VARIETIES
Carolina allspice (*Calycanthus floridus*) is known and sold under a variety of other names – American

EATING

You can use the bark of Carolina allspice in exactly the same way as cinnamon – and as with that spice, a gentle toasting in a dry pan or slow drying in the oven works wonders in developing the intensity of fragrance and flavour.

Depending on how you intend to use it, you can keep the bark whole – it usually dissolves with long cooking or pound it to a powder if you prefer. As with cinnamon, once dried it loses its potency after a few months – so harvest in small quantities. Once dry, store in an airtight container and use within a few months.

Hot, buttered toast is good: hot toast bubbling with a mixture of butter, Carolina allspice and sugar is even better. Whisk together 50g Demerara sugar with 1 tsp finely ground Carolina allspice. Spread your toast with a generous amount of softened unsalted butter, making sure the butter goes all the way to the edges of the bread then sprinkle with the sugar/allspice mixture and pop the toast back under a hot grill until the sugar starts to melt.

It's not the worst idea in the world to make up a batch of this sugar and keep it handy for cinnamon toast emergencies, to give a bit of a lift to crumbles, sprinkle onto apple pies or add to hot chocolate.

CAROLINA ALLSPICE RICE PUDDING
Carolina allspice makes an aromatic addition to this Spanish-style rice pudding.

SERVES 4–6
250ml water
1/4 tsp salt
100g short-grain pudding rice
1 litre whole milk
25g unsalted butter
35g caster sugar
25g light Muscovado sugar, plus 1 tbsp for sprinkling
1cm x 5cm strip of lemon zest, peeled with a vegetable peeler
1cm x 4cm piece of Carolina allspice bark or 1 stick of cinnamon
1/4 tsp dried ground Carolina allspice bark or 1/4 tsp ground cinnamon

▶

allspice, spice bush, Eastern Sweetshrub and Sweet bubby bush among them – but is most often seen and sold as the generic Carolina allspice.

Of the few varieties available, 'Athens' (named after the city in which it was developed in Georgia, USA) is apparently particularly fragrant.

GROWING
Carolina allspice could hardly be less fussy. Although indigenous to the damp woodlands of the southern USA, Carolina allspice fares much better in full sun in more temperate areas as this helps to ripen the wood more effectively. It is happy in all but extreme soils, is tolerant of shade and needs watering only in times of drought – it really is one of the garden's easy all-rounders. Give it sun, a well drained soil and shelter from cold winds and it will grow healthily and rapidly.

Carolina allspice can eventually form a dense, deciduous shrub around 2m tall and across, occasionally larger, though it can be grown in a large container (60cm across) if pruned back. Carolina allspice can expand its territory if conditions are favourable via seedlings or sucker, although either can be dug up and replanted.

I've never had any trouble from pests or diseases on any of my Carolina allspice plants, nor am I aware of any. The dormant plants are hardy to -20°C or so, but the tender new spring growth can be knocked back by late frosts. Damage is usually only cosmetic.

Although it doesn't require pruning, if you need to shape or restrict the size of your Carolina allspice plant you can cut it back at any time of year – a hugely aromatic and pleasurable task.

HARVESTING
Pruning gives you the ideal opportunity to harvest the bark, although you can snip bits off at any time of the year to use. Look for any drier twigs as these usually have a stronger flavour. Any sticks snipped from the plant can be peeled of bark and used immediately or left for a few days on the windowsill to dry a little.

◄
In a large saucepan, bring the water to a boil, add the salt then stir in the rice and return to the boil. Reduce the temperature to medium-low and cook, covered and stirring once during the cooking time, until the water is absorbed, about 10 minutes.

Stir in the milk, butter, sugars (reserving the 1 tbsp light Muscovado) zest and Carolina allspice bark or cinnammon stick and simmer gently, uncovered and stirring from time to time, until the rice is tender and creamy, about 45 minutes. Remove from the heat. The mixture is slightly soupy at this stage, but the extra liquid is absorbed as it cools so don't be tempted to overcook it.

Remove the bark and zest and serve with a little light Muscovado sugar and ground Carolina allspice or ground cinnammon sprinkled over the top.

CAROLINA ALLSPICE TOAST

CHERVIL

Chervil is a subtle, sophisticated, grown-up herb. It doesn't yell at you in the way rosemary or basil might, but instead gets on quietly with making everything around it shine a little brighter. It gently intensifies the flavour of other herbs and is a traditional backing singer in Mediterranean 'fines herbes', a fine collection of (usually) annual herbs that bring a light zippiness to cooking.

Although most commonly used in the background with others, chervil happily shines on its own when given an opportunity, especially when treated simply. Its flavour is a gentle combination of parsley and aniseed (dominated by the parsley) and works perfectly with seafood, chicken, sorrel, veal and eggs. Once you start using it you won't find yourself short of ideas about where else to add it. A great way to become familiar with its character (as with any leafy herb you're unsure of or unfamiliar with) is to try a few snipped leaves in a mixed leafy salad where you'll notice it here and there without it taking over. It's also perfect finely chopped and thrown over freshly steamed broad beans or peas.

Chervil is a fine fresh summer herb but it also grows well through winter, making it valuable at a time when few other herbs are around. It even has a warming quality that seems to suit the cold weather perfectly – as 17th century herbalist Nicholas Culpepper wrote, chervil '…does much please and warm old and cold stomachs'.

Chervil is one of the Lenten herbs, eaten during Lent for its supposed ability to cleanse the blood and restore the bodily balance. For all its health-giving and generosity in making other flavours shine, chervil is rarely used outside of a few Mediterranean strongholds. The rest of us should put that to rights.

VARIETIES

Chervil (*Anthriscus cerefolium*) is usually sold as a generic rather than named variety. You may however find the curly-leaved variety 'crispum' – I wouldn't recommend this as the flavour is not overly special.

GROWING

Chervil is easy to grow from seed. Sow direct from mid-spring, when the rising temperatures will ensure quick germination and rapid early growth. Alternatively, sow into modules and pot on when the seedlings are large enough to handle easily. Chervil plants get upset if you transplant them more than once, so plant them out into their growing spot as soon as they reach 7cm or so in height. Chervil plants will grow to around 60cm tall and half as wide, so plant them 30cm or so apart.

Chervil favours a moist but well drained spot but is reasonably tolerant of most soils. Shade is critical, especially from the midday sun – chervil can bolt rapidly in sudden hot weather, making the leaves far less succulent and losing that perfectly balanced flavour to a little too much bitterness. This is the perfect herb for intersowing within or under taller plants.

If your plant does bolt, the tiny purple-tinged white flowers that grow in cow parsley-like heads are rather beautiful – they're also rather tasty thrown into salads, giving you at least some small compensation for the lack of succulent leaves.

Greenfly can be a pest but these are easily washed off with liquid horticultural soap or by giving your plant a swift dunk in a very strongly diluted bowlful of eco-friendly washing up liquid.

Chervil grows well in a large container, and makes for one of the finest of all the microleaves (see p.144).

HARVESTING

Chervil can be ready to harvest in six weeks in ideal conditions – although the plant should be at least 10cm tall before you take a few leaves. It's fairly hardy, allowing you to keep harvesting through the winter from a late summer sowing.

EATING

With its curling, lacy leaves chervil has to be one of the prettiest herbs and its sweetly aromatic, slightly aniseedy flavour makes it as useful in the kitchen as it is attractive in the garden. Just make sure you add chervil to any dish at the last minute as heat destroys its delicate flavour.

Chervil is a natural companion to eggs – either simply scrambled or made into an omelette as in the recipe featured here – and potatoes. Add some to a potato salad or a puréed, creamy potato soup and you'll see just what I mean.

Chervil makes a terrific, elegant addition to a simple green salad, added in a generous handful just before dressing with a light vinaigrette. It's also great with asparagus, broad beans, peas and shellfish.

For something a little different, try liberally scattering some chervil over a salad of roasted beetroot, roasted shallots and crumbled goat's cheese lightly dressed with olive oil and apple balsamic vinegar, some flaky sea salt and a few grinds of black pepper – its refined presence combines wonderfully with the other, more earthy flavours.

OMELETTE AUX FINES HERBES

This may seem a little bit fussy for something as simple as an omelette, but it really is best to chop the herbs separately before mixing them together. That way you get each one to the desired level of fineness without over working the leaves.

SERVES 1
2–3 eggs
Salt and freshly ground black pepper
1 garlic clove
1 tsp finely chopped chervil
1 tsp finely chopped chives
1 tsp finely chopped parsley
½ tsp finely chopped tarragon
15g unsalted butter

OMELETTE AUX FINES HERBES

Break the eggs into a medium bowl and season well with salt and freshly ground black pepper.

Cut the garlic clove in half and rub the tines of a fork with the cut sides; discard the clove. Scatter the herbs over the eggs and whisk gently with the fork.

Heat a 20–22cm omelette pan or frying pan over a high heat. Add the butter and sizzle until it just begins to turn a fine golden brown. Pour in the eggs, rattling the pan as it meets the hot butter. Use a spatula to lift the edge of the omelette and tilt the pan so the runny egg runs towards the sides; repeat a couple of times, alternating sides of the pan, until the egg is almost cooked

through – remember it will continue to cook when you plate it up, so be careful not to overcook, you still want it a little bit runny in the middle. Fold onto a warm plate and serve immediately.

You can accompany this omelette with many things, but it is especially good with a green salad dressed with a Classic Vinaigrette (see p.145).

LOVAGE

Every age has its superfoods and two thousand years ago lovage had its moment. It was widely grown for centuries as a source of medicinal and culinary magic, and taken for everything from a sore throat and fever to jaundice and colic. Herbalists declared it effective against 'pestilential disorders', giving them carte blanche to prescribe it for just about anything. It has also been used in bath water and in the shoes as it cleans and deodorises the skin.

Its name may also owe its origins to its reputation for adding a little oomph in the bedroom. In Germany it is known as 'Liebstöckel', meaning 'love sticklet'; its old English name is 'love parsley'; although less romantically it may owe its name to its traditional homeland of Liguria in northern Italy. Either way, it was a common ingredient of aphrodisiac potions. Enough of this, though: this book hopes to add a little spice to your kitchen, rather than the room above.

Lovage is an umbellifer (a family of plants with hollow stems including parsley and carrots) that resembles celery but far outgrows it. By mid-summer it can easily reach 2m tall, lending itself well to a place at the back of a veg patch or border. At this hottest time of the year it is showered with pale green flowers, not unlike fennel flowers. It makes a marvellous companion plant, lifting the vibrancy of neighbouring plants and attracting bees and other pollinating insects into the garden. By winter, lovage will have died back almost completely, as its hollow stems collapse with the frost, which you can cut back close to the ground.

Like many characterful herbs, lovage is either loved and grown enthusiastically or largely ignored. Its musky celery flavour with an undertone of aniseed and lemon is fabulous in stews, soups and stocks and has a particular affinity with pork, chicken, potatoes and tomatoes. You can use it pretty much anywhere you might parsley or celery but in smaller quantities to take account of its stronger flavour.

Every part of the plant is edible, but the leaves and seeds are most commonly used. The seeds have a sweeter, lighter flavour than the leaves and can be used like (and are sometimes sold as) celery seed.

The seeds have been taken since the ancient Greeks for flatulence and indigestion – so keep some on hand if you're susceptible to the downside of Jerusalem artichokes.

VARIETIES
Lovage (*Levisticum officinale*) is sold only as a generic rather than a named variety.

GROWING
Lovage is easily grown from seed. Sow undercover into modules in spring, planting the seedlings out when they are large enough to handle. Hardening them off within five days of keeping them undercover overnight and outside during the day will help them establish well.

If you have a plant already or know someone who does, you can split it with a spade in spring or autumn, ensuring that each segment has a shoot and roots.

EATING

As well as adding a celery edge to cooking, lovage leaves and seeds lend recipes a peculiar savouriness that's hard to put your finger on. It acts like a natural flavour enhancer, and is one of the key ingredients in many of the dried stocks you'll find in the shops. It works especially well in soups, stocks and stews but also surprisingly well in something as delicate as an omelette, or finely chopped and sprinkled sparingly over a leafy salad.

The whole plant is edible: young stems can be candied like angelica (another umbellifer); a tea can be made with the leaves; the fruit and roots are used in liqueurs; and the roots can be used like salsify. Lovage leaves are best used fresh, but if you want to save *some for winter the flavour is better preserved by freezing than drying. Wash the leaves, shake them dry and with chop and freeze into ice cubes or put the handfuls of leaves intact into a suitable plastic food bag for freezing.*

SMOKED FISH CHOWDER
The peppery, slightly lemony flavour of lovage adds a certain bite to this creamy chowder. Try the leaves, combined with other salad greens, in a salad to go with roasted, grilled or barbecued fish too.

SERVES 6
1 tsp groundnut oil
150g unsmoked pancetta or bacon, cut into 1cm cubes
20g butter
2 onions, finely diced
1 small stick of celery, finely diced
1 carrot, peeled and finely diced
500ml fish stock
3 medium potatoes, approximately 550g, well scrubbed, peeled and cut into 2cm dice
Pinch of mace
Salt and freshly ground black pepper
2 very fresh ears of corn
500ml milk
1kg smoked pollock or haddock fillets, skinned and cut into large chunks
4 tbsp finely chopped lovage, plus a little more for garnishing
To serve: Crusty bread

Warm the oil in a large pan over a medium heat and sauté the pancetta or bacon until it just begins to take on a little colour. Remove from the pan with a slotted spoon and reserve.

Add the butter to the same pan and, when it begins to foam, add the onions and sauté

▶

Plant seedlings or divisions at least 60cm from their neighbour in any reasonable soil. Lovage is fine in full sun or partial shade.

Lovage rarely grows taller than 1m, but you can start harvesting lightly once it reaches 40cm in height, taking stems and leaves from the outer parts and letting the centre grow on.

Lovage is a perennial, so while it dies back to the ground in winter, it regrows strongly in spring.

Leaf-miners (the larvae of insects such as moths, flies and wasps which live in and eat the leaf tissue of plants) can be a nuisance. If you see any affected leaves, burn them immediately. For more severe infestations, chop the plant to the ground and incinerate all the green parts and, chances are, it will spring back healthily.

Despite its size, lovage is perfectly happy growing in a large pot or similar – just keep it well fed, refresh the compost and/or feed once in a while to keep it thriving. You may also need a cane or two to support it when at its full flowering height.

Do remember when planting that, fabulous though it is, lovage is a strong, distinctive herb and therefore any more than one plant is likely to be more of an ornamental benefit to your garden than it will be useful for your kitchen.

HARVESTING

Lovage's flavour changes after flowering, becoming slightly more bitter. Early summer is the time to get the young leaves at their best, although you can extend this harvesting window by cutting the flowers as they start to form.

After the flowers come the seeds, which form on a large stalk. They are ready to be harvested when they've turned brown in late summer. Pick the whole heads on a dry day and hang them upside down in an airy spot for the seeds to dry out completely, this should take a couple of weeks. In an airtight container they should last for well over a year.

◄
over a low heat until soft and translucent, about 15 minutes. Add the celery and carrot and sauté for a further 5 minutes. Add the stock, potatoes, mace and a few grinds of black pepper, along with the reserved pancetta or bacon, and simmer until the potato is almost tender, about 10 minutes. Skim off any scum that may form.

While it's cooking, shuck the corn. Chop the bottom off a cob so you can hold it steadily on its end on a chopping board. Run a sharp knife down the ear of corn, working your way around it to cut away all of the kernels. Add the corn and milk to the chowder, bring to a simmer and add the fish and lovage. Cook until the fish is just poached through. Taste and adjust seasoning if necessary. Serve in warmed bowls with some good, crusty bread and a little more lovage scattered over the top.

SMOKED FISH CHOWDER

SWEET CICELY

This rather lovely umbellifer has only recently made it into our garden, and thanks for its arrival go to my father-in-law. His eyes lit up when I mentioned I'd like to grow sweet cicely. Evidently his garden was covered in endless self-seeded plants that were more nuisance than pleasure to him.

Sweet cicely is one of those few herbs that, once you have it on tap, you wonder how you managed without being able to call on its leaves and seeds at will. Its sweet aniseed flavour and fragrance is a loose blend of fennel, liquorice and star anise – all of which share the same pungent essential oil, anethole.

It is fairly full-on eaten on its own but generously complimentary to so many other flavours. As botanist John Parkinson wrote in the 17th century, 'it gives a better taste to any other herb put with it'.

Sweet cicely tends to be either unheard of or relatively popular in a nation's cookery. You'll find it in few English kitchens but the French love its ability

to act as a synergist – enhancing the flavours of any herbs it is cooked with – and commonly couple it with classic herbs such as bay, chives and thyme.

Sweet cicely has another fine quality – it is particularly tolerant of the cold, meaning that even in very northern Europe the leaves can be picked for almost all of the year. In Scandinavia and northern Germany in particular sweet cicely is commonly used, especially cooked with sharp fruits, where its characterful qualities lessen the need for adding as much sugar as might otherwise be used.

With its incised fern-like leaves and small white flowers, sweet cicely looks very similar to cow parsley.

Every part of the plant carries the aniseedy aroma and flavour, from the long taproot to the seeds (where it is most strong when they have yet to fully ripen).

VARIETIES

Sweet cicely (*Myrrhis odorata*) is sold as a generic rather than a named variety. It's not to be confused with *Osmorhiza longistylis*, which is also known as sweet cicely in some parts of North America, and is used in a very similar way.

GROWING

You can start sweet cicely off from seed but it is much easier to get a young plant from a herb nursery as there is only a very short window of viability before sweet cicely seeds become unusable. To sow from seed, collect your own (as they turn dark brown) from a plant at the end of summer and sow immediately. Sweet cicely seeds require a cold spell to germinate, with leafy growth not following until spring.

Whether you've sown seed direct, started them off undercover or planted out seedlings, they'll enjoy a good 50cm from their neighbour, so thin seedlings out if they need it.

You can also create new plants from sweet cicely's long taproot, much as you can with comfrey. In autumn, dig up your plant and slice the root into counters, each with at least one eye, and sink each a couple of centimetres into an 8cm pot filled with good compost. Plant the resulting seedlings out the following year when they've reached at least 5cm tall. Water plants in well and also through any dry spells.

Sweet cicely is fine in most soils, but favours a moist soil in a partially shady position. This happiness in cold, damp, partial shade makes sweet cicely perfect as an understorey plant, beneath trees, shrubs or in that otherwise tricky corner of the garden. It can also be grown happily in pots or containers.

Sweet cicely flowers in early summer, followed by seeds in the hottest months. It self-seeds readily, especially in lighter soils, so unless you're happy for more plants to proliferate either snip off the flowers before they turn to seed or dig up and repot any unwanted seedlings to give to friends.

In autumn, as leafy growth dies back, cut the foliage back to a few centimetres above the earth.

HARVESTING

The leaves emerge from this hardy herb fairly early in spring, so you can be pinching out a harvest from then right the way through to the end of summer.

EATING

Sweet cicely enhances the sweetness and cuts down on the acidity of tart fruits such as rhubarb, redcurrants and gooseberries when you cook them together, so do throw in some of the chopped leaves or green seeds next time you make a crumble or pie. Its seeds and/or leaves are also an intriguing addition to puréed apples.

Sweet cicely's ability to enhance the sweetness of fruit requires you to add perhaps only half the sugar you might normally makes it excellent for those wanting to lower their sugar intake without cutting out on the sweetness.

Its slightly aniseedy flavour also makes it very good with seafood. Try it, too, in egg dishes such as an Omelette aux Fines Herbes (see p.102) or in a yoghurty sauce to dress a cucumber salad.

MIXED ROOT PURÉE
SERVES 8
Salt and freshly ground black pepper
500g carrots, peeled and cut into 2cm chunks
500g parsnip, peeled and cut into 2cm chunks
500g swede, peeled and cut into 2cm chunks
20g unsalted butter
3 tbsp double cream

A few gratings of nutmeg
1 tbsp sweet cicely leaves, finely chopped

Bring a large pan of water to the boil, add a good pinch of salt and the prepared vegetables. Simmer until tender, about 15 minutes. Drain in a colander, reserving about a cupful of the cooking liquid, and leave the vegetables to steam for a couple of minutes. Pass them through a mouli food mill or potato ricer. Warm the butter in a large pan with the cream, tip in the vegetable purée, grate over the nutmeg and a few grinds of black pepper and beat with a wooden spoon until smooth; if it seems a little thick, add a little of the reserved

SCALLOPS WITH SWEET CICELY

cooking water until you get the consistency you like. Taste and season with salt if necessary. Warm through then stir in the sweet cicely just before serving.

ALTERNATIVELY: If you don't have a mouli or food mill, you can certainly prepare this as a rough mash. Just don't purée it in a food processor as it will lose some of its character.

SCALLOPS WITH SWEET CICELY

This dish makes an easy, elegant and delicious starter. If you are in need of a little green accompaniment, serve the scallops with a handful of small salad leaves, dressed with a little oil and lemon juice.

SERVES 4
1 tsp groundnut oil
Salt and freshly ground black pepper
12 scallops
2 tbsp finely chopped sweet cicely
Finely grated zest of ½ small lemon

Warm the groundnut oil in a frying pan over a medium-high heat; wipe out any excess with kitchen paper.

Season the scallops and fry until seared on both sides, about 3–4 minutes.

Mix together the chopped sweet cicely and finely grated lemon zest in a small bowl.

Divide the scallops between 4 plates, sprinkle with the sweet cicely and lemon zest mixture and serve.

SZECHUAN PEPPER

*Native to southern India, the black pepper (*Piper nigrum*) that most of us have in our grinding mills at home is sadly beyond viability away from tropical climes. Fortunately however the livid red berries of the Szechuan pepper grow perfectly happily in most temperate areas and make for a delightful alternative.*

While not botanically related to black or white pepper, Szechuan pepper and a number of other members of the *Zanthoxylum* genus are certainly its culinary cousins. Like the other *Zanthoxylum* peppers, Szechuan pepper forms a naturally untidy, deciduous, spiky bush that grows eventually to about 7m in height and width, though it is perfectly happy being pruned smaller and grown in a large pot.

The leaves of the Szechuan pepper are similar to those of the ash tree, which along with the spikiness gives rise to one of its common names – prickly ash. The leaves emerge in early- to mid-spring, followed quickly by the young flowers that develop through the summer, resembling small elderflower florets. As with elder, once the Szechuan flowers turn into berries through the hotter months they flip over, hanging down and reddening as they ripen.

The red berries of the pepper open as they become fully ripe to resemble miniature beechnuts, 5mm or so in diameter, and for once it's not the present concealed inside you're after it's the wrapping – as that's where the flavour lies. And what a prize it is. It has been the subject of wars and great expeditions to seek the best routes to where it was grown, and its trade is still a hugely important part of the world-food business.

Szechuan pepper, like all peppers, is much more an experience than a flavour. In Chinese cooking there's a beautiful distinction made between the two elements of pepperiness: the numbing pungency ('ma') that sets the tongue and lips tingling, and the spicy heat ('la') more akin to the heat from a chilli. A crucial ingredient at the heart of Chinese cuisine, Szechuan pepper is usually more 'ma' than 'la', and so is often accompanied by chilli in hotter dishes – including the mala sauce made predominantly from Szechuan pepper, chilli, oil, garlic and ginger.

If you're inquisitive about Szechuan pepper and the concepts of 'ma' and 'la' and want to know more before you commit to growing it, it's easy to acquire peppercorns of excellent quality (see pp.184–5 for suppliers). Chances are they'll come with the outer pink casing open and without the black seed held within. But whether you've bought or grown your own peppercorns, it's worth taking a little time to enjoy your first tasting. Split a seed case in two and nibble slowly on a single half at the front of your mouth. Don't rush this, as the flavours and sensations take time to unfold and, the more you chew, the quicker these subtle changes take place. The experience is very much longer and more complex than with black pepper, so let it develop slowly.

This usually begins with a citrusy, lemon sherbet wave that gradually gives way to warm heat (the 'la'). It's a sweet marriage, like the perfect tomatoes with acid and sweet in beautiful balance, but it passes,

EATING

Once under its spell, you'll find endless uses for Szechuan pepper in the kitchen. However you plan to use the peppercorns, a gentle toasting should really bring out those aromatics (and fill your house with its fine perfume) but it's best to toast and create your powder in relatively small quantities – as the peppercorns retain that potent zing for longer than after grinding.

Szechuan pepper is often used in the form of flavoured salt. It is wonderfully simple to prepare. Toast or dry fry equal amounts of coarse salt and peppercorns together until it just starts to smoke. When the mix is cool, use a mortar and pestle or a coffee grinder to reduce it to a coarse powder. You can use it anytime you might salt and pepper: to season meat before, during or after cooking, (try it sprinkled over slow roast belly pork), but my favourite way of using Szechuan salt and pepper is to toss a bowlful of chips in a little of the mix and enjoy it with a cold beer. The combination of the hot chips, the tingling 'ma' and the peppery 'la' quenched by the cold beer is unbeatable.

Chinese Five Spice Powder is very much at the heart of Szechuan cooking and has recently become popular across the world. Making your own is simple, and the results are infinitely superior to even the very best shop-bought jar.

CHINESE FIVE SPICE POWDER

Chinese Five Spice goes wonderfully well with chicken and pork as a marinade, but nothing quite beats it rubbed into the lightly-oiled skin of a duck or goose before roasting. This recipe works perfectly well using already ground spices, but if you can use whole spices and grind them yourself you'll notice a keenness about the flavours that's really special. The resulting blend will be beautifully fresh, alive and bright, without the need for the citrus that's often added to commercial mixes.

MAKES ABOUT 1 x 225G JAR
2 star anise or 1½ tbsp ground star anise
1½ tsp fennel seeds
5cm of cinnamon stick or 2 tsp ground cinnamon
½ tsp Szechuan pepper
6 cloves

▶

almost with the click of a switch, into a strangely numbing, almost anaesthetic feeling (the 'ma') on the lips and tongue. It can be slightly unnerving at first but it is peculiarly addictive, perhaps because it is purported to give you a spiritual lift to go with that sensual experience.

Spiritual or otherwise, there's simply nothing quite like it – it's a delightful window into the hidden world of pepper.

VARIETIES

There are several different species of Szechuan pepper, as well as many more closely related peppers within the *Zanthoxylum* group, each of which lends their own characteristic flavour to their particular regions' cuisine.

Zanthoxylum schinifolium and *Z. simulans* are the two most common varieties of Szechuan pepper. If you have room for just one variety I'd go for the former. I prefer its lighter touch – it's more 'ma' than 'la'. The peppercorns aren't overly powerful but do have a wonderful light wave of heat to accompany their bright lemony overtones and characteristically tingly 'ma'-ness.

GROWING

Buying peppercorns can be expensive, yet the plants are perfectly easy to grow, and by doing so you'll get all those wonderful 'ma' and 'la' qualities at the top of their game. You can grow plants from seed but you'll be a good few years away from harvesting. Plants, by contrast, will afford you a harvest considerably sooner and are relatively cheap, as you'll easily make the outlay back in earlier harvests. Simply plant your bush and prune to the size you like as it grows.

Mulching around the base is vital to minimising competition as the plant establishes. It's also sensible to wind a tree guard around the base of the young bark as it makes easy nibbling for rabbits that are perhaps partial to a sensuous lift too.

As well as the prospect of peppercorns, your plant gives you the excuse to stop every time you pass, to rub the leaves for their heady hit of spice and citrus. Like a tea break, it provides a perfect punctuation to

◄

Preheat the oven to 140°C/Gas 1. Place any of the spices that you are using whole on a baking tray and put them in the oven for 4 minutes, until lightly toasted.

Use a clean coffee grinder or pestle and mortar to reduce the spices to a fine powder. Sieve out any larger particles if you prefer, and store in an airtight jar away from direct sunlight. The spice powder mix should keep its zing for 3 months or so.

FIVE SPICE PORK RILLETTES

Rillettes is as much a way of cooking as it is a recipe. The principle is simple – it is just meat (pork in this case, though it works equally well for rabbit and most poultry) cooked very gently in its own fat. The addition of Chinese Five Spice Powder (see p.111) here adds a warm depth and fragrance to the rillettes that improves with age.

MAKES ABOUT 1KG
300g pork fat or lard
1kg pork shoulder or pork belly,
    cut into chunks
4 garlic cloves
1 tsp Chinese Five Spice Powder (see p.111)
1 tbsp salt
1–2 tbsp olive oil
4 sprigs of fresh thyme
3 bay leaves
10g parsley, tough stalks removed
6 spring onions, sliced lengthways
Salt and freshly ground black pepper
2 tbsp cider apple brandy or dry sherry

Preheat your oven to 70°C/Gas ¼.
    Place your pork fat in a dish at the bottom of the oven and render slowly, pouring the liquid fat off into a bowl every 15 minutes or so. Leave to cool.
    Turn the oven up to 140°C/Gas 1.
    Cut the pork into strips 2cm wide along the

grain of the meat. Crush the garlic and mix it with the Five Spice Powder, the salt and enough olive oil to make a thick paste and rub in into the pork strips. Place two-thirds of the rendered fat or lard in a wide ovenproof dish, pour in 100ml water and add the meat. Tie the herbs and spring onions together in a small square of muslin and add to the water. Place the dish in the oven and let it cook for a minimum of 4 hours. The liquid should be just moving, rather than bubbling hard – turn it down a little If necessary.
    After 4 hours, take the dish out of the oven and carefully take 2 forks to it – if the meat is completely tender and it tears apart easily, it's done. If it's not ready, turn the oven off and return the dish to the oven for a further hour.
    When the meat has cooled enough to handle, take out the herb bag and shred the meat thoroughly with 2 forks. Taste a little, and add salt and pepper if you fancy.

the day, and is up there with popping fresh peas into your mouth as one of the finest kitchen-garden treats.

Keep your Szechuan pepper plants away from any other citrus plants you may have. They are in the same family (*Rutaceae*) as limes, oranges and lemons and Szechuan peppers can carry the canker that attacks citrus trees. In 1968 the US Agriculture Department banned the import of all *Rutaceae* plants as well as their products – including Szechuan peppercorns – sparking off a lively underground market for the peppercorns, especially within Chinese communities where its 'ma la' qualities are so crucial to many dishes. Thankfully the ban was lifted in 2005 for peppercorns that had been heat-treated to kill off any potentially harmful bacteria.

HARVESTING
Harvesting is best done as soon as the pinky red seedcases begin to open and show their dark seed – usually as summer turns to autumn. The outer shell

is where the heat and aromatics are held (the seed is usually flavourless) but pick whole florets, leave them to dry somewhere warm for a day or two, and they should be ready to go into the peppermill.

If the peppercorns are still closed in mid-autumn, pick them and lay them out on a piece of paper indoors. Within a couple of days the heat from the house will dry the outer skins and they'll split to reveal the seeds.

I've read that the dark seeds can be bitter – this is not my experience, but some find the seed a little gritty. If so, you may wish to lightly bash them using a mortar and pestle as this splits the outer cases, releasing the seed for separating.

Store the unground peppercorns in an airtight container away from bright sunlight until you're ready to use them; they should retain their oomph for a year or so if kept in this way.

You can add a little extra Five Spice at this stage if you'd like a stronger flavour, but you probably won't need to as it will develop over time. Add a splash of cider apple brandy or dry sherry and mix everything together.

Transfer the rillette to a sterilised terrine or kilner jar, compacting the mixture lightly to push out air pockets and submerging the meat under the fat. Pour over the remaining third of the warmed, rendered fat. Cool, then refrigerate. The rillette is best left for the flavours to develop for a few days.

Rillettes are good straight from the fridge on crusty bread, better at room temperature, and incredible warmed gently until the fat begins to run.

Serve with something sharp such as pickled gherkins or Jerusalem artichokes (see p.162), or a salad with a lively dressing. Rillettes will keep in the fridge for several months in clean jars, so long as the pork is preserved under 5mm or so of fat.

CHINESE FIVE SPICE POWDER

BEANS & GREENS

Beans and greens have, for too long, sat in the background on the plate – often cooked without the enthusiasm and love they deserve. While beans and greens may be essential food, full of the nutrients our bodies need to do what they do, they don't have to be dull. Although they may not have the same immediate tug on the tastebuds as peaches, Szechuan pepper or alpine strawberries, they still have plenty to offer.

The six foods that follow make that case better than any. The green shoots of asparagus, the leafy ribs of the cardoon, the seeds of the borlotti, the immature flowerhead of the globe artichoke, the flowering whole of Romanesco and the leaves, stalks and flowers of kai lan are all on the list of the top twenty foods I'd advise anyone to grow. Each screams to be allowed space you would otherwise allot to carrots, onions and maincrop spuds. They just need to be let in.

All look incredible too, Romanesco perhaps more than any other edible. Is it a cauliflower, a calabrese broccoli or its own thing entirely? Cardoons and globe artichokes both form great untidy monsters that'll outgrow all but the tallest of gardeners. Both are worth growing just for their looks, many people do, but you'd be mad not to cut some flowerheads and some of the complimentary foliage from either for the kitchen as well.

If you're thinking that asparagus is hardly a taste of the unexpected, think again: unless you have grown your own and have got those perfect shafts of green to your kitchen and into your mouth within an hour or two of cutting, you will not have enjoyed it as it can be, as it really should be. And if you like asparagus, you'll love kai lan. Also known as Chinese kale, kai lan sits on the boundary between asparagus and purple sprouting broccoli. Succulent leaves, stalks and flowers are all delicious and, if you get sowing some this year, you'll be getting in early on what will become a new favourite.

Cardoons, globe artichokes, asparagus and kai lan have another thing in common – they are all perennials. You sow them once and they'll grow again each spring to give you handfuls of tasty food for years after.

There's only one bean in the section. I considered including more legumes – peas, broad beans and French beans are amongst the loveliest sweet harvests you can take from your garden – but they are part of almost everyone's veg patch. I almost squeezed peas in on the grounds of being so utterly fabulous straight from the pod but they really would be pushing 'unexpected' a little too far. I can't, however, pass up this opportunity to urge you to grow them, and suggest you try 'Hurst's Green Shaft' – the finest variety by a country mile.

Of the six foods in this section only kai lan is what might be thought of as a leafy green. This is no reflection on the loveliness of leaves – if this book included all of the finest food (common or otherwise) there'd be more in this section, but most of the leafy greens such as kale, Brussels sprouts and sprouting broccoli are very widely known and commonly grown.

Walking around my veg patch, the River Cottage kitchen garden and many others I visit, I try many new salad leaves every year. I've realised that when I taste them for the first time I'm not only judging them for themselves, I'm imagining how they'd work with other leaves, with simple vinaigrettes, sharp dressings or creamier ones: whatever they might need to shine at their best. It's the way it gets when you do it so often – your mind takes the food to the kitchen rather than just enjoying it there and then in the garden. This is a habit worth nurturing and is one that applies equally well to beans and greens. A few nibbles of kai lan, for example, will tell you that it has enough about it to take some strong flavours, like chilli and garlic, and still stand up, whereas the tender young Red Russian kale leaves are so delicate you can throw them into a leafy salad without fear off toughening up the ensemble.

Sadly, as they are often cooked right at the end of the meal preparation, when stress is at its highest and energy at its lowest, greens are routinely mistreated in the kitchen. Having a few simple tricks in your armoury – such as plunging your vegetables into very cold water after boiling or steaming to fix their colour and texture – will soon see you getting the best out of them. Greens also deserve dressing, just as you would salad leaves. Whether this is a shake of olive oil and a pinch of salt or something more involved is a matter for your mood. The darker greens work very well with garlic, finely chopped chilli, olive oil and a little lemon juice, while cream, chestnuts and bacon may well have been invented to be eaten with sprouts and the nuttier greens. Play around a little and see what takes your fancy.

GLOBE ARTICHOKES

Globe artichokes are worth growing just for that time you have burglars and you need a threatening medieval weapon to hand. Growing rapidly to 1.5m tall, the plants are topped with spiky fist-sized flowerheads born on robust ridged stems thrust from the centre of their silver grey velvet petals. They look like they'd hurt.

They are also an absolute essential in every edible garden. You get to eat the delicious immature flowerbuds, the bees and other beneficial insects get to enjoy any you allow to flower, and your house will be brightened up by the look and divine scent of the cut flowers and the striking foliage.

Cooked whole and served with a good vinaigrette, globe artichokes are a perfect long summer lunch. They make for an eventful meal, but tearing these globes apart is part of the sensuous ritual of eating this high summer harvest. The succulent, sweet heart of the flowerhead is primarily what you're after. It sits deep within the intimidating shell, attached to the fleshy lower half of the hard petals and the base.

Getting at it requires a little merciless destruction. Tear the hard petals off one by one, checking the base for nuggets of delicate nutty flesh – dunk each petal in the vinaigrette and slide the sweet flesh from it with your teeth. Delicious though this may be, it's just the appetiser.

Once all the petals have been dealt with, cut away the mass of inedible, immature florets in the centre, known as the choke. This leaves you with a pale green puck – the artichoke heart – as gloriously happy-making as any food there is.

Once finished and you've drifted back into the real world, you'll wonder how this once-tight globe has managed to create quite such a mad mess during its demolition, but it's worth being this fanatically brutal to get at every last scrap of the heart.

Not only are globe artichokes expensive gourmet food, they're also perfect for the idle or unconfident grower. Plant them once and you have them for years, they're pest and disease free and with their upright jagged foliage and stunning flowers, this tall Mediterranean perennial deserves its place in your growing space on looks alone.

In 16th century Europe, artichokes were largely reserved for men. They were thought to be an aphrodisiac and inappropriate for women to eat, but I have a feeling this may have been a tale spun by the men to get to keep all of them for themselves.

VARIETIES
I prefer the older varieties of globe artichoke – 'Violetta di Chioggia' and 'Gros de Laon' in particular. Their flavour is the best and, grown together, the purple of the former and the green of the latter work together beautifully. 'Green Globe' is also excellent and apparently a little hardier than most, so go for this if you are in a colder or more exposed area.

GROWING
Globe artichokes are easy and cheap to grow from seed. Sow into Jiffy-7s, modules or small pots indoors (a windowsill is fine) in early spring. They usually germinate quickly and with few failures, growing strongly once they get going. Pot them on when they get large enough to handle.

You can then either plant any out in summer or grow them on in pots until the following spring – whichever suits you best.

EATING

Unless you're eating small artichokes, you'll need to cook the globes in plenty of boiling water for between 15–45 minutes, depending on their size.

One of the benefits of growing your own artichokes is that you can pick them while they're still very small, when they're wonderful just as they are, in their raw state, dipped into your favourite dressing. Or try barbecuing them. Simmer them in salted water for 5 minutes, then cut them in half lengthways, brush with olive oil, season

with flaky sea salt and freshly ground black pepper and grill them, cut-side down, over medium-hot coals for 4-5 minutes until they just begin to char. Sprinkle over a minty gremolata made by combining a small handful of finely chopped mint, 2 tbsp finely chopped parsley, a couple of crushed garlic cloves and the zest and juice of a small lemon. The gremolata's also great spooned over roasted asparagus. Add some juicy lamb cutlets, and you've got yourself a feast.

GRILLED ARTICHOKES IN LEMON SAUCE
SERVES 4
2 lemons
4 globe artichokes
6 tbsp olive oil
2 shallots, finely diced
2 garlic cloves, finely chopped
1/4 tsp fennel seeds
1 sprig thyme
1 bay leaf
Salt and freshly ground black pepper
Small handful of chervil, larger stems
    removed and chopped

▶

Globe artichokes thrive in the Mediterranean, so give them a sunny, well-drained spot and they should do the same for you.

Globe artichokes are refreshingly low-maintenance – there's no ongoing care, although a winter mulch of compost around the base will enrich the soil for the following growing season and should result in a bigger harvest of globes.

Aside from dodging the slugs and snails at seedling stage (see p.176), globe artichokes are rarely troubled by pests or diseases.

The plants live for many years but to keep them in top vigour and productivity it's best to divide them every three or four years. If small plants form at the base of the main plant you can detach any that are 30cm tall and carefully separate them from the parent, digging up the roots with it.

Don't be intimidated by what seems like a brutal process – globe artichoke plants are robust and perfectly happy to be given a little resuscitation. You can do this in November, but this necessitates growing them in a pot over winter. It is instead much easier to do this in March and plant them straight out, chopping the foliage down by half. Water them in well and in a year's time you'll have even more artichokes to harvest.

Although they can reach 2m or more in height, artichokes are perfectly happy growing in reasonable-sized pots, although good drainage is vital.

HARVESTING
In return for an easy harvest you'll have to exercise a little patience early on. For the first year you should cut off any flower buds as soon as you see them – this directs the plant's energies into developing a strong root system to sustain it for the following years.

In year two you're into one of the easiest, most flavoursome harvests there is. Depending on variety and your location, the flower buds will appear anytime from May onwards. Take them small and let some grow a little larger – letting you experiment with two very different ways of eating the artichokes (see 'Eating'). You should get at least eight flower buds, often more, per plant.

Although they're predominantly a summertime treat, watch out for an extended wintery haul if you have a mild period. You may find new growth, a little darker than normal and even frost pinched but many find these rarities (known as 'winter-kissed' artichokes) even more tasty.

And do leave some heads to flower – they attract beneficial insects, particularly bees, into the garden and make a wonderful cut flower for the house.

◄

Fill a large bowl with water and squeeze in the juice of 1 lemon. To prepare the artichokes, cut off the stem of an artichoke so that it will stand up straight in the casserole. Cut off the top 1cm of the artichoke with scissors or a sharp knife, then cut off the tips of the remaining large petals with scissors. Prize open the top of the artichoke with your fingers, pull out the purplish and yellowish petals in the centre, then scrape out the furry part of the choke with a teaspoon. Toss the prepared artichoke into the bowl of lemony water (to prevent it discolouring) and repeat with the remaining artichokes.

Warm 3 tbsp olive oil over a low heat in a lidded saucepan large enough to hold the artichokes upright. Fry the shallots for 3–4 minutes, add the garlic, fennel seeds, thyme and bay leaf and cook for a further couple of

minutes, stirring. Add a large strip of lemon zest pared from the lemon with a vegetable peeler, the juice from half the remaining lemon and enough water to fill the pan to the level of about 10cm. Season well with salt and pepper and bring to the boil.

Put the artichokes into the pan, weighted down with a plate, and add the lid. Cook until 1 of the lower petals comes away easily, start testing after 25 minutes. Remove the artichokes and let them cool a bit while you make the sauce. Heat the grill as high as it will go.

Reduce the cooking liquid until you have about 400ml remaining. Strain into a clean pan, add 1 tbsp olive oil and the juice from the rest of the remaining lemon and boil again, whisking, until reduced by about a quarter. Halve the artichokes lengthways, removing any furry choke that remains,

brush with the remaining oil and grill until charred slightly (you can do this on the barbecue instead if you would rather). Divide the artichokes between 4 plates, stir the chervil into the sauce and trickle over. Serve immediately.

ARTICHOKES STUFFED WITH WALNUTS AND GOAT'S CHEESE
Steamed artichokes dipped into a Classic Vinaigrette (see p.145) or melted butter stirred with a spritz of lemon juice eaten slowly, one sparkling petal at a time, are one of summer's greatest, slowest pleasures. But if you want to turn artichokes into a spectacular and substantial starter, do try stuffing them. The prep may be a little fiddly, but the results are most certainly worth it.

ARTICHOKES STUFFED WITH WALNUTS AND GOAT'S CHEESE

SERVES 4
2 lemons
4 large globe artichokes
100ml dry white wine
65ml fruity extra-virgin olive oil

For the stuffing:
60g walnuts
100g fresh breadcrumbs
100g soft goat's cheese
40g Parmesan, grated
1 egg yolk
3 tbsp finely chopped parsley
Salt and freshly ground black pepper

Preheat the oven to 180°C/Gas 4.

Prepare the artichokes as per the previous recipe. Place the walnuts on a baking sheet and bake for 8 minutes, stirring once, until fragrant. Cool the walnuts but leave the oven on.

Pulse the walnuts in a food processor until coarsely chopped, then add the breadcrumbs, goat's cheese, grated Parmesan, egg yolk and parsley. Season generously then pulse a few times until the mixture is well combined.

Remove the artichokes from the water and divide the mixture between them, spooning it into the cavity and pressing it down well with the back of a spoon, and press or sprinkle some into the gaps between the larger petals. Cut 4 thick slices from the remaining lemon and place them in the bottom of a heavy, lidded casserole. Stand the artichokes on the lemon slices, pour over the white wine and enough water to cover the bottom of the artichokes by 2.5cm. Trickle the olive oil over the artichokes. Bring to a bare simmer, cover tightly and bake for 40–50 minutes – start testing after

35 minutes to see if one of the larger petals near the base of the artichoke comes out easily. Serve immediately.

ALTERNATIVELY: For a deliciously different stuffing, try making a paste of the breadcrumbs with 3 anchovies in oil, 2 finely chopped garlic cloves, the finely grated zest of a lemon, an egg yolk and 1 tbsp capers; season well with salt and pepper and use it to stuff the artichokes as before.

ASPARAGUS

You're in a restaurant, you've studied the menu, drooled over the description, made your order and the waiter tells you that your meal will be served in three years. It's hardly ideal, but when it comes to sinking your teeth into your first homegrown asparagus every single one of those 1000-odd days you've waited from sowing will seem a perfectly happy price to be paid. This is the taste of spring and, for me, few other veg come close.

The secret to developing the necessary patience for asparagus – and believe me, it doesn't come naturally to me – is to think of your asparagus bed not as part of your veg patch, but instead as a sort of mini-orchard. While most of a typical veg patch is made up of annuals – plants that are sown, grown, picked and eaten within a year, often much less – asparagus is a perennial, producing year after year from the same plant. Although it has a developed and robust root system that enables it to get growing swiftly and strongly as spring arrives, it needs time to establish early on if it is to give you years of blissful harvesting. In this way, it is much the same as with most fruit and

nut trees and bushes, and most of us can live with the idea of waiting for them to get producing.

The good news is that you can chop off one of the three years that it takes for asparagus to establish before you begin simply by starting with young plants rather than sowing from seed. That's not an end to the self-restraint, however. For two years you'll have to put the knives out of reach when you see the first perfect green spears appear, leaving them to grow uncut so that the plant can develop the underground engine room that will keep you in delicious green fingers for 20 or more years to come.

Even after this long 'hands off' you'll still have only a very short, special season in late spring to early summer in which to make happy hay each year, but this is an essential part of the pleasure. I am awfully impatient and naturally much happier when surrounded by the things I like best to eat, yet I will happily avoid asparagus for 48 weeks of the year. I never buy it. Those four short, sharp weeks (six if you're lucky with the weather) are heaven, and like the football World Cup or the Ashes series in cricket, all the more special for their occasional arrival.

The flavour of your own asparagus will be enough to convince you that you are a genius grower. In truth, asparagus pretty much grows itself but you can top anything that another grower or the shops can offer simply by having the shortest journey to your kitchen. The secret to the best asparagus in the world is to get everything else ready in the kitchen before you go outside to harvest. Asparagus is a naturally sweet, succulent vegetable but both of these essential characteristics slide away rapidly from the second you separate the spears from the plant.

It really is a rapid decline – not to unpleasantness, but from the best that the vegetable world has to offer to something that is just perfectly ok. Thankfully this garden crime is entirely avoidable.

To eat asparagus at its best, boil the water before you pick. Make the dressing or the sauce, or assemble any ingredients you want to use before you take the knife to your garden. It really will make a difference and, if you're going to wait all that time until harvest, why dilute the perfection?

If you're short of space, not sure you'll be living where you are for long, or if you simply can't wait for that fantastic asparagus flavour, you might want to try one of two alternative ways of bringing that delicious flavour to your kitchen.

Asparagus peas (*Tetragonolobus purpurea*) look a little like miniature green loofahs and will give you something of the delicious taste of asparagus without the wait. There's something about these bedraggled plants that never quite convinces you they're doing as well as they could, but they're hardy and grow in pretty much any soil, do well in pots and require little in the way of attention. Their brick-red flowers are followed by a tangle of pods which you should never allow them to go beyond an inch or so before picking, as they quickly become fibrous and bland.

Asparagus lettuce is another annual that produces a tasty loose-leaved lettuce when sown in spring, but sown in the hotter months you can take advantage of the plant's tendency to bolt by harvesting the delicious shooting stems which give you the asparagus taste without the wait.

VARIETIES
'Connover's Colossal' and 'Mary Washington' are two old varieties that I particularly love. They are reliable producers and their flavour is exceptional.

Asparagus plants can be male or female, either can be delicious but male plants usually offer you a larger yield, with female plants tending to produce larger spears. Female plants produce seed that can grow into seedlings that deprive your best plants of resources, so collect the seeds before they have the chance to fall.

Many of the newer varieties available are F1 hybrids that produce all male plants, so you can expect more spears of fairly consistent dimensions. 'Jersey Knight', 'Backlim' and 'Gijnlim' are excellent varieties, should you choose to go down this avenue.

Personally, I prefer non-F1 varieties and the range of size, diameters and degrees of perfection that come with them. I also think that the older varieties have a depth of flavour I've yet to experience in any of the newer varieties.

GROWING
As with many perennial plants, asparagus is as simple to grow as it is to eat.

You'll need to choose a good spot for your asparagus bed – a well drained site that's entirely clear of perennial weeds is ideal. If you don't have a well drained site you can always create the perfect conditions for yourself by building a raised bed.

If money is more of an issue than time, you can start asparagus from seed. Sow individual seeds into modules in late winter for transplanting into pots in early summer or planting out direct into a well prepared site. You'll have three years until your first harvest, but this does make for a very cost-effective route to your own asparagus.

If you can, I'd recommend you start a year into this cycle, planting young dormant plants known as crowns. Hopping a year nearer to delicious lunches will cost you more than starting from seed but an earlier crop of asparagus is worth every penny.

Early spring is the time to plant your crowns or seedlings. Dig a trench a little deeper than the depth of your spade's blade, allow around 80cm or so if you are creating more than one row. Shovel in a little compost or well rotted manure with some of the excavated soil so that you have refilled around 10cm. Shape this refilled material into a ridge along the bottom of the trench.

Place the crowns at least 50cm from each other along the ridge, teasing out the roots evenly on either side. Shovel in the rest of the excavated soil carefully, covering the top of each crown by 10cm or so. Water well.

The key to easy asparagus is in keeping an occasional eye on your asparagus bed for the 11 months when it is being unproductive, and not allowing weeds to take hold. It's pretty much all that stands between you and the best asparagus you can eat – so it pays to get ahead on this task immediately by applying a mulch. Grass cuttings, straw or manure all work well

to suppress weeds, and will help retain moisture through the summer months. Use a hand hoe or trowel to carefully remove any weeds without disturbing the asparagus roots.

It's worth a few minutes of your time to support the plants as they grow tall after harvesting: place canes along either side of the rows and link them together with string to create a supporting boundary that prevents your plants swaying in the breeze too much. This stops the stems snapping or creating a hole at the base of the plant which can fill with water, which leads to the roots rotting.

In autumn, cut the stems back to 5cm above ground as the foliage turns yellow.

Almost every plant has its pests, but with asparagus at least they are mostly cosmetic and easy to spot.

EATING

Your own asparagus is a luxury that, once tasted, is hard to live without. For a month you'll be able to eat the best a veg patch has to offer, and happily it is at its best when treated with a light hand in the kitchen.

With asparagus, time is your most precious commodity. Cut the spears as you need them – the aim is to eat them within the hour.

Boiled or steamed until just tender, asparagus falls into a happy partnership with any (or all) of butter, salt, olive oil, black pepper, anchovies, lemon and Parmesan, as well as any number of dressings, mayonnaises and sauces. I particularly love asparagus with hollandaise. And the driest white wine or cider makes the best accompaniment.

ASPARAGUS WITH WASABI MAYONNAISE
Asparagus – boiled, steamed, roasted or grilled – I can't get enough of it in spring. Its season is so short, I like to eat it as often as I can, either dipped into a mustardy vinaigrette (see p.145) or alongside this marvellous pale green mayonnaise.

SERVES 4 AS A STARTER
2 garlic cloves
Salt and freshly ground black pepper
1 egg yolk
1 tbsp lemon juice or lime juice
1 tbsp wasabi powder, freshly grated horseradish or prepared hot horseradish
225ml light olive oil or a mixture of olive oil and groundnut oil
800g asparagus
2–3 tbsp olive oil (if you are going to roast or grill the asparagus)

First, make the mayonnaise. Pound the garlic cloves into a paste with a pinch of

salt in a pestle and mortar, or on a chopping board with a sharp knife. Place the garlicky paste into a bowl with the egg yolk, lemon juice and wasabi or horseradish and whisk together until smooth. Begin to trickle in the oil, a couple of drips at a time to begin with, whisking as you go. As it begins to thicken you can add the oil a little more quickly, but keep whisking all the time. You can, of course, do this in a food processor, but you won't get to experience quite the heart-stopping thrill of waiting for the mayonnaise to come together.

When the mayonnaise is ready, prepare the asparagus. The best way to ensure you're going to enjoy the tenderest of spears is to take hold of each one and bend it until it snaps. You can, if you are a perfectionist who enjoys practising your knife skills, remove some of the skin at the base of each spear too.

There are several ways to cook asparagus. Boil until just tender in lots of salted water, about 3 minutes for thickish spears, less for

Asparagus beetles rarely get above nuisance status, and, with their black-and-white striped back and red rim, they are not hard to identify. It's worth checking your plants regularly to ensure numbers never get too high: pick them off and dispose of them as you see fit. Chickens love them. And although I've never tried it, tomatoes planted nearby are supposed to deter the beetles, as are aromatic annual herbs such as basil, dill and parsley.

Slugs and snails will usually help themselves to more leafy suppers nearby but occasionally can become a pain: use slug pubs (see p.176) if they start to make a serious impact on your crop.

HARVESTING

In England the asparagus season makes mid-April through May a very special time. When the wait is almost over you'll find me (and many other asparagus lovers) on their hands and knees looking for the first green fingertips breaking the surface. When the temperature and light crosses a critical threshold growth is strong and spears can appear suddenly overnight. Stones, even a half-brick, can be lifted and edged aside by the light-hungry spears' push for the sky. There is sex going on in your garden. These fingers are stems topped with flower buds driven by the urge to blossom and produce seed, to reproduce. You, the hungry voyeur, need to interrupt this indecent activity before it goes too far.

When the spears reach 15cm or so in length take a knife and, holding the spear carefully, saw a centimetre or two below the soil to separate the fingers from the roots. You can buy specialist curved asparagus knives for this, although a serrated bread knife works perfectly well.

Each crown will throw up perhaps a dozen spears each season. Although you should take only half or so from each in the first year of harvesting, you can slice away like Zorro after that, but only for a month or so. After that, leave any spears to carry on their untidy journey to flowering – this top growth allows the plant to develop resources for subsequent harvests, and more meals for you in the years to come.

skinny ones, or steam for the same amount of time. Or try roasting them. Place them in a single layer on a baking sheet, trickle over some olive oil and sprinkle liberally with salt and pepper. Roll them about a bit to ensure they're well coated, and roast in a hot oven, 200°C/Gas 6, for about 10 minutes, turning once. On sunny days, asparagus is wonderful cooked on the barbecue over medium-hot coals. Brush with olive oil, season and grill, turning frequently, until cooked through and slightly charred.

ALTERNATIVELY: This mayonnaise is also delicious if you omit the wasabi powder and fold in a fines herbes mixture (see Omelette aux Fines Herbes p.102), or a small handful of chopped basil at the end. Serve it with shellfish, spoon it into a sandwich with cooked chicken or grilled fish, or tumble a couple of spoonfuls into some just-cooked asparagus, peas and broad beans. Try, too, omitting the wasabi and adding lots of chopped capers, cornichons and dill to serve with grilled fish.

ASPARAGUS WITH WASABI MAYONNAISE

BORLOTTI BEANS

Why would you not want to grow the world's most beautiful bean? Even if you don't eat them borlottis are worthy of their place just for the livid splash of their speckled red-cream pods they will add to your garden. They look like they may have been planted by Cath Kidston. The beans inside the pods are loyal to the same red-cream colour scheme too, although in my experience in almost exactly opposite proportions to the pod they come from. Or perhaps I'm imagining things.

Borlottis have become almost a cult: passionately loved by some, virtually unknown to others. In their spiritual homeland of the Veneto region of Italy, classic recipes such as radicchio and borlotti soup are at the core of the area's cuisine. The brightly coloured beans arrive right at the heart of summer and have a happy way of working well with virtually everything that's ready in the garden at the same time. They have a starring role in one of my favourite dishes, ribollita, that most adaptable of soups which uses handfuls of tomatoes, courgettes, chard, kale, herbs, garlic and whatever else may be around to go with the borlottis. It is summer in a bowl.

Borlottis look more like broad beans than most other climbing beans. Their long, plump, strikingly beautiful pods are as elegant as the beans within, and as with broad beans you split them along the seam to get to their sweet beans. While their vines can grow to 2m, borlottis are less productive than some climbing beans. Yet while the yield may be lower, you'll get your hands on a flavour and texture that money can't buy. You'll also get to eat far more of your harvest: while many climbing French beans can hide away in the leaves and become large and tough, borlottis stand out proudly, begging to be picked. Besides, the very few that you miss can always be dried to eat in the winter months.

Borlottis are slow food. Out in the garden the plants are slow to grow and the beans take time to mature, while in the kitchen they benefit most from relaxed, unhurried cooking. You don't even have to be in a rush to use them. While borlottis are classic Mediterranean food that look and taste of summer, they are hearty enough to keep you going through autumn and winter too: any you don't eat in the sunny months can be dried for winter use, and if you don't use them all in winter they can be sown for next years crop.

Be gentle with borlottis in the kitchen. Simmer them slowly, as if you're trying not to wash off the speckles. I've taken to Anna Del Conte's preference for cooking them in the oven rather than on the hob. Get them just boiling on the top before transferring them into an oven preheated to 150°C/Gas 2. They'll take easily over an hour, perhaps nearer two, to cook properly.

Gentle as you may be, those livid speckles will fade with cooking but the texture will be perfect. Perhaps having enticed you into sowing them, caring for them and picking them, their decoration has served its purpose. Luckily their nuttiness and texture compensates in spades, as does their ability to take on the taste of whatever flavours are around them.

VARIETIES
'Lingua di Fuoco' is reliable, delicious and is widely available. It can also be found as a dwarf version for very windy locations, but the yield is much reduced.

GROWING
Start borlottis off undercover (a sunny windowsill is fine) from early spring until mid-summer.

Like all beans and peas, borlottis like a long root run, so give them room to develop. You can buy root trainers in which to start them off but cardboard toilet roll inners work just as well. Fill them with compost and bury the seed to a knuckle's depth. You can sow borlottis direct, but it's an invitation to birds to winkle them up, and to slugs and snails to graze off the new green growth as it comes through.

Plant your seedlings out when they are at least 5cm high, keeping them at least 25cm apart. Keep an eye out for slugs and snails early on as they can munch away all you've been waiting for. Growth isn't as rapid as many of the peas and beans, but don't be deterred, they're reliable – the pods and their fine beans will get there in the end.

You'll need to support your plants as they grow with canes or similar. A tepee with an open section will allow you to get to the beans hanging inside, or a framework of canes crossed halfway up (to form an 'X') will leave the beans hanging accessibly.

EATING

Borlottis have a meaty texture and quality about them that sets them apart. While robust and able to stand on their own two feet in a recipe, they also take on the flavours and subtleties of the other flavours around them. It makes them perfect for soups, casseroles and stews (see below), but don't overlook their ability to be the star themselves. Try a fabulous late summer borlotti hummus: purée cooked borlottis with a couple of anchovies, a little lemon juice, garlic, and olive oil and eat with olive bread.

They also make for a fine alternative to the usual baked beans when cooked in a tomato sauce and served on toast, or when served alongside a salty goat's cheese in a salad.
Cook them in gently simmering water or herb-infused stock – timing varies with size and if they'd started to dry a little on the plant, so testing the largest bean regularly is the best way to get it just right.
Cooked, fresh borlotti beans are wonderful simply tossed in some good, fruity extra-virgin olive oil and dressed

with a little apple balsamic vinegar. They are also delicious dressed with a little Classic Vinaigrette (see p.145).
Once they have been dried, borlotti beans should be soaked overnight before cooking.

WARM BORLOTTI AND CHORIZO SALAD
If you're after something that will, on tasting, transport you straight to the Mediterranean, look no further. The borlottis take on some of the punch of the spicy sausage and garlic, while still retaining their own distinct flavour. A hearty lunchtime treat.

▶

You'll need to water borlottis through dry periods. If you have the time, use comfrey tea (see p.183) every fortnight or so from flowering onwards; the potassium it contains will boost your harvest.

Like all peas and climbing beans, borlottis are ideal for those with limited space – their footprint is small as they climb upwards, giving you a healthy haul without using up much floor space.

Peas and beans have a magical ability – they can take nitrogen (one of the main nutrients for plant growth) from the air and make it available in the soil through nodules in their roots. It's a way of self-feeding that also benefits any plants grown in their vicinity. If you're feeling creative, why not plant something near to your peas and beans that will not only enjoy the nutrient boost but will offer the legume something back. The classic 'Three Sisters' method of growing a legume, sweetcorn and squash is an ancient way of growing favoured by Native Americans that pairs characteristics of each plant to benefit (and benefit from) the others. The beans make nitrogen available to the sweetcorn and squash, while the sweetcorn acts as a scaffold for the bean to climb through. The squash takes advantage

of the nitrogen too, while cooling the roots of the other two and retaining water with its large leaves. It's a brilliant way of growing three delicious foods together, and you can take the principle in any direction your tastebuds choose – borlottis climbing through a dwarf peach with nasturtiums at the base works equally, deliciously well.

Borlottis grow perfectly happy in a good-sized (60cm) container, but keep extra-vigilant about watering.

HARVESTING
If you sow borlottis successively (every three weeks or so), you can pick your beans from early summer through to the start of autumn. The core of your harvest will be in the height of summer.

Pick regularly, when the pods feel plump with beans. You'll need to keep your eyes open to get them before they start to dry too much but they are slow to develop, so this is not the blink-and-they're-over way of runners, peas or some other French beans.

Do leave some beans for using through winter. Let pods stay on the plant until winter is about to hit. On a dry day, cut the plant down (leaving the roots in the ground to give up their nitrogen as they decompose) and hang it upside down somewhere light, where the air can move around it. The pods and their beans will slowly dry out, after which you can pop the beans from the now crusty pods. Let the beans dry for another day or two spread out on paper, and store them in an airtight jar or a paper bag.

◄

SERVES 4
1 tsp olive oil
1 cooking chorizo, about 150g, broken into chunks
1 onion, finely diced
2 garlic cloves, halved and finely sliced
1 bay leaf
400ml chicken stock
180g borlotti beans, podded weight
Salt and freshly ground black pepper
2 large, ripe tomatoes, cored, deseeded and roughly chopped
A big handful of parsley, tough stalks removed and roughly chopped
To serve: Crusty bread

Warm the olive oil over a medium-high heat in a saucepan. Add the chorizo and cook until starting to brown slightly. Remove with a slotted spoon, reduce the heat and add the onion. Sauté until translucent, about 15 minutes, add the garlic and bay leaf and sauté for a couple of minutes.
    Return the chorizo to the pan with the chicken stock and borlotti beans, season with black pepper and simmer, partially covered, until the beans are tender, about 25 minutes. Remove from the heat, discard the bay leaf, adjust the seasoning and, when just warm, stir in the chopped tomatoes and parsley.
    Divide between 4 plates and serve straight away with crusty bread.

BORLOTTI BEAN STEW
This hearty borlotti bean stew is wonderful with tender fillets of fish, but if you would prefer a heartier meal, substitute spicy sausages for the fish. Just brown the sausages then add them to the stew along with the beans.

SERVES 6
60ml olive oil
2 leeks, white and pale green parts only, halved and thinly sliced
1 stick of celery, diced
1 carrot, peeled and diced
1 fennel bulb, quartered, cored and finely sliced (reserve any leafy fronds for garnish)
2 garlic cloves, crushed
1 bay leaf

BORLOTTI BEAN STEW

3 small sprigs of thyme
700g ripe tomatoes, peeled* deseeded and
   finely diced
1.2 litres chicken or vegetable stock
600g fresh borlotti beans, podded weight
   about 350g
2 tbsp fresh oregano, chopped
2 tbsp fresh parsley, chopped
Salt and freshly ground black pepper

For the fish:
6 sea bass or sea bream fillets, skin on
2 tbsp olive oil
2–3 tbsp fruity, extra-virgin olive oil for
   trickling over the top

Pour the olive oil into a large casserole dish
and warm over a medium-low heat. Add

the leeks, celery, carrot and fennel, partially
cover and sauté gently, stirring from time to
time, until everything is very soft, about 15
minutes. Add the garlic, bay leaf and thyme
sprigs and stir for a further minute. Add the
tomatoes, stir and simmer for 5 minutes. Pour
in the stock, bring to a simmer and add the
beans, oregano and parsley and some salt and
pepper. Simmer, partially covered, until the
beans are tender, about 50 minutes. (If you
are using dried beans, soak them overnight in
plenty of cold water, drain and add them to
the recipe now, but double the cooking time.)
Taste and adjust the seasoning, then remove
from the heat. Remove the bay leaf and any
woody thyme sprigs.
   In a large frying pan, warm the olive oil
over a fairly high heat. Season the fish fillets

and slash the skins a couple of times with
a sharp knife. Place in the pan, skin-side
down, and fry for 3 4 minutes until crisp,
turn and fry just until cooked through,
1–2 minutes. Spoon the borlotti bean stew
into 6 warmed bowls, place a fish fillet on
top of each one and sprinkle on the reserved
fennel fronds.
   Serve immediately, with some good olive
oil trickled over the top.

* To peel the tomatoes, cut a small cross
in the base with a sharp knife and plunge
them, 1 or 2 at a time, into a bowl of boiling
water. Leave for 30 seconds and plunge into
iced water. If the tomatoes are properly ripe,
the skins should slip off easily.

KAI LAN

When I have grown something out of the ordinary and it has succeeded I often find myself caught in two minds. A part of me wants to keep this new discovery to myself (perhaps so that I may eat all the world has to offer of it), while the rest of me wants to shout to everyone that'll listen that I think I may have found a real classic.

This is only the second year I've grown kai lan, so rather than shouting yet I'm whispering it loudly – I am quite blown away by this wonderful plant.

Simply put, kai lan is a dreamlike combination of three of the finest flavours you can take from the garden, all in one plant, looking and tasting very much like an untidy cross between sprouting broccoli, kale and asparagus. And if that doesn't get you interested I'm not sure what will.

Kai lan grows as a succulent, fleshy bush, anything up to a metre tall if left uncut, but once you get your teeth into it you'll be more likely to keep it to half the height as you chop away at it for meal after meal.

The whole plant is edible – from its thick, generous blue-green leaves, fat stems and the scattering of small flower heads. Slice some off and it just keeps on coming back: the more you cut the more quickly the sweet succulent shoots grow back through the summer months. Every inch is tender from top to toe.

And its timing is perfect. As the sprouting broccoli begins to tail off so comes the first asparagus, followed by the early peas, then kai lan picks up the baton through the summer.

Leafy greens are rather undervalued I think, perhaps due to that old association with them being 'good for you' rather than particularly tasty. If you've grown some for yourself you'll know purple sprouting broccoli, asparagus and kale as the equal of anything that you can grow – and while it is certainly 'good for you', kai lan is right up there with the other three when it comes to the kitchen. It can have a slightly more mustardy edge than other leafy greens but its nutty sweetness allows you to pair it with pretty much anything that takes your fancy.

Cut it young and you'll find it needs next to no steaming, loves all the sauces, dressings and other treatments that go so well with asparagus and purple sprouting broccoli and, no matter how much you eat, you never tire of it.

VARIETIES
Although it is also known as Chinese broccoli or Chinese kale, I've only ever seen it sold as generic kai lan or kailaan.

GROWING
You can start kai lan off in modules or Jiffy-7s any time from March through to September, planting out the seedlings 40cm apart when they've established. Or, for an easy life, sow the seeds direct, sprinkling a light covering of compost or soil over the top. Be prepared to thin your seedlings as they emerge to the required 40cm spacing if necessary.

Although mostly grown as an annual, with new seed sown each year, kai lan is perennial and tolerates

EATING

Sitting between the springtime liveliness of asparagus and the wintery heartiness of kale and sprouting broccoli, kai lan works equally well in light or heavier recipes. Steamed kai lan is every bit as good as asparagus when used as the 'soldiers' with a soft-boiled egg and it takes beautifully to the barbecue when slathered in olive oil. You can slice off, tempura batter and deep fry the heads (either when flowering or before) – they're perfect with a sweet chilli jam. Or you can use any part of the plant in place of Romanesco in the pasta recipe on page 135 (shorten the roasting time

to around 20 minutes), or instead of cardoons in the gratin recipe (p. 133). The flowers, like many brassicas, carry a lovely mustardy flavour, and add a delicious punch when thrown into a leafy salad.

I particularly love kai lan steamed with hollandaise or olive oil, Parmesan and black pepper if it's warm outside, or given the classic stir fry treatment with lots of ginger, a little sugar, a little garlic, a glug of rice wine vinegar and a little oyster sauce if the weather's not so good.

Lightly steamed kai lan is delicious dipped into a deeply savoury anchovy,

mayonnaisy dressing. Chop together 6 anchovy fillets in oil with 1 crushed garlic clove until you have a fine paste. Tip the paste into a bowl with 1 egg yolk, 1 tbsp lemon juice and 1 tsp Dijon mustard and whisk everything together until smooth. Start to trickle in some light-flavoured olive oil, a mixture of olive and groundnut oils, or rapeseed oil – about 150ml should do it – a few drips at a time at first, whisking as you go and adding the oil more quickly as it starts to thicken. Taste and adjust the seasoning if necessary and thin with a couple of tablespoons of hot water if it's a little too thick.

frost, so with luck you grow it all year round, but it slows down in productivity from late autumn onwards. I prefer to let it run fully to flower (they are also edible) after a few months of cutting – kai lan means 'mustard orchid' and its creamy white flowers add a late summer splash to the veg patch. When they start getting a bit ragged as the cold arrives, I cut the plant back to 5cm or so above the base and leave it to resprout in spring.

Theoretically kai lan can suffer from the same range of pests and diseases as any other brassica, but in my experience it seems remarkably untroubled by them. Cabbage white caterpillars may take the occasional munch (though this will be much lessened by sowing nasturtiums as a sacrificial crop) and flea beetles are liable to punch the odd pinhole through the leaves, but I've never seen damage beyond the lightly cosmetic. It is a brassica though, and as such is susceptible to clubroot – a practically untreatable disease of brassicas which persists in the soil for years – so if you plan to grow kai lan plants for more than a year it may be worth resowing in a different position after a couple of years to minimise the potential for the disease to take hold.

HARVESTING
For once you don't have a long wait for your reward – two months or so after sowing you can start to pick lengths (up to 25cm) of stem and small upper leaves and flower buds.

STIR FRIED PORK WITH KAI LAN
Kai lan is a great addition to stir fries. Try this speedy supper with beef or chicken in place of the pork if you prefer.

SERVES 4
3 tbsp dark soy sauce
1 tbsp rice wine or sherry
1 tbsp toasted sesame oil
400g pork tenderloin, cut into
   1cm x 5cm strips
1 tbsp groundnut oil
3cm piece of fresh ginger, peeled and cut
   into thin strips
1 red chilli, halved lengthways, deseeded,
   membrane removed and cut into thin strips
2 garlic cloves, halved and finely sliced
200g young kai lan, trimmed
60ml chicken stock
4 spring onions, trimmed and cut on the
   diagonal into 1cm pieces
Juice of 1 small lemon
Small handful of coriander leaves
To serve: Rice or egg noodles

STIR FRIED PORK WITH KAI LAN

Whisk together the soy sauce, rice wine and sesame oil in a bowl. Add the pork strips, stir, cover and marinate for 20 minutes.

In a large frying pan or wok, heat the groundnut oil over a medium-high heat. Drain the pork of its marinade and fry in batches until browned. Remove to a warm plate while you prepare the rest.

Reduce the heat to medium and sauté the ginger, chilli and garlic for a minute. Stir in the kai lan and chicken stock and simmer, partially covered, until the kai lan is tender, about 2–3 minutes. Return the pork and any juices left on the plate to the pan with the spring onions and lemon juice and stir until heated through, about 4 minutes.

Sprinkle on the coriander and serve with rice or egg noodles.

CARDOONS

If you're not familiar with cardoons, imagine a thistle and celery having a gigantic child with a wild hairstyle and rather ragged (if beautiful) clothes. They are hugely impressive plants, often growing much larger than the closely related globe artichoke, though grown for very different reasons.

Although the immature flowerheads of cardoons and globe artichokes are similar, the size and anatomy of cardoon flowerheads make them a fiddle too far. Even if you did have the necessary time on your hands to whittle away to get to the heart, their flavour and texture is to globe artichokes what baseballs are to oranges.

The edible prize with cardoons is their crisp, succulent, ribbed leafstalks and stems which can be eaten either raw or cooked in endless ways – mostly commonly blanched like celery, stewed or roasted. Their flavour is gentle, sweet but not without a little bitterness, and closest to that of globe artichoke hearts.

As with rhubarb, cardoons can be grown without light to sweeten and tenderise the stalks and leafribs (a process known as 'blanching') by binding the leaves tight to the main stem to exclude the sun. Traditionally this was done with a rope made of twisted straw but sheets of cardboard tied in with string work perfectly well. After six weeks or so you'll uncover paler, tenderer, less bitter cardoon stalks. I find the edge of bitterness delicious, but being able to blanch the stalks and leafribs gives you another flavour to play with too.

Cardoons are native to Mediterranean Europe and North Africa where they grow wild. They became

a favourite of the Ancient Romans and Greeks and subsequently spread to become a popular vegetable throughout Europe, until around a century ago, when widespread growing decreased dramatically. Cardoons are, however, still popular in Portugal, where an enzyme extracted from the plant is used as a traditional vegetarian rennet in the making of many regional cheeses, including Nisa. In neighbouring Spain, cardoons are an ingredient of the chickpea stew 'Cocido madrileño', one of the national dishes.

The fact that there is a little bit of a fiddle to preparing cardoons (though no more than, say, chard) can put some people off. Don't be one of them: not only do cardoons possess a unique and fine flavour, they are worth growing if only to make everything else you grow look fabulous. Their silvery green jagged foliage seems to compliment every other garden colour (including bare earth), while the whole plant will add some structure to your space, as well as much winter interest. The flowers are extraordinary too and (along with the foliage) work very well as a cutting flower. Grow them at the back of your patch and you've instant impact, instant height and a backdrop that will make the rest of your space that little bit more impressive.

VARIETIES
Cardoons are usually sold as a generic unnamed variety in vegetable seed catalogues, but look out for 'Gigante di Romagna' – it grows large, healthily and has a fine flavour.

GROWING
Many people grow cardoons just to form a striking perennial tower or informal hedge in their herbaceous border, and why not – they are impressive in size (up to 2.5m in height and similar spread), colour (with their silvery-green foliage and vibrant purple flowers), and have the ability to lift a winter garden, adding the third dimension through the less productive weeks of the year.

EATING

As with salsify and globe artichokes, cardoon's flavour is distinctive but not overpowering. Young and small, the ribs are good raw, but are perhaps best when cooked – braising or blanching in stock before being battered and fried, or used in a gratin.

However you choose to use them, trim off any spiky or leafy bits to leave the central main rib. Chop the ribs into whatever sized pieces suit and drop them into acidulated water to prevent them discolouring. Use a potato peeler to peel the cardoon ribs, removing the shallow ridges along the main-rib as you go, and return them to the water. Parboiling for a few minutes is advisable prior to roasting.

Cardoons are great simply boiled and tossed in melted butter and flaky sea salt, Classic Vinaigrette (p.145) or garlicky mayonnaise.

For a real treat, serve raw, tender young stems dipped into bagna cauda, that deeply savoury and highly addictive Piedmontese sauce. Make it by gently heating 200g unsalted butter with 200ml olive oil until melted. Crush 4 or 5 garlic cloves and add them to the pot – you don't want them to fry, just to poach gently and infuse the sauce with their pungent aroma. Finely chop 5 or 6 anchovies in oil and add them to the pan, stirring until they dissolve. Add a few grinds of black pepper and the zest of 1 lemon and keep stirring until everything is well combined. Serve warm. In fact, if you're making this for a crowd, it might be time to drag out that dusty wedding present fondue kit to keep the sauce warm as people tuck into it. It's also fantastic with raw or blanched cauliflower. Tear some chunks of bread to dip in it too

– if you don't you can be certain your guests will.

The cardoon root is also edible, though harvesting it kills the plant. If you're particularly inquisitive, dig it up and prepare as you would parsnips. It tastes like celery, but sweeter.

CARDOON GRATIN
This is a wonderful, rich side dish to serve alongside a roast.

SERVES 8
Juice of 1 lemon
About 1kg cardoons, small or medium inner stalks only
1.25 litres chicken or vegetable stock
250ml double cream
1 bay leaf
Grating of nutmeg
Salt and freshly ground black pepper
120g Gruyère cheese, grated

Cardoons are as fail-safe, pest resistant and low-maintenance as any edible plant gets. They aren't overly fussy about soil type and they make good windbreaks once mature, but do stake them early on if they're on a windy site. Take your time when considering where to plant cardoons – they are large perennials, so envisage the mature plant when deciding on location. If you're planting a few cardoon plants together, allow them around a metre or so from each other.

Start cardoons off from seed either in individual cells or small pots in early spring (germination is usually quick and good) planting them out when they reach 10cm or so tall. You will need to avoid slugs during the first few week after planting out your cardoons, but therafter pests shouldn't be a problem.

If you know someone with plants or wish to expand your own cardoons you can separate the smaller plants that develop at the base of the mother plant as winter arrives, growing them in a pot undercover before planting out in mid-spring. You can even separate small plants from the main plant as late as mid-spring, and plant them immediately in their new home but they will be a little smaller than those separated in winter.

Although the flowerheads are too much of a fiddle to bother with eating, do let them flower. The large purple heads are gorgeous, make for perfect and long-lasting cut flowers for the house and bring beneficial insects such as bees into the garden.

HARVESTING
Cardoons are ready for blanching in late summer, with harvest around six weeks later. You can cut unblanched stems and ribs from the leaves at any time but do ensure that you go for the more succulent newer growth. The stalks quickly flop when cut, so be sure to harvest them when you're ready to cook.

Fill a bowl with cold water and add half the lemon juice.

Trim the cardoon stalks of any leaves and cut them into 10cm lengths, putting them into the bowl of water and lemon juice as you go to prevent them from browning.

Drain the cardoons and simmer them in the stock to which you've added the rest of the lemon juice until tender, about 35–40 minutes. Drain, reserving the stock. Cool the cardoons then peel away their spiny skins and strings, just as you would with celery.

Preheat the oven to 180°C/Gas 4.

Return the stock to a clean pan with the cream, bay leaf and a few gratings of nutmeg and boil to reduce to about 300ml. Season with salt and pepper.

Butter a gratin dish of approximately 35cm x 22 cm, spread the cardoons out in the dish and pour over just enough of the stock-and-cream mixture to cover. Sprinkle over the grated Gruyère and bake until browned and bubbly, about 35 minutes. Leave to stand for a few minutes before serving.

CARDOON STEMS WITH BAGNA CAUDA

ROMANESCO

Romanesco seems a little lost. In France it's a cabbage, in Germany it's the pyramid cauliflower, in Italy it's Romanesco broccoli. It is sold as any of those depending where you look for seeds, although given that it was first described in Italy 500 years ago perhaps we should go with Italian judgement. And by 'broccoli' I mean 'calabrese', although wherever we pigeonhole it, Romanesco shouts its individuality visually and gastronomically.

If it tasted like my shoe I'd grow Romanesco entirely for its beauty, but luckily it's delicious. It has the fresh, lively crunch of the best cauliflower but a sweet, gently spicy nuttiness that's not found in calabrese. It's also jammed with vitamins A and C, iron, fibre and is a particularly rich source of antioxidants.

And Romanesco's conical dome hides a quietly spectacular secret: its pattern of spiralling heads repeats, looking broadly the same whether you look from your garden chair, on your knees in the veg patch or with your nose against its leaves. A whole head of Romanesco is a rough conical spiral, itself comprised of spirals of conical buds, which are each in turn made up of smaller conical buds ordered into a logarithmic spiral. This visual pattern of self-repetition is known as a fractal.

Although self-similarity occurs elsewhere in nature – river courses, veins in leaves, mountain ranges, branching plants etc – it's a comparatively rare occurrence in the vegetable world. It makes Romanesco look a fussy brassica, fancy even, but when you tuck into its florets you'll be eating a delicious slice of mathematical magic.

For some reason Romanesco feels the need to take advantage of this mathematical possibility where other cauliflowers and calabrese don't seem bothered. There is no nutritive or reproductive benefit, so why is should be as it is, is a mystery. It's utterly pointless and entirely beautiful and I like that.

VARIETIES

Until the last few years Romanesco was a little tricky to track down in seed catalogues. Now you shouldn't have so much of a problem, as people are beginning to catch on to this deliciously different brassica. The only thing you'll have to ensure is that you look at both the calabrese and cauliflower pages – it can be classed as either. It can can also appear on its own.

I've only ever grown generically named Romanesco, although there is a variety, 'Veronica', which apparently produces slightly more individual florets rather than the more usual denser head.

GROWING

There are some critical steps to growing healthy brassicas such as Romanesco. So long as you follow these you'll give yourself every chance of getting your hands on some very fine veg.

Start your Romanesco off in modules undercover anytime in mid-spring, potting them on as soon as they're easy to handle. Brassicas like to grow steadily, without hesitation, so make sure they don't have to pause by having overgrown their module or pot.

I like to let Romanesco get to around 8cm tall and to wait until I am sure the last frosts are gone before I plant it out – this means that the plants usually sidestep the worst of the damage slugs and snails can do and have enough of a root system to grow on happily. Romanesco can grow into quite large

EATING

Romanesco is no less of a joy in the kitchen than it is on the plot. There are few vegetables more impressive than a whole head of Romanesco simply steamed, cut-side down, and served with a sharp, spicy dressing.

Otherwise, cut or harvest as smaller florets that show off that fabulous fractality. Steaming preserves both colour and texture better than boiling. Once cooked, plunge the Romanesco into iced (or at least very cold) water – this will encourage it to keep its fine sharp colour.

You can use Romanesco in the same way you would cauliflower or calabrese, but its particular tenderness lends itself to softening in stock or tomatoes and being used as the base of a pasta sauce, either with stronger flavours such as garlic and chilli, or other more gentle companions, which will allow its distinctive nuttiness to shine through.

ROASTED ROMANESCO PASTA WITH PINE NUTS AND RAISINS

Salty anchovies, sweet raisins, toasted pine nuts and roasted romanesco are a marriage made in heaven or, more precisely, southern Italy. Roasting the cauliflower gives it a wonderful depth of flavour which works perfectly not only with the pasta, but also with the romesco sauce which follows.

SERVES 6
1 small romanesco cauliflower
80ml olive oil
Salt and freshly ground black pepper
25g fresh breadcrumbs
450g dried spaghetti
3 anchovy fillets in oil
40g pine nuts
40g raisins
Small handful of parsley, tough stalks removed and coarsely chopped
Juice of ½ lemon
¼ tsp chilli flakes
To serve: Parmesan

▶

plants so allow 60cm or so between your seedlings and tread the soil down well to anchor the shallow-rooting plants.

Steady availability of water and nutrients is particularly important to brassicas. Add compost a few months before planting your brassicas and/or grow them where you previously grew peas and beans. The legume family (to which peas and beans belong) take nitrogen from the air and via root nodules make it available in the soil – the hungry brassicas will be especially happy to take advantage of any excess.

If you are after Romanesco at the very top of its game pick a spot for it with alkaline soil. If you don't have such a spot, add a little lime to your intended growing area. Though it may seem a bit of a fiddle, it will make your Romanesco particularly happy.

In dry periods a little light watering regularly will pay dividends. Living in the south west of England where we're rarely able to complain of lack of rain this is only occasionally something I have to do, but it is still critical nonetheless. If your Romanesco

(or other head-forming brassicas) stop their steady progress to perfection they will not fully recover however well you treat them subsequently.

Like most brassicas, Romanesco is affected by clubroot – an especially tedious disease of the roots which is almost impossible to eradicate from the soil. The only remedy is not to get it and this is best ensured by not growing brassicas in the same place in consecutive years, longer if possible.

Bolting – where the Romanesco burts its globe skywards in little florets, can be a problem. Although bolting tends to be caused by the extra light and heat that comes with long summer days, watering seems to arrest this urge, so get ready with the watering can if you've not had too much rain.

HARVESTING

Romanesco is usually ready to harvest in late autumn by which time it should have formed a dense head 20cm or more across. You can cut the whole head or snap off smaller heads – whichever suits you best. Harder frosts will burn the heads, so don't delay when the cold weather comes.

◄

Preheat the oven to 180°C/Gas 4. Break the romanesco cauliflower into florettes and toss in 60ml of the oil. Spread out on a baking sheet, sprinkle with salt and pepper and roast for 35–40 minutes, stirring a couple of times, until they start to turn golden and caramelise a bit. Toss with the breadcrumbs and return to the oven until they are toasted, about a further 5 minutes.

While the romanesco is cooking, put a large pan of water on to boil (you need at least 4 litres of water) to which you should add 1½ tbsp salt when it comes to the boil. Add the spaghetti and cook according to the instructions on the packet until just al dente.

While the pasta is cooking, chop the anchovies to a paste on a chopping board. Warm the remaining oil in a large saucepan over a medium heat and sauté the pine nuts

until just toasted, add the anchovies and stir until they are well combined, then stir in the raisins.

Drain the pasta well, reserving 100ml of the cooking liquid. Stir this into the pine nuts, anchovies and raisins. Toss the pasta into the sauce with the roasted romanesco cauliflower, toasted breadcrumbs, parsley, lemon juice, chilli flakes and a few grinds of black pepper. Divide between 6 warmed bowls and serve immediately, with the Parmesan and a grater passed around so everyone can serve themselves.

ROMESCO SAUCE

Romesco sauce, that most vibrantly hued Catalonian delight, is most traditionally served with seafood but it works wonderfully well as a dip for warm, middle eastern

flatbreads, with grilled meats and roasted vegetables. It is, in fact, very good served alongside or trickled over romanesco cauliflower roasted as in the preceding recipe. It really is. I'm not just saying this because serving up a plate of Romesco Romanesco sounds too good to resist.

MAKES ABOUT 350G
3 dried ancho chillies
2 red peppers
120ml extra-virgin olive oil
50g blanched whole hazelnuts
50g blanched whole almonds
1 thick slice of slightly stale good white bread, crusts removed
5 garlic cloves, finely sliced
1 large juicy tomato, peeled (see p.127), deseeded and roughly chopped
½ tsp smoked paprika

ROASTED ROMANESCO PASTA WITH PINE NUTS AND RAISINS

1 tbsp finely chopped parsley
1 tbsp red wine vinegar
Salt

Soak the chillies in warm water for an hour. Preheat the oven to 200°C/Gas 6. Core the peppers and cut them into quarters so they lie almost flat. Trickle over 1tbsp of the olive oil and roast until the skins blister and darken, about 35–40 minutes. Place in a bag for 5 minutes to steam, remove and peel off the blistered skins.

Scatter the nuts on a tray and roast in the oven until just beginning to turn golden, 5 minutes. Remove from the oven and cool.

Warm 4 tbsp of the olive oil in a small frying pan over a medium-high heat. Fry the bread until golden on both sides. Remove from the pan, lower the temperature and sauté the garlic for a minute until softened.

Drain and deseed the chillies and place in a blender or food processor with the peppers, tomato, garlic, nuts, bread broken into chunks, smoked paprika, parsley and red wine vinegar. Blitz, with about 3 tbsp oil, until you have a smoothish paste. Taste and add salt if necessary.

LEAVES & FLOWERS

There are few things less inspiring than a ropey salad. An average supper can at least fill a hole, but a leafy disappointment isn't worth the effort of eating on any front. I'm not going to eat a limp, undressed lettuce just because it's supposed to be good for me and I don't expect you are either. Even when it's good, a salad is not likely to result in you kicking back, hunger abated, with cigars and brandy. Neither will the wealth of antioxidants you've just taken on board leave you bathing in a post-meal rosy glow. Salad satisfies in another way, and only if the flavour and texture is spot on.

The secret to truly wonderful salad is in the varieties you sow and the combinations you put together. Although there are days when all I want from a salad is a perfect 'Buttercrunch' lettuce dressed with just a little good olive oil and salt, salad needn't start and finish with lettuce.

More often than not I want something a little more varied, and if you want a mixed salad, you have to grow that way. One of the biggest changes in how I grow has been in growing fewer whole lettuces every year and more and more leaves to cut young and lush. By sowing patches of many different leaves I can put together a mixed salad that suits me. 'Green Oak Leaf', 'Cocarde', 'Bionda Foglia', 'red salad bowl', 'Freckles' and 'Bughatti' are amongst the lettuce leaves I have growing to cut before they grow to maturity. The cut-and-come-again approach is simple: sow lines or blocks of leafy salads and cut them when they are perhaps 10cm tall, leaving 3cm or so at the base. This remaining core has the roots and enough above-ground green to quickly resprout for you to take another picking. Gone is the tiresome waiting for the plants to heart up without bolting and the waste that often comes with rows of lettuce being ready at once. You will also get to eat weeks rather than months after sowing, and then come back for second, third and fourth helpings shortly afterwards.

If you're not familiar with them, oriental leaves reward a little investigation. Every year I grow mizuna, mibuna, green in snow, chop suey greens, giant Indian mustard, red frills mustard and Shungiku. Each has its own personality yet almost all have an underlying pepperiness that increases the larger the leaves are. I love them on their own and in combination. Try a few small leaves cut from any of the oriental family of leaves thrown into an otherwise plainer leafy salad and you'll see how they lift and lighten it.

Salads are all about flavour and texture rather than volume, and nothing demonstrates this better than microleaves. In a few pages time I'll be trying to convince you to chop down a whole forest of seedlings when they're scarcely a few centimetres tall. You may think this a dreadful waste of plants that'll grow a hundred times taller, until you taste them. Microleaves are a revelation of clean clear flavour and you don't even have to wait to get them – try them ten days after sowing and you may never grow these leaves any other way again.

I'll also urge you to eat a few flowers. Although they may not be enough to keep body and mind together, edible flowers do add a little glitter to what might otherwise be a plainer parade. I was unenthusiastic when I first heard about them but I exercised my own advice of trying to find a way in which everything is delicious and ran to the garden to throw a nasturtium flower into my mouth. I'm glad I did. Courgette flowers followed shortly afterwards. Stuffed with soft cheese and herbs and deep fried in tempura batter, they make a fabulous lunch. From there, I'd be surprised if your inquisitiveness didn't get the better of you and drag your tastebuds towards the daylilies, the herb flowers and on to violas, calendulas and beyond.

When you've gone to all the trouble of growing your own salad leaves and flowers, when you've nurtured them, weeded around them and protected them from all manner of flying and creeping predators, you don't want to fall down at the last minute when you finally get them to the kitchen table. Treat them gently. Pick through the leaves, discarding any less-than-perfect ones, and place them in a sink or bowl filled with cold water to remove dust and grit. Unless I've got all the leaves absolutely at the top of their game I like to let the leaves stay in the water for at least an hour, often two. This perks them up, conditioning them perfectly for you to use immediately. When you're ready, lift them a handful or two at a time into a salad spinner – don't overload it as you'll bruise the leaves. Spin them, place onto a clean tea towel and pat them very gently, tenderly, to remove any remaining water. Your dressing won't cling seductively to damp leaves, so it's worth taking a little extra trouble to ensure a perfect result. Any that you're not eating straight away can be kept undressed in a tied plastic food bag in the bottom of the fridge. Conditioned like this they should last most of a week, perhaps longer.

DAYLILIES

The challenge with eating daylilies is cultural as much as anything: there's no getting around the fact here that you are eating a 'flower' flower, rather than a 'vegetable' flower. And yet, while it might seem another leap entirely from courgette flowers, or even nasturtiums, it really is one worth making.

Daylilies are not true lilies (which are inedible), they belong to the *Hemerocallis* species which originate in eastern Asia, where they have a long history of kitchen and medicinal use. You'll find the flowers sold as gum jum (or 'golden needles') fresh or dry throughout the region where they are commonly used in soup (especially hot and sour soup) and pork dishes such as moo shu.

The daylily's species name derives from the Greek 'hemera kallos' meaning 'day beauty' and, as the name implies, the flowers tend to last only a day. A blossom usually opens at dawn, brightens the garden for the day and fades with the sun. However beautiful and ephemeral this might be, don't let it cause you to

hesitate: it's an excuse to feel better about eating them. While each blossom may only last a day, the plant produces a succession of flowers, usually over a number of weeks.

Enjoy the show of their blossom and pick them late in the day before they wilt, knowing that you haven't harvested anything that hadn't fully enjoyed its moment in the limelight. They'll be delicately sweet from their nectar, retaining a crisp vigour that can even have a crunch to it, as well as being at their most nutritious.

Daylilies offer far more than just beautiful edible flowers, however. You can eat all parts of the plant, presenting you with something to nibble on for months – the early leaves in spring, the buds as well as the flowers in summer and then the rhizomes when the cold weather comes. As well as daylilies' ability to take to most soils, this steady supply made them such an attractive proposition to early settlers to America, who brought them to the country and sucessfully cultivated them in large numbers.

Daylilies' unique characteristics have (unsurprisingly) attracted enthusiasts, specialist experimentation and endless societies dedicated to their loveliness. Their long history of hybridisation has given us over 60,000 cultivars, many of which are rather unpleasantly gaudy. As with fuchsias, it can all get a bit anoracky with daylilies, but I find it best to just think of them as a food crop like any other. They just happen to be rather beautiful too.

VARIETIES

There are so many daylily varieties to chose from that it's worth being nosy and asking suppliers for their recommendations, and (if you can) trying a few. With a little planning you can grow early-, mid- and late-season varieties, resulting in a flower harvest that will last for months on end.

Although by no means a hard and fast rule, bear in mind that it is usual for varieties with yellow flowers to be the sweetest, with more likelihood of bitterness found in the red daylilies.

'Hyperion' is an excellent daylily to start with. It grows strongly to a metre or so in height and is hardy and robust. It also throws out many yellow flowers over a fairly lengthy period each year. At only 40cm or so tall the yellow flowering 'Stella d'Oros' is the perfect smaller variety for those wanting to grow daylilies in pots.

If you want to add a splash of colour to your garden, try growing 'Red Rum' – one of the tastiest red flowering varieties. Although it grows to only 50cm (and so is also a good choice for growing in pots) it is especially hardy, flowers over a long period and has excellent disease resistance.

You may want to consider the spreading *Hemerocallis fulva* if you're looking for a vigorous understorey crop for a forest garden or orchard. It grows to about a metre high, and will take up any space it's allowed to root into. This is the type most widely cultivated in China and Japan, where the flowers are picked as they start to droop, before being dried for sale.

GROWING

Daylilies are extremely easy to grow, are hardy and perennial. They need very little care and will tolerate everything but extreme conditions. Give them something a little more favourable – full sun, and a little well-drained room to expand into – and they'll grow happily and flower abundantly.

Daylilies can be grown from seed, but to ensure they grow true to type you would be much better off buying them as young plants. Once you have have them growing (or if you know someone else with plants) you can divide them in late winter or early spring in order to create new specimens.

EATING

Daylily flowers are delicious at all stages of their growth, raw or cooked. The flower buds and pods taste a little of French beans and are best stir-fried or steamed, but it's their blossoms with their succulent sweet crunch that I favour. These blossoms are fabulous from the point of half-openness, but if you try nipping them from the plant towards the end of the day when they're near to (but not actually) wilting, you'll get to enjoy them in their sweet prime in the garden as well as in the kitchen.

Try a few thrown into leafy salads, or just raw as a simple gardener's treat. If you miss picking some before they start to go over you can use a handful or two of withered flowers to thicken soups and stews.

You can even eat the daylily's crisp, nutty tubers. While I have yet to try these, their taste is apparently similar to salsify (which I love) and they can be prepared in much the same way. Try serving them as a side to something like a slow roast shoulder of lamb. Be sure not to take big hauls of tubers though – these are the engine room of the plant, so think of them as an occasional underground treasure.

Daylily shoots make a fine alternative to asparagus, and one that doesn't take 3 years to materialise. Pick them while they are still small – 12cm at most in length – and strip away the

Dividing daylilies is simple. Lift the clump and either chop it into quarters using a sharp spade and plant each immediately, or (for more, smaller new plants) break off new shoots with a portion of root and pot each up to get them away to a good start. The new plants may need some time to regain vigour, perhaps even a year, so you may prefer not to divide all your plants at once.

Once planted they rapidly form a clumping heart from which they grow and flower each year. Avoid non-clumping varieties unless you're happy for them to spread rapidly – the Tawny daylily has naturalised in some areas to such as extent it is also known as the roadside or railroad daylily. Ask your supplier for advice if you're not sure about the variety to get.

Slugs and snails are usually the only pests to battle. They love the fresh new growth, but most varieties are vigorous enough to grow away from any nibbling. Do take whatever measures you prefer (see p.176) to protect young plants though.

Pick off and incinerate any buds that become unusually swollen and fail to open – they may house the grub of the hemerocallis gall midge which attacks and destroys the lilly.

HARVESTING

Daylily flowers and buds appear in summer. Once the patch is established you'll find a clump throws out new flowerheads fast enough to keep up with all but the most enthusiastic harvesting. You can pick and eat the buds any time along their journey to opening.

Daylily leaves are edible, as are the tubers (though I've yet to try either). If you fancy giving the leaves a go, they apparently best in early spring. Try frying 10cm lengths of the tender, young outer leaves gently in butter – they have a mild oniony flavour. In late autumn into winter, when the tubers have grown well through the summer, you can dig up the plant (perhaps to divide into more) and harvest a few of the sausage-shaped roots, replanting the rest.

outer leaves before eating in any way that you might asparagus. As with the tubers, remember to be gentle in your enthusiasm for harvesting if you want the plant to thrive.

A classic tempura treatment works well for the flower buds and even better for the whole daylily flowers, which make great, wildly shaped fritters. To make the batter, whisk together 120g plain flour with a good pinch of salt, an egg yolk and about 170ml chilled sparkling water, enough to make a batter the thickness of double cream. Don't worry if it's a bit lumpy – this is one occasion when that doesn't matter,

it's even desirable. Dip the flowers into batter and deep fry them 1 or 2 at a time in groundnut or vegetable oil heated to 180°C (if you don't have a thermometer, a cube of bread dropped into the oil should turn golden brown in just under a minute). Fry the flowers until golden, drain on kitchen paper, sprinkle with sea salt and serve immediately with chilli dipping sauce.

HOT AND SOUR DAYLILY SOUP
Don't be put off by the long list of ingredients – this hot and sour soup is simplicity itself to throw together, just put the dried mushrooms into soak while you

assemble everything else and you're ready to go. If you'd like to make it meat-free, just leave out the chicken and add more mushrooms in its place.

SERVES 4–6
25g dried shitake mushrooms
1 tbsp groundnut oil
1 tsp sesame oil
4–5 kaffir lime leaves, roughly chopped
2.5cm piece of fresh ginger, peeled and very finely sliced
3 garlic cloves, halved and finely sliced
2 sticks of fresh lemongrass, tough outer layers discarded, and finely chopped
2 small green chillies, halved, deseeded, membranes removed and finely sliced
150g fresh shitake or wild mushrooms, sliced

DAYLILY FRITTERS

1 litre chicken stock
3 tbsp nam pla or fish sauce
1 tbsp soy sauce
1 tsp soft brown sugar
About 270g boneless, skinned chicken breast,
    cut into thin strips, or leftover cooked
    chicken
Salt and freshly ground black pepper
6 spring onions, trimmed and cut into 2cm
    pieces on the diagonal
Small handful of daylily buds
3 tbsp Chinese black vinegar, or 2 tbsp apple
    balsamic vinegar
1½ tbsp Chinese rice vinegar
Juice of 1 lime
Small handful of daylily petals
30 or so coriander microleaves (see p.144) or
    a few regular coriander leaves

Put the dried mushrooms into a bowl and cover them with boiling water. Leave to soak for 30 minutes, then drain through a fine sieve, reserving the liquid. Pat the mushrooms dry and slice them.

Warm the groundnut and sesame oils in a large saucepan over a medium heat and sauté the lime leaves, ginger, garlic, lemongrass and chillies for a couple of minutes, then add the dried and fresh mushrooms and sauté for another couple of minutes. Pour in the stock, nam pla or fish sauce, soy sauce, 65ml of the mushroom soaking liquid and the sugar. Bring to the boil, simmer for 5 minutes, then add the chicken and a few grinds of black pepper and simmer for 5 more minutes. Add the spring onions, daylily buds and vinegars.

Simmer for 2 minutes. Remove from the heat, stir in the lime juice, daylily petals and half the coriander microleaves or regular coriander. Taste and adjust seasoning if necessary. Throw over the remaining coriander leaves and serve immediately in warmed bowls.

MICROLEAVES

If you try nothing else in this book, I urge you to try planting some microleaves. These tender, flavourful veg and herb seedlings, harvested almost before they've had a chance to start growing, will transform the way you grow and eat some of your favourite foods.

Fennel, rocket, chervil, sorrel, coriander and radish in particular are a revelation harvested as microleaves. Their characteristic flavour is all there, concentrated in miniature, and it comes with a punch every bit as powerful as when they're fully grown. And you don't have the wait.

Seven days is all it takes in the summer to sow, water and then nibble on a few miniature harvests – you'll wonder why you used to wait so long to enjoy their flavour at full size. It's a way of growing that can take some getting used to. We harvest almost everything we grow at its largest, ripest and most tender. We seek volume – it tells us we've been successful. Microleaves are the complete antithesis of

this traditional way of growing but give them a whirl and, I promise, you'll soon find them taking over your windowsills.

Growing microleaves couldn't be easier: you simply sow seeds in a seed tray or guttering and in seven to twenty days (depending on variety and time of year) you snip sensational seedlings. This is all the time it takes in the spring and summer for the seeds to germinate and start to grow. All you have to do is interrupt this journey to adulthood when the seedlings are no taller than 8cm.

You may need to adjust your perceptions a little to feel comfortable with hacking down a plant so early in life. You won't be the only person to have the scissors at the ready and wonder if it's not better to let the seedling grow on to a full sized plant, but ask yourself this; what will give you most pleasure – volume or flavour?

Coriander is the perfect example of a herb that excels when grown as microleaves. If you grow coriander to full size before you harvest its fragrant leaves you'll have to wait for a few months and then run the risk of it bolting (going to seed) in the sun. The growing leaves also lose their tenderness and liveliness of flavour very quickly as the plant ages. Instead, try sowing a few coriander leaves in a pot on a sunny windowsill. When they're no more than a few centimetres tall, pick out one seedling. Not two, not a handful, just one. Wipe any compost from the roots and put the single seedling in your mouth. Chew very slowly at the front of your mouth and let the coriander flavour take over. It's as if you have a handful of 'regular' coriander in there, only a fresher, livelier coriander than you may be used to.

Microleaves are ideal for anyone with limited space. The more restricted your growing area, the more you should prioritise transformers – those punchy flavours that liven up your meals – and microleaves fit the bill perfectly. All you need is a short length or two of guttering filled with microleaves on your windowsill to bring their intense flavour into your

kitchen without taking up too much of your valuable space.

As well as offering a revelation in familiar flavours, microleaves breed confidence. Many first-time growers fail in their first year because they grow the usual suspects – a square of potatoes, a patch of cabbages, a block or two of carrots and a line of onions – that often taste very close to what they're used to buying. There's no feeling of 'success' for months and when it finally comes the taste isn't so sweet. Successful growing is about confidence and momentum. Microleaves will tell you within a week that 'you can grow' and you'll taste the difference that sowing a few seeds can make.

VARIETIES
It tends to be the stronger, distinctive flavours which carry their flavour best in miniature. The leafy herbs, along with radishes and fennel are my favourites. The oriental leaves are also well worth investigating – giant red mustard, red frills mustard and mizuna in particular – their mustard edge comes through even in miniature, and a little goes a long way.

EATING

The intensity and clarity of flavour in many microleaves will be a surprise to those new to them. They seem to possess all the flavour potential of the adult plant in their infant state. Flavours are typically cleaner and brighter and this encourages a simple treatment. Don't let them get lost.

A small handful cast into a leafy salad will set it alight with a lively punch, but do let microleaves stand on their own two feet as well. While a simple small salad of well-chosen microleaves creates a flavoursome and dainty accompaniment to a simply grilled piece of fish or meat, they have other uses too.

Dress just-cooked pasta with a slug of really good extra-virgin olive oil, a squeeze of lemon, some grinds of black pepper and a few gratings of Parmesan then, at the very last minute, toss through a handful of microleaves and serve immediately, when they're just wilted. Or try using them in the poshest-ever version of that childhood favourite, an egg and 'cress' sandwich.

Remember: with microleaves it's not about volume, it's about flavour.

CLASSIC VINAIGRETTE
Creating a perfect vinaigrette is the work of minutes and so easy, you wonder why supermarket shelves are crammed with

expensive, unpleasant, entirely lesser versions of the real thing. The art of dressing a salad, especially when it is composed of something as tiny and precious as microleaves, is to use a large bowl and the merest slick of dressing. Pour a few droplets of vinaigrette into the bottom of the bowl, add the leaves and turn them over gently with your hands until they're glistening with the barest shimmer of dressing.

MAKES ABOUT 250ML
1 tsp Dijon mustard
2 tbsp red wine vinegar, cider vinegar or lemon juice
Good pinch of flaky sea salt
6 tbsp good fruity, extra-virgin olive oil or extra-virgin cold-pressed rapeseed oil
Freshly ground black pepper

▶

Purple and red leaved veg such as 'Red Drumhead' cabbage and amaranth are also worth growing simply for their looks, to accompany the other more intensely flavoured microleaves and add a colourful flourish to all that green.

Most veg and herb varieties are largely indistinguishable at the seedling stage so you can sow any you fancy apart from parsnips, as their seedlings are poisonous.

GROWING

Sow into guttering or seed trays with a 3–4cm of seed compost, leaving around 8cm at either end to prevent any spilling out when watered. A sunny windowsill or greenhouse is the ideal location.

Watering is important to ensure good swift growth, but regular light watering is best – just a gentle sprinkling, across (rather than along) the guttering minimises the risk of compost being washed out.

I use two metre-long pieces of guttering, each of which I sow in quarters of radish, coriander, rocket and giant red mustard. This gives me a blast of contrasting flavours to throw into salads, to eat with fish or just to nibble on for the pleasure of it. Sowing them seven days apart means that I'm harvesting

from one piece of guttering while the other grows replacement microleaves. In winter, germination and growth is slower but the warmth of your home will still be steady enough to give you microleaves right the way through the colder months. With the slowing down of growth, I double up the number of gutters and sow them in pairs, a fortnight apart, to keep up a good supply.

One of the great advantages of growing microleaves is that they aren't around long enough to attract the attention of pests and diseases. With a turn-around time of one to three weeks between sowing and picking and with the plants being grown and harvested indoors, the odds are stacked much more in your favour than in that of the slugs and snails.

HARVESTING

Microleaves are ready to harvest when they have formed their first true leaves. They are best cut around 5–8cm tall. When you're growing them for the first time, try some very small and let some grow larger to see where you most enjoy their flavour and texture.

Microleaves are best harvested with scissors, giving you a clean cut and avoiding the need to wash the compost from the roots.

◀

In a small bowl, whisk together the mustard, vinegar or lemon juice and salt until the salt has dissolved. (Once you add the oil, the salt won't dissolve, so do make sure the crystals are amalgamated into the mustardy mixture first.) Now trickle in the oil, a couple of drops at a time at first and then more quickly as it begins to emulsify, until you have a thick, glossy dressing. Stir in a few grinds of black pepper to finish.

ALTERNATIVELY: You can adapt this recipe, adding more mustard if you'd like it to be a little more fiery, a clove of garlic mashed to a purée with the salt first, and/or herbs, of course (try it with the fines herbes mixture used in Omelette aux Fines Herbes, see p.102), but add any herbs just before you want to use the vinaigrette so they're at their perky best. Without the herbs, you can seal the vinaigrette in an airtight jar and keep it in the fridge for up to a week.

MICROLEAVES SALAD

MIZUNA

Oriental leaves are a deliciously diverse family of leaves that inhabit that space where salad ends and cabbage begins. Getting to know this missing link will help you to bring punch and life to your salad bowl and a lightly cooked green zip to your stir fries.

If you're unfamiliar with oriental leaves, mizuna (also known as Japanese mustard, potherb mustard or Japanese greens) is as good a starting point as you'll find. It looks like a more deeply, sharply incised rocket, and while they share a lively pepperiness, there's a bright grassiness that adds to mizuna's distinctive flavour.

Like its close cousins mibuna, green in snow and many of the other oriental leaves, mizuna has only recently become popular in Europe (although it was originally introduced from China and Japan in the 18th century, but to no great applause). Now it is one of the most common leaves in supermarket mixed salad bags – so you may be more familiar with

mizuna than you are aware – but is still rarely sold on its own. To enjoy it at its best then, you'll have to grow you own.

And there are so many good reasons to do so. Mizuna is prolific, tolerant of most soils, happy in pots, grows its beautiful rosettes of leaves all year round and adds spice, colour and visual interest in the kitchen and the garden in winter, when those qualities can be in short supply.

Mizuna is also surprisingly good for you, being high in vitamin C and folic acid. It's also packed with antioxidants and glucosinolates which are

thought to inhibit the development of cancers of the lungs and alimentary tract. These compounds give mizuna (and other brassicas) its characteristic mustardy depth. I find leaves around 10cm long bright but mild and ideal for eating raw, while the larger leaves have a greater concentration of the compounds and therefore a stronger mustard flavour.

These larger leaves are perfect for stir-frying, having the substance to stand up to brief cooking which also moderates their mustardy heat a little. Try a handful of leaves thrown in late to a stir fry for a minute or two next to garlic, ginger, prawns and a few sploshes of soy – and you'll see what I mean.

VARIETIES

You'll almost always find mizuna sold under it's generic name, but there are few other varieties out there – the finely divided 'Early mizuna' and 'Fine-leaved mizuna', and the broader leaved 'Waido'. All are equally delicious.

GROWING

There are few plants easier to grow than mizuna. It is happy growing in most soils, it's tolerant of all but the coldest weather yet slow to bolt in full sun, and while it grows more slowly in winter you can still cut a harvest once in a while. It's a real all-year-round easy-winner: grow it once and it'll become a permanent fixture in your veg patch.

This tolerance of temperature extremes makes mizuna invaluable in the height of summer when many lettuces tend to run to seed, making it a great follow-on from peas, beans and early summer crops such as lettuce and carrots.

I sow mine any time between March and October straight into the soil, but you can start mizuna off undercover in modules if you prefer. Plant seedlings out when the first true leaves emerge – usually within a fortnight, often much sooner.

Although you can grow mizuna as individual plants in lines as you might lettuce (allow at least 20cm between plants), I prefer to cut most of my leaves when they are small, so I sow it in swathes. Sprinkled in a block, they'll grow into a green mass of leaves that will smother out most weeds and retain moisture. It's a beautifully low-maintenance way of growing all the oriental leaves (and many other salads), and makes a perfect edible understorey for taller plants such as sweetcorn.

EATING

As an addition to a mixed leaf salad, mizuna comes into its own. Go for smaller, less mustardy leaves initially and explore your preferences from there. If you're making a salad of mizuna only, try a little honey in the vinaigrette – it sits very happily against the mustard of the leaves.

Don't be afraid to branch out with mizuna – it can turn its hand to any recipe in place of rocket, it's fabulous thrown late into a stir-fry and makes a deliciously different variation on the usual basil pesto.

MIZUNA PESTO

Dotted onto a bowl of soup at the last minute (such as the Cream of Jerusalem Artichoke Soup, see p.162), spooned onto pizza and, of course, swirled into pasta, this punchy pesto adds a huge hit of flavour. It works brilliantly with rocket too.

MAKES 1 x 250ML JAR

30g whole, skinned almonds or hazelnuts
1 small garlic clove
Salt and freshly ground black pepper
100g mizuna leaves, roughly chopped
30g finely grated Parmesan or hard goat's cheese
Finely grated zest of ½ small lemon
1 tbsp lemon juice
5–7 tbsp extra-virgin olive oil or extra-virgin cold-pressed rapeseed oil

Preheat the oven to 180°C/Gas 4. Spread the nuts out onto a baking sheet and bake for 8 minutes, until they just begin to take on some colour. Tip onto a plate and cool. When they're cold, pulse them in a food processor until quite fine.

On a chopping board, chop the garlic clove, add a little pinch of salt and combine the two with the flat of your knife into a paste. Put into a food processor with the nuts, mizuna leaves, cheese, zest and lemon juice. Pulse a few times until coarsely chopped and combined. Add the oil slowly, pulsing as you go, until you get the consistency you like. Be careful not to over-process.

Test and add more salt, lemon juice and some ground black pepper, according to your own taste.

Although mizuna is a brassica it's not vital to respect its place with the rest of that family in a traditional crop rotation; I tend to grow it with the salad leaves, and in a different place each year to minimise any risk of disease.

Flea beetle and slugs are the only real nuisances you may have to deal with. Flea beetles are small (1–2mm) black beetles that rarely do more than leave a few tiny perforations through the leaves. I usually leave them to it, but if they're making more than cosmetic damage I use a tip of organic gardener Bob Flowerdew's, smearing treacle on a piece of card and brushing it across the tips of the mizuna leaves – it disturbs the beetles, making them jump (like fleas) onto the treacle. Slugs can be disposed of as you see fit (see p.176).

HARVESTING

One of the great pleasures of mizuna and many of its close relatives is that rather than wait for a set time to pick its leaves, you get to develop a relationship it, getting a feel for when the balance of flavours and the relative intensity of the mustard suits you best. In warmer parts of the year this can easily be within three weeks of sowing.

Pinch off the odd leaf as they grow: if it tastes good, get harvesting. You can pull the whole plant up if you wish, but why not take a cut-and-come-again approach, allowing you to harvest from one sowing for months.

There are two approaches to cut-and-come-again harvesting. You can pinch leaves off a couple of centimetres above the base, or (as I prefer) snip them off with sharp scissors. Either way, harvest with care as the roots are shallow and easily dislodged. The roots and leaf stubs that remain act as the engine room for growth. Within a few days you'll notice leaves resprouting, and within a couple of weeks you'll be harvesting again.

If you have a cloche, greenhouse or polytunnel, you'll find mizuna grows fairly steadily through autumn and winter, although you'll not be able to harvest so frequently. As soon as there's a hint of spring warmth, growth speeds up again, helping you fill the otherwise lean weeks of spring.

There are two ways of ensuring that you never run out of mizuna. You can sow mizuna (and any other of the oriental leaves) in at least two instalments, at least a week apart, as the second sowing will be ready after the first, or sow some seed undercover (in the polytunnel or under a cloche) and some outside for the same staggered development.

Harvesting often keeps the leaves tender, but eventually, after a few months, they'll start to become slightly less succulent when they resprout. As soon as you get the first inklings of this, sow a replacement batch to take over.

ALTERNATIVELY: This pesto is wonderful as it is, simply tossed through pasta, but you can give it an extra kick by gently sautéing three or four chopped anchovies and a finely chopped red chilli until the anchovies melt into a pulp, then tumbling it through cooked pasta, about 350g uncooked weight to serve 4, with 3 tbsp of the pesto and a small handful of fresh breadcrumbs, fried in butter until just golden. Pass some more Parmesan or goat's cheese around the table with the grater so people can help themselves.

MIZUNA PESTO

NASTURTIUMS

Much as Jerusalem artichokes are the most generous vegetable plant, nasturtiums are the edible flower equivalent. Sow them and you're sowing the equivalent of five plants in one go: you get delicious flowers, fine young leaves for salads, a living mulch growing between your brassicas, the perfect companion plant, and then late in the season you have the seeds to enjoy in any number of ways. And, as with Jerusalem artichokes, sow them once and you have them for life: they self-seed prolifically giving you more next year for no effort or expense.

Along with courgette flowers, nasturtiums are the best passport to the world of edible flowers. If you're trying one for the first time, don't be a wuss and nibble at a petal, throw a whole flower in your mouth – the experience and the gradual unravelling of flavours is quite unlike anything else in the garden.

Imagine a handful of rocket dipped in honey and dusted lightly in mild chilli powder and you'll be somewhere near the flavour. Often as the more gentle flavours fade a wave of pepperiness takes over right at the end: nasturtium means 'nose-tweaker', alluding to this pepperiness which (while it varies) can get up there with watercress for bite in some varieties.

The seeds, which develop in huge numbers in late autumn, are purported to stave off colds if taken by the handful at first inkling that the sniffles are on their way. I haven't tried this remedy although I know plenty of people who swear it works, but it's far from easy to get many of the little devils down as they seem to take the moisture out of your mouth. I tried a few and felt like I was in the egg-eating scene in *Cool Hand Luke*.

Nasturtiums are as good a companion plant as there is. They repel a number of cucurbit beetles and bugs, and act as a sacrificial plant – offering their leaves for the cabbage white caterpillars to feast on rather than your brassicas, while also attracting black fly away from your less vigorous and more susceptible harvests. Their flowers also attract pollinating and predatory insects, helping to maintain the ecological balance vital to a healthy organic garden.

Nasturtiums' rambling vigorous habit allows them to fill the spaces between your other plants, mulching out the weeds, retaining moisture and protecting the otherwise bare earth from erosion. They also look quite beautiful while they go about their caretaker duties, making them the perfect companion for you too.

patch and thin any cramped areas as they grow.

You don't need to give nasturtiums the best seat in the house. They will thrive very happily in poor soil as well as good.

Nasturtiums will grow happily in pots. If you are growing in posts, they will welcome the odd comfrey feed (see p.183) and be sure to water them frequently, through any extended periods without rain, to ensure that they do not dry out

VARIETIES
The two finest varieties I've found for flavour and looks are 'Black Velvet', (which will happily clamber if you give it a structure to grow up) and 'Tip Top Mahogany', which has particularly peppery leaves.

GROWING
Nasturtiums ability to self-seed prolifically is (at least to me) a very desirable trait: I love the fact that I don't have to worry about sowing or buying more seed, and just tear up any plants that come up where I don't want them.

Sow the seed in spring, either in lines 10cm apart if you are just sowing a few, or broadcast them in a

HARVESTING
Having planted your nasturtiums in early spring you'll be in for a delicious harvest of peppery, colourful trumpets from late spring all the way through to well into autumn. Nasturtiums are very productive, so you'll be hard pushed to make much of a dent in their stocks – but do leave at least half of the flowers unpicked for the bees and other pollinating insects to take advantage of.

You can pick the young new nasturtium leaves at any time through the growing season. The seeds too, while the source of your supply of plants for next year, can be picked reasonably freely through late autumn and into winter as they are produced in such profusion.

EATING

Nasturtium flowers make a fabulous pick-me-up plucked from the plant and eaten as you wander about the garden, but they're even better scattered into a mixed leaf salad where their spicy heat and sweetness makes a peppery punctuation to the plainer leaves. Try them in tempura batter too (see p.141), where their peppery honey comes through beautifully.

Although far from appetising as a cold cure, nasturtium seeds can be pickled into an outstanding and very English version of a jar of

Mediterranean capers.

Nasturtium leaves, picked small, are far better subjects for your kitchen time. Like the flowers, they work well added sparingly to leafy salads, and make a deliciously different pesto. Blitz a cup each of pine nuts, olive oil and pecorino with 2 cups of small nasturtium leaves and a clove of garlic in a blender and use just as you would any pesto.

Nasturtium leaves also make a wonderfully savoury butter to serve with steaks or grilled fish. Beat 200g

softened butter until smooth then stir in half a dozen finely shredded nasturtium leaves, the zest of half a small lemon, 1 tbsp lemon juice and a few grinds of black paper. Place the butter on a sheet of cling film and shape into a sausage about 3cm thick. Wrap well in the cling film and refrigerate for at least 4 hours. Cut into slices and place on top of the hot meat or fish just before serving. If you don't use it all at once, leftover nasturtium butter can be frozen, well wrapped, for a month or so.

NASTURTIUM RISOTTO

NASTURTIUM RISOTTO

Golden saffron risotto threaded with
peppery nasturtium leaves and scattered
with fiery orange petals is as dramatic to
look at as it is simple to make.

SERVES 4

12 threads of saffron
900ml chicken or vegetable stock
1 tbsp olive oil
1 tbsp unsalted butter
1 medium onion, finely diced
1 garlic clove, crushed
260g arborio or vialone nano risotto rice
100ml dry white wine
25g finely grated pecorino or Parmesan,
  plus extra (ungrated) for serving

Salt and freshly ground black pepper
40g nasturtium leaves, shredded
Some calendula or nasturtium petals

Put the saffron in a small bowl with a
tablespoon of hot water and leave to infuse
as you get on with making the risotto.

Put the stock in a saucepan over a low
heat to warm. In a risotto pan or large
frying pan, warm the oil and butter over a
medium-low heat then add the onion and
sauté gently until softened and translucent,
about 15 minutes. Add the garlic and
stir for a further minute, then add the
rice, stirring until well coated, and tip in
the wine. Stir until the liquid has almost
completely evaporated.

Pour the saffron threads and their golden
liquid into the pan containing the stock.
Begin to add the stock to the rice a ladleful
at a time, stirring constantly until the
liquid is almost completely absorbed before
adding another ladleful. Begin to taste the
rice after about 25 minutes – the grains
should be tender but not mushy.

When it is cooked, stir in the cheese until
it is melted and coats the grains. Remove
from the heat, taste and add salt and
pepper if needed. Stir in the nasturtium
leaves and scatter the calendula or
nasturtium petals over the top.

Serve immediately, passing the pecorino
or Parmesan around the table with the
grater so everyone can help themselves.

SORREL

Make a little corner in your garden for sorrel. It pretty much looks after itself and even a small patch of it will give you regular handfuls of sharp, lemony leaves that will extend the palate of flavours you have to play with in the kitchen.

Sorrel takes its name from the French surele: sur meaning 'sour'. It is a distant relation of the similarly sharp rhubarb, both owing their edge to high levels of oxalic acid. Its pointed leaves are almost spinach-shaped but smaller and green, or silver-green for buckler-leaved sorrel.

We don't really do 'sour' or 'bitter' as much as we should, certainly here in Britain. There are exceptions such as rhubarb, gooseberries and lemons, but perhaps because sorrel is a leaf and so easily comparable to other sweeter salads it hasn't gained widespread popularity here. In France it's quite different, and last time I looked they knew a thing or two about cooking.

The secret in welcoming sorrel into your kitchen is to use its bite wisely. Other than a reviving nibble as you work in the garden, sorrel's not one to be savoured on its own. The leaves inhabit that middle ground between being a salad leaf and a herb, and overuse of the distinctive, lemony flavour detracts rather than enhances. Raw and used sparingly, the leaves add perfect punctuation to plainer salads; cooked, they work beautifully with simply flavoured foods like potatoes and eggs and give a pleasant edge to oily fish.

Sorrel is closely related to wild dock, and like its cousin you'll have little problem foraging for it, particularly throughout Europe and North America.

In its wild form sorrel has been used for many centuries. It was popular amongst the ancient Egyptians, Greeks and Romans who enjoyed it as a digestif before and after meals. In England it was used as much for medicinal purposes as it was for culinary. It grows wild in woodlands and open fields, and varies between deliciously tender to harsh and fibrous.

As with dock, sorrel has the ability to ease stings and soreness. Perhaps its soothing effects extended to those who ate it, as 17th century herbalist John Evelyn noted that sorrel seemed to make 'men themselves pleasant and agreeable'.

Sorrel is a tough, reliable cropper but it can become a nuisance if you let it self-seed. It has naturalised in many areas, North America especially, so keep it in a corner, grow it in a pot or prevent it from flowering. The best way to achieve this is to grow it as a cut-and-come-again leaf, harvesting all but the lower 3cm of the leaves. It will quickly regrow ready for your next cutting. It also ensures that what you take to the kitchen is lush and tender and constantly at the top of its game.

Sorrel leaves are rich in vitamins and minerals, and as well as being nutritious for you they can improve the health of your garden. Sorrel is deep rooting, accumulating minerals from the lower levels as it grows. Harvest regularly and either lay any leaves you'll not be eating on the soil or add them to the compost, and they'll enrich it with nutrients as they decay.

VARIETIES

New varieties for domestic cultivation have brought a consistency of flavour and texture superior to that of wild sorrel. 'Buckler-leaved' sorrel (*Rumex scutosa*, also known as 'Silver Shield' sorrel) has a particularly fine, delicate taste and tenderness to its leaves. It can be slightly less productive than other varieties, but this shouldn't be a problem – this is not a crop you want to be harvesting in barrowloads anyway. Named after the medieval shield it resembles, this is the best one to try if you have limited space and can grow only one variety. It has much smaller, arrowhead leaves than other varieties – full of sorrel's characteristic lemony zing but with a much more succulent texture.

EATING

Young, small sorrel leaves add a wonderful sharp zing to salads, but use them sparingly – you're after a trace of punctuating zip rather than a dominating flavour. Cooked, sorrel makes a happy companion for oily fish, potatoes and eggs in particular. As with spinach, you'll need a raw skipful to make a cooked handful, but what it loses in volume it makes up for in easiness. Chop or tear up a few handfuls of leaves, throw them into warm butter and a few prods of the wooden spoon is all it needs to create the smoothest of sauces. However you choose to cook sorrel, do avoid aluminium or cast iron pans as the oxalic acid reacts with the metal and taints the flavour, and if you're using larger leaves, do strip out the main rib as this will cook more slowly and not collapse so readily as the main part of the leaves.

SORREL TART
Lemony sorrel and tangy crème fraîche combine beautifully in this creamy tart, perfect for a springtime lunch or picnic. If you like, add some hot smoked trout, salmon or pollock to the filling in place of some or all of the potatoes.

SERVES 6
For the pastry:
125g plain flour, plus extra for dusting
½ tsp salt
75g unsalted butter, chilled and cut into
   small pieces
1 egg yolk
3–4 tbsp cold milk
1 egg white

For the filling:
30g unsalted butter, plus a little extra for
   greasing
4 shallots, finely diced
150g sorrel, stalks removed and roughly
   chopped

170g new potatoes, cooked and halved
2 eggs
1 egg yolk
150g crème fraîche
Salt and freshly ground black pepper
170g Gruyère cheese, grated

To make the pastry, pulse together the flour, salt and butter in a food processor until it resembles coarse breadcrumbs. Tip the mixture into a bowl and add the egg yolk; combine with a knife and then add just enough milk to bring the dough together. Turn out onto a lightly floured surface and pat together into a flattened disc. Wrap in cling film and chill for 1 hour.

   Butter a 20cm x 5cm loose-bottomed Victoria sandwich tin, dust with flour and tap to remove any excess. Roll out the pastry and line the tin, letting excess pastry hang over the sides and chill for a further 30 minutes.

   Preheat the oven to 180°C/Gas 4. Place the tart tin on a baking sheet, prick all over

Being a non-flowering variety 'Profusion' never bolts, giving you a fine flavour all through summer and autumn without the risk of self-seeding.

The wild variety of sorrel (*Rumex acetosa*) resembles a narrow small-leaved dock. It's worth a forage but its cultivated cousin is usually a considerable improvement.

GROWING

Sorrel is relatively unfussy about soil and situation, tolerating all but maritime exposure and a waterlogged site. A well drained but moist soil in a sunny or semi-shady spot should see it perform at its best.

Sow sorrel seed direct from spring through to the end of summer, in two or three staggered batches to ensure a seamless, year-long harvest. You can sow in rows (a little more than the width of your hoe apart) but I prefer to sow in blocks or swathes to form a self-mulching patch that needs little weeding or watering.

Although watering is important early on, sorrel is fairly drought resistant, making it perfect if you live in an area of low rainfall or with sandy soil.

Sorrel is also pretty much problem free, its sharp taste deterring the attentions of slugs and snails.

Sorrel is a perennial, so you can grow it on year after year, and even snip a small harvest through the winter, but it is best grown as an annual (sowing afresh every year) to keep the leaves succulent and tender.

HARVESTING

Sorrel can be harvested all year round when grown outside in mild climates, or undercover in less favourable areas. It grows well late into winter and if grown as a perennial it appears early in spring when there are few leaves around.

Sorrel takes very well to the cut-and-come-again treatment. You can start harvesting sorrel leaves when they are 12cm or so high – around two months after sowing. Cutting the leaves leaving 3cm or so above ground allows the leaves to regrow from the roots and stems that remain. It's worth being careful to cut regularly even if you aren't going to use all the leaves as this encourages tender new growth and prevents the plant going to seed. The quality of flavour and texture tends to decline after three months or so, but if you sow successionally you'll have new plants ready to harvest from.

As with spinach, sorrel shrinks dramatically when cooked, so pick more than you think you need.

with a fork and line the shell with baking parchment or foil weighted down with ceramic baking beans, rice or dried pulses. Bake the shell for 18 minutes, remove from the oven and take out the baking parchment or foil and baking beans. Beat the egg white with 1 tsp water, brush the base with the egg wash and return to the oven for about 8 minutes until the base is golden and dried out. Use a sharp knife to remove the excess pastry from the sides of the tin.

For the filling, melt the butter over a medium-low heat and sauté the shallots until soft and translucent, about 10 minutes. Add the sorrel and stir until wilted, stir in the potatoes, remove from the heat and cool.

In a large bowl, whisk together the eggs, yolk and crème fraîche and season well. Stir in the cooled sorrel and potatoes, and half the Gruyère. Tip the mixture into the tart shell, smooth the surface and sprinkle on the remaining cheese. Bake at 160°C/Gas 3 for 30–35 minutes until puffed up and golden.

SORREL TART

BURIED TREASURE

When we start out growing some of our own food for the first time, most of us are a little nervous. Despite the evidence of millions of years of plants growing perfectly happily, we suspect we are uniquely incapable of watching over them as they do what they have evolved to do. We will kill them. At the very least we will be anxious for most of the time they grow.

Strange then that many of us choose to dedicate much of our patch to crops that keep their edible parts hidden. You'll find potatoes, parsnips and carrots in almost all allotments and veg patches, with first-time growers watching nervously for harvest time to roll around and excavation to begin. Perhaps we like the mystery.

I've said it before and I'll say it again: I can't understand why we give up so much room to maincrop potatoes, onions, winter carrots and parsnips that are cheap to buy and taste identical to those in the shops. If you're keen to grow some of the usual suspects, you can still lift your harvest into the heavenly clouds by going for only the very best varieties – there's a world of difference between a maincrop masher and a sweet, nutty 'Belle de Fontenay' or a waxy 'Pink Fir Apple'. Why not buy the rest and invite a few other flavours you'll rarely find for sale into your kitchen instead?

Buried treasure crops aren't the most glamorous. The edible part seems to grow without the sun and there are no brightly coloured flowers turning into succulent fruit. There's no sex about them. That isn't to say, however, that these plants aren't beautiful in their own, less flashy way. Yacon's foliage is unlike any other, albeit a steady-eddie green in colour, while salsify's grassy leafiness gives way to nigella-like flowers that are beautiful cut for the house. Jerusalem artichoke's wonderful flowers are even more impressive. Yet, while you could conceivably grow them for their looks alone it's what's happening underground that'll keep you happiest.

The buried treasure in this section is truly special. All but salsify are essentially perennial: you sow them one year and any tubers you allow to grow on will ensure a future harvest the following year. It's a more sustainable way of growing than sowing entirely annual crops as the energy stored in the tuber allows the plant to get growing quickly, without much delay or input. They're also each very low-maintenance crops, so are particularly good for the less confident or those with less time to dedicate to growing. They're pleasingly unattractive to most pests and diseases, although slugs and burrowing worms can make a dent in your crop. Happily any damage is almost always cosmetic… but you're never quite sure what you are going to get until you pick up the fork.

What you do get with many tubers and roots is a different kind of flavour to those grown above ground. There's typically an earthiness that tells you where they've come from, as well as a sweetness that is less saccharine than that which you might be used to from other vegetables and fruit. Roasting and slow cooking often bring out their best, and you'll find most are very happily paired with cream.

Behind this commonality lie some surprising flavours. Yacon has a clean, subtle, sweet celery and pear flavour, oca has a lemony sharpness that turns sweet and mellow with a few days in the light, while salsify sits on the fence between globe artichoke hearts and oysters. Yacon and oca originate in South America where a wide variety of tubers have been at the heart of local diets for thousands of years. They make a great starting point for investigating the many other South American favourites, mashua and Madeira vine amongst them.

Where buried treasure crops really add value beyond their flavour is in their timing and resilience. While peas, asparagus and sweetcorn are among the scrumptious foods whose freshly picked sugars are delicate – slipping away from the moment they're picked, much of the harvest we pull from the earthy darkness sits at the other end of the scale. Tubers and roots take time to mature, using the energy from the whole growing season to reach their peak. It means you tend to dig for buried treasure in the winter but, happily, most roots and tubers enjoy this extra time in the cold soil to develop their flavour.

Unlike most potatoes, which are at their prime when lifted, some tubers and roots change for the good when left exposed. Yacon, for example, can develop a deeper, more intense sweetness and oca moves from sharp to sweet and mild after a couple of days lapping up the sunlight.

This changing intensity and character of flavour allows you to develop a relationship with your food even after it's picked – to use it when the flavour and texture suits you best. All you have to do is be prepared to give it a go.

EGYPTIAN WALKING ONION

I didn't think it was possible to fall in love with an onion. Asparagus, a peach fresh from the tree, and even that first (or last) handful of raspberries of the year, but onions? Do me a favour. Yet here they are, Egyptian walking onions, in this book.

I like onions in that reliably useful, cosy-jumper kind of a way, they provide the backdrop to many of my favourite dishes. And yet, when I want some of that intense, oniony flavour up front I would have previously opted for shallots or spring onions any day.

That is, until I discovered Egyptian walking onion, that unusual onion which sows itself every year and offers the best of all worlds. These fabulous perennials form a clutch of small, mild shallot-like onions at their centre, throwing hollow leaves like spring onions into the air at the first sign of warmth.

The soft blue-green spikes poke out of the soil as spring's starter gun fires and nothing holds them back,

late snow included. They can grow up to a metre, but I find half that is more usual. The leaves can be snipped off and used as you would chives or the green part of spring onions, but don't eat them all – let some grow on and they'll produce miniature onions (known as bulbils or topsets) in clusters at their tips.

If left to grow, each of these clusters can form anything up to 20 mini-onions at the end of each leaf (though I would expect half a dozen or so and treat any extra as a bonus). New leaves may also grow from each new set of bulbils which can in turn form other 'child' clusters. With such rampant, branch-like growth you can see how the Egyptian walking onion came upon its alternative name of 'tree onion'.

As the topsets grow their weight becomes more than the hollow leaves can support and they bend lazily towards the ground. If they touch the soil they may root, forming another new plant a little away from its parent, which is the plant's way of 'walking' around your garden.

I like these topset onions either early and small (before they need peeling) or later in the season when their size (3cm or so) makes the mini-palaver very much worthwhile. I like to have new plants growing every year as that gives me a larger resource that I can pick a little from, so I usually leave some topsets on each plant to grow on and produce new plants, either where they land naturally or tear them off to plant where I fancy.

At the end of summer I usually lift the most congested clumps out of the ground and separate them out a little. This gives me a good haul of delicious shallot-like onions plus a few extra plants invigorated by the splitting.

Egyptian walking onions are thought to originate from India and Pakistan where they've been cultivated for over 5000 years, but it was the Egyptians who made them their own, hence the name. They revered them, believing their smell would not only protect them and ward off diseases but could also awaken the dead. They feature in tomb paintings as far back as the Old Kingdom of Egypt in 3000BC, so I guess I'm not the first to develop an affection for them.

VARIETIES

There are no named varieties of Egyptian walking onion, but some have brown skin, others pinky-red. I've only eaten the pinky-red ones so I've no idea if the brown taste any different, but I wouldn't think so.

GROWING

Egyptian walking onions are extremely easy to grow. Other than keeping the weeds at bay, there's nothing you need to do to tend to your Egyptian walking onions throughout the whole growing season.

Start Egyptian walking onions in a little corner of your growing space and let them expand as little or as much as you like. They will tolerate all but waterlogged soils and fare best in good soils in full sun.

Occasionally you'll find Egyptian walking onions as plants, however bulbs are more commonly available. They can be planted in spring or autumn – just sink individual bulbs into the soil so that their tops are just covered. Allow 30cm or so between bulbs.

At the first sign of spring, green growth will emerge. By mid summer flowers may form on the tips of some of the leaves, most of which fade as the onions that develop compete for energy.

Towards autumn the weight of the topsets will cause the stalks to bend and lower the bulbils to the ground, where they are likely to root and form new plants. You can snip the green cord that attaches

EATING

The joy of Egyptian walking onions is that you get a few fabulous harvests that take from the best of the onion family. Their green growth can be used like spring onions or chives, while you also get 2 chances of tasty sweet mini-onions – these form at the tips of the leaves and can also be broken off from the base. Use them as you would onions or shallots, and don't be afraid of giving them some room to shine on their own, as in the fabulous soup that follows.

The peeled bulblets are also perfect pickled, where they make for a delicious addition your ploughman's lunch. Alternatively, for an excellent

accompaniment to roast chicken, simmer a few handfuls of bulblets in chicken stock until tender, add a handful of peas and a slug of cream and simmer until the peas are cooked through and the sauce is slightly thickened, and finish with chopped chervil.

EGYPTIAN WALKING ONION SOUP

It's essential to caramelise the onions properly in order to give this soup its addictively delicious depth of flavour. Don't let this put you off – although it takes a while it's a rather soothing activity which makes the kitchen smell wonderful.

SERVES 4–6
1 litre light chicken or vegetable stock
50g butter, plus a little more for buttering the bread
About 1kg Egyptian walking onions, bulblets halved and very thinly sliced and stems thinly sliced
Salt and freshly ground black pepper
4–6 slices of sourdough bread
1 garlic clove, halved
150g Gruyère cheese, grated

Put the stock in a saucepan over a low heat to warm.

Warm the butter in a large saucepan over a medium-low heat. When the foaming subsides, lower the heat and add the sliced

▶

the bulbils to the mother, or leave them to let the winter's cold do the job for you instead.

As well as these topsets, the plant forms plump bulbils at its heart at ground level. Don't be shy of breaking these up to give you some onions for the kitchen as well as more plants for the following year. Both these individual bulbs and the plants themselves transplant well, so feel free to move them around the garden as you fancy.

Egyptian walking onions can suffer from the same pests and diseases as all onions but rarely acquire them – probably due to their ability to colonise new ground so inventively before diseases have a chance to build up. However, to minimise the likelihood of disease, avoid planting them where onions, garlic or leeks have recently been grown.

HARVESTING
The whole plant is edible. The green leaves may be cut and harvested at any time, but do leave some on each plant to grow if you want to harvest shallot-like bulbils either for the kitchen or to form new plants.

The leaves will quickly regrow, and if you are in a mild climate, may even continue to grow slowly through the winter.

The topset bulbils are usually ready from mid-summer into autumn. Pick them from where they land on the ground, or pinch them off the plant to eat or sow to create new plants.

You can also take mini-onions from the base of the plant and autumn is the best time to do this. You can be fairly rough with the clumping heart – just lift the whole thing and break it up into smaller pieces to replant or to eat.

If you want to store any of these mini-onions, shake the soil free from each bulb but don't wash them as moisture may soak in and lead to rotting. Let them sit outside in the dry to set a little before removing the roots and all but a couple of centimetres of stalk. You can plait them if you like or just keep them in an onion net, in a cool, dry place for winter. Check regularly for any that are starting to rot or sprout and remove them immediately.

◀

bulblets and a good pinch of salt. Cook the bulblets very gently, covered, stirring occasionally, for about 35 minutes.

Remove the lid, increase the heat a little and continue cooking, stirring often, until the bulblets are very soft and form a rich, caramel-coloured mass in the pan, about 15–20 minutes. Add the chopped stems and continue cooking for a further 10 minutes, stirring frequently.

Pour over the warm stock, season with salt and pepper and simmer for 15 minutes.

Heat up the grill and lightly toast the bread. Butter each slice and rub them with the halved garlic clove. Spoon the soup into heatproof bowls. Place a slice of toast on top of each one, sprinkle the toast with Gruyère, trickle a little of the soup liquid over the cheese and grill until golden and bubbling. Serve immediately.

EGYPTIAN WALKING ONION SOUP

JERUSALEM ARTICHOKES

I'm mildly evangelical when it comes to Jerusalem artichokes. Rarely in the shops, their fabulous tubers have a delicious, sweetly earthy flavour that's very much its own. You get a generous double-handful of delicious winter tubers for every tuber you plant in spring and any fragments of tuber you leave behind will regrow the following year, giving you more for even less work. They are a complete no-brainer as far as I'm concerned: everyone should grow them.

Jersualem artichokes' generosity goes far beyond the kitchen. Their flowers bring hoverflies, ladybirds and bees into the garden, which will happily sort out some of the more tedious pests you might have around. They also make fine cut flowers for the house. Grow a few rows together and they'll form a seasonal windbreak that will shelter your fruiting and flowering plants, as well as giving you a little privacy behind which you can enjoy the late summer sun. Come the autumn, you can cut them down and add the stalky material to your compost bin to contribute to next year's fertility. So many uses, and that's without mentioning their taste.

Despite sharing a name, Jerusalem artichoke's flavour bears little similarity to that of the globe artichoke – it's earthy, sweet and tastes very much of the ground in which it grows. Jerusalem artichokes are also full of vitamins, fibre and minerals and store some of their starch as inulin, which most of us can't digest readily. This gives rise to their famed ability to stoke up intestinal gas in some people. Luckily the more Jerusalem artichokes you eat, the better your body deals with inulin. So if you're a sufferer (or happen to live with one) it's a fine excuse for eating more of them.

If you're short of space or want to keep their spread limited, Jerusalem artichokes will grow perfectly happily in large tubs filled with good compost, which you should refresh every couple of years.

And if you're wondering about how to care for them, relax: there's nothing to do. Jerusalem artichokes are the ultimate low-input, high-output crop, where every centimetre, from the tops of the flowers to the subterranean tubers, is beautifully useful. They may be the most generous plant in your garden and are so undemanding and productive that it almost feels like cheating to grow them. And when much of our food takes ten times the energy to produce than you gain from eating it, Jerusalem artichokes teach us a fine lesson. Growing simply doesn't get any more sustainable than this.

VARIETIES
All varieties I've tried are equally delicious, but I go for 'Fuseau' every time as it is less knobbly than the others, which makes preparing your artichokes easier.

GROWING
Jerusalem artichokes belong to the sunflower family, taking their name from the Italian for sunflower, 'girasole'. They are native not to Jerusalem but to the river basins of the USA, which explains why they love their flowers in full sun and their feet in a fertile, moist, but not waterlogged soil.

Buy your Jerusalem artichokes as tubers and plant them direct into the soil, 15cm down, and 60cm at least from their neighbour. Choose your spot well, as once you have Jerusalem artichokes they are difficult to remove. You'll see stems emerging in summer, growing rapidly to 3m before forming small, though very beautiful, sunflower heads in late summer. They make excellent cut flowers for the house and, the more you pick, the more energy goes to the tubers developing underground.

You can grow Jerusalem artichokes in pots, but make them large, 100cm in diameter, and make certain to keep them well watered, particularly through summer.

I've never experienced or heard of Jerusalem artichokes having any pest or disease problems.

HARVESTING
The arrival of the first frosts in winter will take care of any remaining flowers and most of the foliage, but will also stir the tubers into converting starches into sugars, improving the flavour of your harvest.

The earthy tubers are cold hardy and poor in storage, so they're best lifted anytime in winter, as you want to use them. You'll get a fine return – a couple of kilos for every tuber planted in spring is perfectly usual. Be sure to leave a few tubers behind for next year's growth (in practice it will be pretty hard not to).

EATING

Roasted Jerusalem artichokes are a fantastic addition to your Sunday roast and are delicious in warm salads. Heat the oven to 190°C/Gas 5, scrub your artichokes and cut into biggish chunks, about 2cm is good, toss with olive oil, salt and pepper and roast in a single layer on a baking tray for about 35 minutes, turning halfway through the cooking time. Toss them with some toasted walnuts or hazelnuts, a handful of mizuna, microleaves, rocket and some goat's cheese or shavings of Parmesan.

Uncooked Jerusalem artichokes have a texture similar to water chestnuts

and can be used as a great, unusual pickle to go with boiled ham, roast pork or duck. To make, simply pour 300ml white wine vinegar into a saucepan with 150ml water. Add 2½ tbsp caster sugar, ½ tbsp flaky sea salt, 2 tsp coriander seeds, 1 tsp mustard seeds, 1 tsp black, white or green peppercorns, ¼ tsp turmeric, a pinch of chilli flakes and a bay leaf. Bring to the boil. Layer about 450g peeled, thinly sliced (use a mandolin or a sharp knife) Jerusalem artichokes in a Kilner-type jar, pour over the hot liquid, cool, then cover and refrigerate overnight. Eat within a week.

CREAM OF JERUSALEM ARTICHOKE SOUP
Let's face it, Jerusalem artichokes aren't going to win any beauty contests: gnarled, knobbly and rather mean-looking, they are rivalled only by salsify and celeriac in the not-entirely-gorgeous veg stakes. All the more astonishing then that these humble little roots can transform themselves into this luxuriously velvety and altogether very sophisticated soup.

SERVES 6
1.2kg Jerusalem artichokes
Juice of ½ lemon
80g unsalted butter
320g leeks, white part only, washed and finely sliced
1 medium potato, peeled and cubed

PICKLED JERUSALEM ARTICHOKES

1 medium onion, diced
1 stick of celery, diced
2 garlic cloves, crushed
1.8 litres good chicken or vegetable stock
100ml double cream
Salt and freshly ground black pepper

To finish: A trickle of rapeseed oil and/or a spoonful of Mizuna Pesto (see p.148); a swirl of cream and some finely chopped chives; some croutons and a scattering of finely chopped parsley; finely chopped chives and crisp bacon

Begin by peeling the artichokes. As you peel them, slice them thinly and toss them into a large bowl of water to which you've added the lemon juice. This will stop them going brown.

In a large, heavy-bottomed saucepan melt the butter over a low heat and gently sweat the artichokes, leeks, potato, onion and celery until soft, about 25 minutes. Add the garlic and sweat for another couple of minutes.

Add the stock, bring the soup to the boil and then lower the heat and simmer, partially covered, for about 20–30 minutes, until everything is very soft and can be easily mashed against the side of the pan with the back of a wooden spoon. Leave to cool slightly.

Liquidise the soup in batches until it is very smooth, then return to a clean pan. Warm over a medium heat, add the cream and season well with salt and pepper. Serve in warmed bowls finished with 1 of the suggestions above.

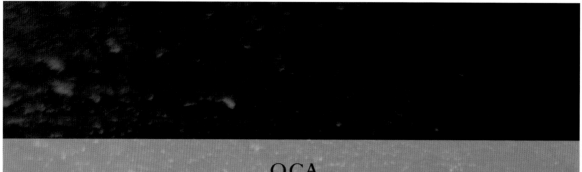

OCA

Oca looks rather like a blind cobbler's thumb — all pink tinged and knobbly with pump rolls like ill-fitting, stacked tyres. If you are familiar with 'Pink Fir Apple' potatoes, an oca tuber is like one of those that has been all made up for a party.

Thankfully oca is not only 'interesting' to look at, it also has a rather intriguing flavour When the pink tubers are first dug out of the ground they taste lemony and sharp due to their oxalic acid content. However this eases off after a few days in the light, when their natural sweetness comes through. This characteristic gives you two very different flavours to play with from a single harvest.

Whether lemony or in their sweeter form, you can eat oca raw – when they're crunchy like a carrot – or cook them unpeeled for ten to fifteen minutes, when they develop a texture very much like a salad potato. Sharper or sweeter, raw or cooked, this variety makes oca particularly versatile – try it grated into salads, sliced thinly as you might radishes, as part of a selection of crudités or with mint and butter as an alternative to new potatoes. However you try it, oca takes well to salt, chilli, or with lemon if it has been allowed to sweeten in the sun.

Oca is a perennial tuber, enormously popular in parts of South America, especially around the Andean highlands where it has been a staple for centuries. It has also been grown in parts of New Zealand (where it is known as the New Zealand yam) for 150 years or so, but given its versatility and fine flavour its popularity is surprisingly patchy away from these areas. I find that a bit of a mystery. As with potatoes, its simplicity makes it perfectly suited to

being dressed up in so many ways and, when you combine that with the variation in flavour between the lemony or mellow sweetness, it seems all the more appealing. So why not drop half a row of potatoes and try a little oca instead? You'll be glad you did.

VARIETIES
Though you'll find oca in endless varieties of colour in their native South America, I've never found oca sold as anything other than a generically named variety with red-pink tinged tubers.

GROWING
Oca is a tender perennial. It grows new plants from each of its tubers that in turn produce a wealth of tubers. The top growth dies back rapidly when the frosts arrive, and if the ground freezes it may well kill off the tubers. For that reason it is grown as an annual (sown, grown and harvested within a year) in many cooler areas.

You can order oca tubers from a supplier for delivery in winter. Keep them somewhere cool and dark. In

EATING

Oca gives you many opportunities to use it in different ways. It is great raw or cooked, lemony or sweet. Try it raw or cooked rolled in Szechuan salt and pepper (see p.111), and with a little lemon squeezed over if you've left the tubers to sweeten in the sun.

Oca is also excellent roasted as you would potatoes, or used as an addition to stews (toss them in during the last few minutes of cooking).

In Mexico they enjoy raw, thinly sliced oca dressed in lemon juice with a sprinkling of salt and chilli flakes. Or why not try cooking it until tender and dressing it in Mizuna Pesto (see p.148)?

To make an unusual starter, try cutting raw oca into very fine matchsticks and dressing them in a mustardy mayonnaise, as you would if you were making a traditional celeriac remoulade. You could also try adding some chopped capers and a few small cubes of cured ham if you want to make the salad a little more substantial.

OCA SAAG ALOO
This is my take on saag aloo, using oca instead of the 'aloo' (or potatoes) and is delicious served with a dollop of yoghurt. If you have any left over, it makes an unusual and tasty filling for an omelette the next day.

SERVES 4
1 tsp groundnut oil
40g unsalted butter
1–2 green chillies, halved and finely sliced
½ tsp cumin seeds
½ tsp mustard seeds
¼ tsp asafoetida (optional)
2 medium onions, halved and finely sliced
2cm piece of fresh ginger, peeled and grated
3 garlic cloves, halved and finely sliced
2 tsp ground coriander
1 tsp garam masala
½ tsp turmeric
650g oca, scrubbed and cut into chunks
300ml chicken or vegetable stock
250g spinach, stalks removed and chopped
Juice of ½ lemon
Salt and freshly ground black pepper

▶

very early spring bring them into the light to initiate sprouting – this is very much like chitting potatoes, where the light stimulates growth of sprouts.

When the sprouts appear you can either plant them into your patch direct, or start them off in 10cm pots if you're concerned about frosts. They may well take a few weeks or a month to come through – they are slow-growing to begin with. Once the foliage is about 10cm tall, plant them out into a good tilth, as this will allow the roots to get away rapidly. Oca tolerates most soils, although avoid very wet sites.

Each oca tuber can be surprisingly productive, so give them a little space. Allow at least 60cm between tubers, though a metre would be better if you have the room. It's worth using a mulch to help retain moisture and suppress weeds early on – if you use compost or well rotted manure the nutrients will act as a slow-release feed, seeping down to the roots and nudging development along.

Oca foliage is rather attractive – rather like an upright clover – and flowers may develop in late summer. At this point, the foliage can get a little long for itself and lean over, however this is perfectly normal.

Oca can be very light sensitive and tends to start making its tubers only as autumn nears – don't be nervous if they haven't developed before this point.

Oca tubers won't turn green like potatoes as they don't contain the troublesome chemical solanine. Equally importantly, they aren't susceptible to blight and seem to be less attractive to slugs.

Oca can be grown perfectly well in a pot, but make it a reasonable size (at least 50cm) and ensure you keep it well watered through dry periods.

HARVESTING
Oca isn't ready to harvest until the first frosts arrive as it produces tubers quite late in the growing season. If frost is forecast, protect the plants with horticultural fleece or sheets of newspaper. Wait until the foliage has died away before harvesting as the tubers will continue to grow. You should expect a few dozen tubers per plant, often more.

◀
Warm the oil and half the butter in a large saucepan over a medium heat. Once the butter stops foaming, add the chillies, cumin, mustard seeds and asafoetida, if using, and cook until the mustard seeds pop. Add the onion, stir until well coated and sauté over a medium heat until starting to turn golden, about 15 minutes. Add the rest of the butter, the ginger, garlic, coriander, garam masala and turmeric and cook, stirring, for a further couple of minutes. Add the oca and stir for 5 minutes. Pour in the stock and cook, covered, until the oca is tender, about 12–15 minutes. Stir in the spinach and cook for a minute until just wilted. Pour in the lemon juice, season if necessary and serve in bowls with a dollop of yoghurt, if desired.

OCA SAAG ALOO

SALSIFY

Salsify is a reward for the nosy. You won't find it in the shops and probably not even in farmers' markets. You will be hard pushed to find it in many restaurants either. Indeed, you could be forgiven for concluding that it's not up to much, but nothing could be further from the truth.

Salsify was the first plant I grew that I'd never tasted before I sowed the seed. The descriptions I'd read were so alluring – the taste supposedly somewhere between asparagus, globe artichoke and oysters – that I couldn't not grow it. On that first wet, cold day out in the patch lifting the roots I wondered if I'd done something wrong; the root took a while to dig up and when it came up there was an equal weight of earth attached. Much like a paler parsnip, but with horizontal side roots like cotton threads, taking nutrients and water from the surrounding soil, salsify can be a bit of a nuisance, it's true. Yet a moment's messabout washing and bashing to relieve the root of its soil is a small effort to make compared to, say, earthing up potatoes. So don't let your inquisitiveness be dulled – the fiddle is part of the fun.

That first taste of salsify was quite an experience. I couldn't pick out the famed oyster flavour but the sweet earthiness was unlike anything I'd tasted before. It has similarities with globe artichoke, Jerusalem artichoke and asparagus but it retains culinary independence. I now grow it every year but more than that, it has convinced me of the importance of challenging your tastebuds to new flavours.

Salsify (like the Jerusalem artichoke) belongs to the sunflower family. It originated in the Mediterranean area, and is grown in pockets throughout the world but for some reason doesn't enjoy widespread appreciation. The flavour is distinctive but delicate and it needs a gentle hand in the kitchen. Boiling the backside out of salsify will not bring out its finest qualities. In every instance where someone has told me they don't like it, without fail they have prepared it like a carrot – boiled and served bald. Salsify is best served with cream, which perhaps explains why it is so popular with the French, the slender, creamy-coloured root taking beautifully to the cream, garlic and butter so much at the heart of their cuisine.

VARIETIES

Salsify seed is often sold as generic rathern than named varieties, although you may find 'Mammoth' and 'Sandwich Island' occasionally – both of these are delicious and crop reliably well.

GROWING

Salsify couldn't be easier to grow. It will grow ok in almost any soil but prefers a stone-free soil, dug deeply to allow the roots easy development as they grow. Don't add manure to the soil in the months leading up to sowing – as with most root vegetables, this will only encourage unwanted forking.

In early spring, sow your seeds 15cm apart from each other and 1cm deep into soil. Water the developing plants in dry periods and keep the area well weeded.

If you live in an area unlikely to freeze hard over winter you can even try growing a few salsify roots on for another year – just cut the leaves back to a couple of centimetres above the ground and form a mound of earth at least 20cm over the root in autumn. You'll get blanched new growth like chicory leaves coming through in spring which can be steamed or served raw in salads.

HARVESTING

Salsify roots may be ready to lift as soon as early autumn but can be left in the ground until needed, as long as a hard freeze is not forecast. As with parsnips, I think a little light frost improves their flavour so I leave most of my salsify in the ground a little into winter.

You'll need a good fork to harvest salsify. You'll find the process much simpler if you remind yourself that you are not digging them up, so much as lifting them. A little excavation maybe called for, especially if the ground is wet. You'll have to go down a bit, to loosen all the surrounding earth and, while pulling a little on the strong leaves will help you, don't be tempted to wiggle and twist too much – the roots don't take much encouragement to snap.

Salsify flowers are also edible, either as flower buds eaten lightly steamed in salads, or with the petals sprinkled onto salad leaves once the flowers have opened. I don't personally find them that remarkable either way, but it is worth trying them as they may be to your taste. Whether you eat them or not, you should definitely cut some of these pretty flowers for the house.

EATING

However you intend to use salsify, there's an easy way of starting things off. Wash the root, slice off the side shoots and boil for around 8 minutes (depending on the size of the roots) until tender. After being rinsed in cold water to make the roots handleable, you can easily slip the skins off, using a knife to slice off any more stubborn areas. The raw roots discolour quickly when peeled or sliced, so to prevent this happening throw them into acidulated water (a little lemon juice in water is ideal). Now they're ready to use however you choose.

There are few better accompaniments to roast beef or lamb than salsify in cream – on its own this dish should be enough to make you order the seeds for next year straight away.

Preheat the oven to 180°C/Gas 4. Prepare and peel 400g salsify as for the rösti recipe (below) and cut it into 5cm batons. Butter a gratin dish of approximately 24cm x 18cm and spread out the peeled salsify evenly in the dish. Warm 120ml strong chicken or vegetable stock and 200ml double cream in a pan with a few gratings of nutmeg; taste and add enough salt and pepper to make a well flavoured liquid. Pour it over the salsify, dot with a little butter and bake for 45–50 minutes until bubbling and golden.

If you wanted to make an optional crunchy topping, in a small bowl, combine 40g chopped pecans, 20g fresh breadcrumbs, the zest of ½ small lemon and ½ tsp finely chopped thyme leaves. Sprinkle the mixture over the salsify before baking.

Salsify leaves look almost identical to wide-bladed grass and, while they are edible in salads and so on, they are far from remarkable, but if you're the inquisitive (or disbelieving) sort, why not give them a try?

SALSIFY RÖSTI

It can take a bit of practice to perfect your rösti technique, but it's worth it. The key is to let the salsify and potatoes cool completely

SALSIFY RÖSTI

before mixing them into a cake, and waiting until the bottom has formed its wonderful golden crust before attempting to turn it. And butter, plenty of melted butter...

Serve your rösti with fried eggs and bacon as part of a very indulgent breakfast, or turn it into a luxurious starter with a dollop of crème fraîche or sour cream and some slices of very good smoked salmon or trout.

SERVES 6
370g salsify (unpeeled weight)
Salt and freshly ground black pepper
200g floury potatoes, such as King Edward or Maris Piper (unpeeled weight)
70g unsalted butter
1 small onion, finely diced
1 tsp fresh thyme leaves, chopped
2 tbsp olive oil

Scrub the salsify thoroughly then rinse them to remove as much grit as possible.

Bring a large pan of water to the boil, add some salt and boil the salsify (keeping them as long as you can, just cutting them enough to fit in the pan) for 10 minutes. Drain and rinse under cold water, then peel off the skins.

Cook the potatoes in their skins in boiling, salted water for 10 minutes, rinse under cold water, then peel. Leave to cool completely, then chill both the salsify and potatoes in the fridge, uncovered, for at least 4 hours. Grate the cooled vegetables with a box grater, trying to keep the strands as long as possible.

Warm 15g of the butter in a frying pan over a medium-low heat and sauté the onion until softened and translucent (don't let it colour), about 15 minutes. Put the onion, salsify and potato in a bowl with the thyme leaves and season well with salt and pepper. Mix gently with your hands until well combined.

Heat a heavy-bottomed frying pan over a medium heat, warm 40g of the butter and the olive oil. Tip the rösti mixture into the pan and spread it out into a round. Cook for a few minutes and turn over in sections with a spatula. Form it into a round no more than 1.5cm thick. Turn the heat down slightly and cook until the bottom of the cake is golden brown, about 12–15 minutes. Invert the rösti onto a large plate. Melt the remaining butter in the pan, then slide the rösti back in so that the golden side is uppermost. Cook over a moderate heat until the underside of the rösti is golden and the centre cooked through, about 12 minutes.

Slide onto a serving plate and cut into wedges.

YACON

I first heard of yacon a couple of years ago. I was sat by the fire on a very cold winter's evening, beer, pencil, paper and the TV for company, scribbling the coming year's wishlist. The presenter of a gardening programme was visiting a nursery in southern England and being treated to what sounded like an unmissable taste: an underground 'pear'.

I rang the nursery next morning; engaged. I rang every five minutes for the next two hours before I finally got through. Sold out that morning, I was told. No matter. I immediately ordered for the following year, and have been growing this beguiling tuber ever since.

Fresh out of the ground yacon is very much like a baking potato to look at. However its flavour is a little strange for what you might expect from an underground tuber – it's like a sweet cross between early apples, watermelon and very mild celery, with a touch of pear. Mildly flavoured raw when first dug, it's the texture as much as the taste which sets yacon apart. The tubers have that fine texture of water chestnuts. They don't quite collapse as such – they've more resistance than that – but, like a very fine sorbet, they do sort of give in.

Yacon is also refreshingly juicy. 'Yacon' means 'water root' in the Inca language and its tubers were historically highly valued as a wild source of thirst-quenching refreshment for travellers. The liquid can also be drawn off and concentrated to produce yacon syrup. As with Jerusalem artichokes, yacon tubers are rich in an indigestible sugar – inulin – meaning that the syrup they form has all the sweetness of honey or other plant-derived sweeteners like maple syrup, but without the calories.

Yacon also benefits the bacteria in the intestinal tract and colon that boost the immune system and aid digestion. This potential as a dietary aid and as a source of sweetness for diabetics has led to yacon being grown more widely, especially in the USA.

VARIETIES

Yacon tubers (*Smallanthus sonchifolius*) can be red, orange, yellow, pink and purple but most of the more colourful ones are found only in South America, where yacon originates. The rest of us are likely to find only white varieties.

GROWING

Yacon is a perennial plant, so once you have planted it, so long as you look after it, you will have it forever.

Yacon is pleasingly easy to grow in most soils where there is reasonable rainfall and moderate heat. The plants do require a long season to grow – forming their tubers in autumn – but anywhere that parsnips and Jerusalem artichokes thrive will suit yacon perfectly well.

You can either buy plants or if you know someone who has them you can divide the crown including the smaller roots that grow above the main tubers.

Yacon can be slow to get growing in spring but quickly puts on lush, leafy growth through the summer to a height of 2m, occasionally a little more once established. It flowers some years towards autumn, but it's what's happening under the surface that's of most interest.

EATING

Yacon has a crunchy texture, slightly reminiscent of water chestnuts, and a sweet flavour, so it's rather good simply peeled, sliced and eaten as a snack.

It's great in salads too, though its tendency to brown means that you should add it at the last minute, once everything else is assembled and ready to be dressed, or sprinkle with a little lemon juice to prevent it discolouring as it's peeled (and do peel it, the skin can be a little bitter).

Yacon also has a delightful tendency to absorb sauces and dressings, which make it a fantastic vehicle for other flavours. Try it grated with carrots in a mustardy vinaigrette with a handful of sunflower and pumpkin seeds, or in the traditional South American fruit salad, salpicón. Combine peeled, chopped yacon with chunks of pineapple, chopped papaya and mango and dress in freshly squeezed orange juice and a spritz of lemon.

You could also use yacon instead of apples in a Waldorf salad. Just peel and dice the yacon and toss it in lemon juice to stop it from going brown, then combine it in a bowl with chopped celery, some raisins and walnuts. Dress with mayonnaise thinned with a little sour cream and serve immediately on crisp lettuce leaves.

Yacon makes for a juicy, refreshing munch in the garden – just dug and brushed free of soil, or washed if you have water to hand. Otherwise get your tubers into the kitchen and try them with a little lemon juice and honey sprinkled over.

And don't waste an opportunity with the leaves – they make a delicious wrap, in much the same way as vine leaves or cabbage leaves do, for any number of fillings.

Nose below the surface in late autumn and you'll see that yacon produces two sets of roots – the large edible tubers that act as the energy storage facility for the plant, and the smaller propagation roots (resembling Jerusalem artichokes) which grow just under the soil surface and are the seeds for the following year's growth.

When you lift your yacon plants to harvest the tubers, cut the stems back to about 10cm long and store the crowns covered in damp compost in a cool frost-free place where they won't dry out.

In early spring plant the crowns into large pots and wait for shoots to start growing from each small tuber. Split the crowns into individual shoots with their tubers attached and plant into smaller pots.

Yacon plants are quite sensitive to temperature, so plant them out when you would tomatoes, a metre or slightly more from their neighbour, in a sheltered, sunny spot. Any compost you add to the planting

hole and watering through dry periods will ensure good growth throughout the season.

Yacon is very rarely troubled by pests or diseases, but they are hungry plants so either add much compost and/or rotted manure between growing seasons or move their growing site altogether.

HARVESTING

Yacon tubers develop into autumn, and as the frosts approach it's worth putting a little straw around the plant to protect the tubers. The leafy growth is withered by the cold – as soon as this happens, use a long fork to gently lift the tubers. It helps to have another person pulling on the stems of the plant at the same time to get the whole plant up.

Snap the large tubers from the crowns. They're crunchy, tasty and refreshing immediately, but a few days in the sun can add to their sweetness.

Yields can be variable – in the first year I had around six tubers the size of very large baking potatoes per plant, in the second year considerably more.

A cool, dry shed or garage is perfect for storing yacon tubers until you're ready to eat them. They may well sweeten a little over time, and (if you're lucky) they can last many months in storage.

YACON AND BLUE CHEESE SALAD

It's not easy to improve upon the famously fabulous combination of walnuts and blue cheese but the addition of yacon, with its succulent sweet crunch, really lightens and freshens this deliciously different lunch.

SERVES 4 AS A STARTER
Small handful of shelled walnuts
    or pecans
Juice of 1 lemon
1 medium-large yacon
Handful of salad leaves
180g blue cheese, such as Dorset blue
    vinney, roquefort or gorgonzola

For the dressing:
1 tbsp apple balsamic vinegar
Pinch of flaky sea salt
3 tbsp extra-virgin olive oil

Preheat the oven to 180°C/Gas 4.
    Spread the walnuts or pecans out onto a baking tray and toast in the oven for 8–10 minutes, shaking halfway through, until lightly coloured – keep an eye on them to ensure they don't burn.
    Fill a bowl with water and add the lemon juice. Peel the yacon, cut into slices and toss into the lemony water to prevent them from discolouring.
    In a small bowl, whisk together the vinegar with the salt before adding the olive oil a little at a time, whisking all the while until smooth. In a bowl, lightly dress the salad leaves in a little of the dressing and divide between 4 plates. Arrange the sliced yacon on top, crumble over the blue cheese, then trickle over the rest of the dressing. Scatter the nuts over the top and serve immediately.

YACON AND GREEN BEAN SALAD

Crunchy yacon can be grated into salads, julienned and tossed into stir fries, roasted with other root veg or steamed. It adds pleasing bite to this flavoursome salad – serve it as it is as a main course, or wrapped in little gem lettuce leaves as a starter.

SERVES 4 (OR 8–10 AS A STARTER)
Juice of ½ lemon
1 medium-large yacon
300g green beans, topped (and tailed if you
    like, but the tails look rather nice)
15g sesame seeds
250g cooked chicken breast, torn into long
    shreds
Small handful of Vietnamese or regular
    coriander (Vietnamese coriander has a
    slightly hotter, more peppery flavour),
    stalks removed and roughly chopped

YACON AND GREEN BEAN SALAD

Small handful of mint, stalks removed and roughly chopped

For the dressing:
2 tbsp chunky peanut butter
1 tbsp Chinese rice vinegar
1 tbsp soy sauce
1 tsp sesame oil
1 small red chilli, halved, deseeded, membrane removed and finely diced
Juice of 1 small lime

To serve:
Little gem lettuce leaves (optional)

Fill a bowl with water and add the lemon juice. Peel the yacon and cut it into batons, about 5mm x 5mm x 5mm, tossing them into the lemony water as you go to stop them from turning brown. Bring a pan of salted water to the boil, add the beans and boil until they just lose some of their crunch, about 2 minutes. Drain and refresh under the cold tap. Pat dry with kitchen paper.

In a small frying pan, warm the sesame seeds over a medium heat until they just begin to turn golden. Tip them onto a plate to stop them cooking any further.

In a small bowl, whisk together all of the ingredients for the dressing until smooth.

Drain the yacon and combine in a large bowl with the green beans, chicken, sesame seeds, coriander and mint (save some of the herbs and seeds for garnishing the salad). Pour over half of the dressing and toss the salad with your hands until everything is well combined. Serve on a platter, trickled with the rest of the dressing and the remaining seeds and herbs or wrap in little gem leaves and serve as a starter.

The directory

Now that you have made your wishlist and read about the crops in detail, this is where you will find the additional information necessary to make your garden into a reality. The skills — how to sow seeds, plant a tree, make great compost and prepare liquid feeds to ensure you maintain healthy nutrient levels year after year — are all covered here, along with a list of sources and suppliers which will put you in touch with some of the best places to source your plants, seeds or tools from. And of course, no book can contain all you'll ever want to know about growing and eating food. I've been lucky enough to be inspired and informed by many many people, so I've also included some of their books which I believe are well worth looking into should you want to explore a little further.

Tools

Tools are an investment – spend your money well and they'll pay you back for years, take shortcuts and you'll regret it every time you pick them up. Take time to try some, ask around, borrow a few and buy them for how they feel in your hands and how they perform in the soil, not for how they look.

There are a few tools that are essential:

- A SPADE For digging, cutting straight edges, and turning compost.
- A FORK For loosening or breaking up ground and lifting root crops.
- A HOE For weeding between plants or larger areas.
- A RAKE For levelling and working your growing surface.
- A DIBBER For making holes in the ground to plant seeds.
- A TROWEL For digging small areas for planting into and spot weeding.
- SECATEURS For pruning hard branches of tress and shrubs.

The cost can mount up, so do investigate secondhand shops, the recycling centre, online auction sites, or the possibility of sharing tools. A wheelbarrow and two buckets (if they can be considered as tools) are also indispensable.

DEALING WITH SLUGS AND SNAILS

Wherever you are and whatever you grow, slugs and snails will be a nuisance. Here are a few strategies for minimising their impact.

- Make up slug pubs – by filling the bottom 8cm of a plastic bottle, sunk into the ground, with cheap beer. This will atract the slugs, who will fall into the beer and perish.
- Go for a walk around your garden at dusk with a drink and pick any you see. Dispatch as you see fit.
- Use organic slug pellets – new types are available that interrupt the slug's feeding enzymes rather than poisoning them.
- Nematodes (specific microscopic organisms) can be introduced to the area to kill and feed on slugs. This can be expensive but is well worth it for smaller areas such as your most precious plants and seedlings.
- Create a small pond to attract frogs and toads. These predators will keep the slug population very much under control.

Planting a tree

Planting a tree may seem like a simple business and it is, but it's also very particular. You need to get a few basics right as this is one of the key factors in how good a start your tree gets away to. Ask three people how to plant a tree and you'll get four opinions but having planted thousands of fruit and nut trees, I'm confident of this method:

- Put your tree into a bucket of water to ensure the roots get a good pre-planting soak.
- Clear off any turf so that you have 1m² of bare ground.
- Dig out a hole 10cm or so below the depth that the roots will go to.

PRUNING

Trees are usually pruned, especially early in life, to establish and maintain the desired shape. There are many shapes and forms you can choose, too many to include here, but the principles for most freestanding trees are simple:

• Always use sharp secateurs to ensure a clean cut
• Almost all trees and bushes bar the stone fruit (plums, peaches, apricots etc) are pruned when dormant in winter
• Stone fruit should be pruned in spring when the sap is rising
• Prune into a goblet shape to let in light and air – unless you have a good reason to do otherwise
• Prune a few millimetres above an outward-facing bud to encourage growth away from the centre
• Remove and compost or incinerate all prunings.

Developing an espalier, fan or stepover shape involves a few years of gentle training and pruning. I'd usually recommend buying these trees already partly trained as the initial framework will be established, leaving you with the task of maintaining it as it grows.

• Place a cane across the hole and test your tree in the space to ensure that the graft (where the rootstock joins the upper part of the tree) is at least 10cm above ground level and that the root system is below.
• Put your tree back in the bucket to prevent the roots from drying out.
• Loosen the sides and the base of the hole to improve drainage and help ensure that the roots have broken earth to grow into.
• Plant your tree at the same depth at which it was growing in the nursery.
• Take handfuls of soil and crumble them into the centre of the root system – your aim is to try and fill the main air spaces between the roots.
• Once done, chop the turf you lifted into small pieces and lay them grass-down in the hole then back fill with the loose soil, treading in well.
• Thoroughly water your tree immediately after planting. Some suggest using compost and fertiliser at this point, I don't. Better that the roots have an incentive to grow away.
• Unless your tree is particularly tall, use a short 1m stake with 60cm knocked into the ground – the 40cm above ground is tied to the tree. This secures the base of the tree, preventing it from lifting up in strong winds and leaving the top to move in the wind, developing its own resilience.
• Check to ensure the graft and roots are at the right depth.

Sowing

Much of what you grow is likely to come from packets of seed. Don't panic about sowing seeds. Almost always they have instructions printed on the reverse of the packet and almost without exception they'll be perfectly worth following.

The seed has all the information inside it to become the plant – all you have to do is place it in the right environment at the right time to allow it to realise its potential.

Some seeds are more successful grown (or at least sown) undercover – where the conditions are more sheltered, warmer and where they maybe less vulnerable to pests. For all of the foods mainly started from seed I've outlined where this is an option, but whatever you're starting from seed, even if it's not included in this book, there are some good pointers for success.

SOWING OUTDOORS

From mid-Spring there should be enough warmth in the soil and the air for sowing most vegetable, herb and flower seeds straight into the ground it will grow in. This is known as direct sowing. Almost anything can be directly sown if the weather is suitable and the time of year right, but most leafy herbs, salads, leafy greens, beans, peas and many of the roots take to this way of sowing best. To give these seeds the best chance of success:

• Prepare a fine tilth – i.e. a fine-grained topsoil. This allows the delicate roots of newly germinated seeds to grow easily into an environment that suits them.
• Sow a little earlier than the packets say if you're in the south of the country or wait a little if you're in the north. Similarly, if the weather is unseasonably cold or wet, you can usually hold fire until the conditions are better.
• Lightly water the ground before you sow rather than afterwards – this reduce the risk of your seeds being washed away.
• Sow thinly – with finer seed this usually means sowing quickly to ensure good spread.
• Cover the seed with the same depth of compost as their size – a dusting for salads; a couple of centimetres for broad beans.
• Thin out some of the seeds that germinate too closely together. These thinnings make good eating.
• Water your seeds a little every few days if there's no rain.
• Keep an eye out for weed seedlings – they will enjoy these delightful conditions every bit as much as your seeds. Weed them before they establish too well as they will divert water and nutrients from your precious seedlings.

SOWING UNDERCOVER

Some of the more tender plants prefer warmer conditions to begin life in – in Britain tomatoes, chillis and aubergines are among those that you can't start outside and have much confidence that they'll grow to perfect fruiting. It makes sense then to start these plants undercover – in a polytunnel, on a windowsill, in a greenhouse or under a cloche. It is also a good way of ensuring a staggered, successional harvest from a crop that you have sown direct at the same time – as those sown undercover will grow more quickly than those sown direct.

There are many ways of starting your plants off indoors and most work well. I do however have favourites for particular foods that I believe get them away to the best possible start:

• Use root trainers or toilet roll inners for peas and beans - they like a long root run. Plant them out when the roots begin to emerge from the bottom, cutting the toilet roll inners down the side to allow it to open up as the roots expand.
• Use guttering for any leafy herbs, leafy greens, microleaves and salads – leaving a good few centimetres either end so that when you water the compost doesn't pour out. Water lightly.
• I find many of the Mediterranean favourites such as tomatoes and chillis grow well in Jiffy-7s – small counters made from coir (coconut fibre) which expand to around 6cm tall and 4cm across when dropped in water. Pot your plants on into peat-free pots when they are 10cm or so tall.
• I sow courgettes, squash and melons in pots as they need a good reservoir of nutrients and water to draw on straight away.
• Module trays are excellent for brassicas and any others that prefer not have their roots disturbed to much.
• In general, I am no fan of seed trays. You will usually kill one seedling for every one you successfully extricate from the tangle of roots. However, pea tips and microleaves grow perfectly well in reasonably dense sowings in seed trays.

Before you plant your seedlings out, first take them outside in the daytime and bring them back undercover for the night for at least five days to allow them to adjust to the daytime temperatures. Water your seedlings well prior to planting, choose a day when the following night isn't unusually cold, and plant out in the morning to give your seedlings the benefit of a whole day's light and warmth. Dig each hole for your seedlings just before you put the seedling in to avoid the seedling or the soil drying out. Finish by gently firming the soil around your seedling after planting, and water well.

Growing in limited space

Don't be put off by what you might view as too small a space – *everyone* thinks they have too little space. It is far more likely that it is a lack of imagination and invention that are limiting your possibilities.

TIPS FOR MAKING THE MOST OF A SMALL SPACE
• Look for dwarf varieties of larger plants – an ever-increasing range is available, including many fruit trees
• Look to train fruit almost flat against a wall using an espalier or fan shape. Even a north facing wall is fine for morello cherries
• Let a sunny window take care of undercover seedlings if you haven't the space, money or inclination for a greenhouse or polytunnel.
• Look to integrate plants inventively - the classic Three Sisters planting of sweetcorn, a climbing bean and a squash works equally well with a dwarf apricot, borlotti beans and nasturtiums.
• Maximise cut-and-come-again crops for repeated harvests from one sowing.
• Invest in a cloche or use water bottles with the bottom cut off to act as mini-greenhouses.
• Look for tall varieties, climbers or trailing plants to make the most of vertical space without taking up valuable floor space.

CONTAINER GROWING
Almost anything can be grown in a container of some kind. Pots, hanging baskets, raised beds and planters come in any size to suit your space. When growing in a container, remember to:

• Give your plants enough room – choose containers they can grow into.
• Make sure your containers have holes in the bottom to ensure good drainage and be vigilant about watering.
• Maintain nutrient levels with the occasional nettle or comfrey feed (see right) and replace, or at least regularly top dress, the compost every year. If you're growing right next to where you spend much of your time then this is hardly an inconvenience.
• As well as taking advantage of what's already there, use canes, mesh, tepees, netting and wires to provide vertical support to climbing beans, peas, nasturtiums, cucumbers and climbing fruit such as kiwis and grapes.

Making the best compost

Compost is the secret to next year's harvest and the harvests after that. Your compost bin takes all the 'waste' and recycles it into a nutritious feed for the soil, replenishing the nutrients depleted during the growing season.

The ingredients of good compost fall into two main groups, Greens and Browns. Greens include nettles, comfrey leaves, vegetable peelings and annual weeds. Browns include shredded waste paper, cardboard, shredded woody prunings and hedge clippings, bedding from herbivore pets such as rabbits and fallen leaves.

COMPOSTING RULES
• Use equal volumes, intermixed, of Greens to Browns.
• Activators such as grass cuttings and urine accelerate the breakdown of the slower rotting Browns.
• Chopping or shredding the woodier Browns helps speed up their decomposition.
• Ideally, have three bins side by side and add only to the first, turning each into the next bin as it fills.
• If you have room for only one bin, turn the compost regularly to add air to the mix, speeding up decomposition. The compost will be ready in nine months to a year, depending on how often it is mixed.
• Don't add any of the following to your compost – meat, fish, dairy, non-wood ash, cooked food (including bread), cat litter and dog faeces, nappies, perennial weeds or annual weeds with seed heads.

LIQUID FEEDS
Comfrey and nettles make the perfect natural liquid feed for your plants. These feeds are simple to make; start by filling an old onion net or similar (to stop the tap getting blocked) with shredded leaves of either nettles (which will encourage leafy growth) or comfrey (which will promote flowering and fruiting). Next, suspend the bag in your water butt, and leave to decompose over the next fortnight to create your liquid feed or 'tea'. Use comfrey tea fortnightly from flowering until harvesting and nettle tea fortnightly as required. As comfrey can be invasive, sow the sterile Bocking 14 variety if you have no local wild source. Comfrey tea works equally well as a foliar feed (sprayed on the leaves) or watering the ground.

Sources & suppliers

There are many many fine sources of plants, seeds and other supplies – there are also plenty of perfectly average ones. The selection below offers great places to investigate but don't discount your own favourites or more local suppliers. The best suppliers treat you as an individual, listening to your requirements rather than simply trotting out their stocklist or fobbing you off with whatever is around. Many of these suppliers have advised me to go elsewhere for what I need rather than sell me what they have. These are the people with whom it's worth nurturing an ongoing relationship.

PLANTS AND SEEDS

Agroforestry Research Trust
www.agroforestry.co.uk
Excellent range of plants (including most trees and soft fruits, nuts, etc.), seeds, courses, publications from the leader in all things to do with Forest Gardening and Agroforestry.

Cool Temperate
http://cooltemperate.co.uk/index.shtml
01159 162673
Wide range of plants including quince, medlars, peaches.

Crûg Farm Plants
www.mailorder.crug-farm.co.uk
mailorder@crug-farm.co.uk
01248 670232
Exceptional range of edible and non-edible plants, many collected by the owners. Including Szechuan pepper, fuchsia, etc.

Edulis
www.edulis.co.uk
01635 578113
Wide range of unusual edible and non-edible plants, including yacon, oca, etc.

Jekka's Herb Farm
www.jekkasherbfarm.com
01454 418878
The Queen of herbs. Excellent supplier of plants and seeds, including sweet cicely and lovage.

Burnt Ridge Nursery
www.burntridgenursery.com
36098 52873
US nursery with a wide range of fruit and nuts, plus ornamentals.

Grimo Nut Nursery
www.grimonut.com
+1-905-YEH-NUTS (934 6887)
Canadian nursery with a great range of nut trees (including pecans and mulberries) plus some fruit.

Rolling River Nursery
www.rollingrivernursery.com
53062 73120
USA nursery supplying edible trees, bushes (including Chilean guava and Autumn olive) and vines.

Perry's Fruit and Nut Nursery
www.perrysfruitnursery.com.au
61883 830268
Australian nursery supplying a wide range of nut and fruit plants including peaches and pecans.

Reads Nursery
www.readsnursery.co.uk
01508 548395
Excellent range of fruit trees, bushes and nuts, including medlars, apricots and nectarines. Good source of trained fruit trees.

Thompson & Morgan
http://plants.thompson-morgan.com/
08442 485383
Very wide range of fruit plants and veg seeds – including dwarf fruit trees.

Trees For Life
www.frankpmatthews.com

The Heritage Seed Library
www.gardenorganic.org.uk/hsl
02476 308210
Suppliers of edible seeds, who conserve and make available many heirloom and lesser-known varieties.

Thomas Etty
www.thomasetty.co.uk
01460 57934
Seed suppliers, many heritage varieties and lesser-known edibles.

Garden Organic
www.gardenorganic.org.uk
02476 303517
A charity (formerly HDRA) for veg and herbs seeds as well as advice, etc.

Delfland Nurseries
www.organicplants.co.uk
01354 740553
Specialising in high-quality organic vegetable seedlings.

The Real Seed Catalogue
www.realseeds.co.uk
01239 821107
Excellent supplier of seeds, no F1s

Sarah Raven's Kitchen and Garden
www.sarahraven.com
08701 913430
Great supplier of edible and non-edible seeds, meticulous about excellent choice of varieties. Particularly good for edible flowers and salad leaves.

Rocket Gardens
www.rocketgardens.co.uk
01209 831468
Organic vegetable and herb seedlings, and fruit bushes to create instant gardens.

Baker Creek Heirloom Seeds
www.rareseeds.com
41792 48917
Excellent North American source of perennial vegetable seeds.

Seed Savers Exchange
www.seedsavers.org
56338 25990
North American seed-saving network.

Sow Organic Seed
www.organicseed.com
88870 97333
Excellent range, including South American tubers.

B&T World Seeds
www.b-and-t-world-seeds.com
00330 468912963
Hugely extensive range of seeds.

OTHER SUPPLIES

Fertile Fibre
www.fertilefibre.com
01432 853111
Organically certified peat-free compost and more.

The Natural Gardener
www.thenaturalgardener.co.uk
01568 611729
Coir and biodegradable pots, compost and sustainable pest control.

The Little Veg Patch
www.earthwormlandscapes.co.uk
01202 882993
Instant raised veg patch.

Wriggly Wrigglers
www.wigglywigglers.co.uk
01981 500391
Worms, wormeries and general garden supplies.

The Green Gardener
www.greengardener.co.uk
01603 715096
Extensive range or biological pest control, plus general supplies.

West Riding Organics
www.wrorganics.co.uk
01484 609171
Organically certified compost.

LBS Garden Warehouse
www.lbsgardenwarehouse.co.uk
01282 873370
General garden supplies, including mulch mat/ground cover.

Link-a-bord
www.linkabord.co.uk
01773 590566
Instant raised beds made from recycled plastic

Implementations
www.implementations.co.uk
08453 303148
Bronze/copper tools – hardwearing and beautiful.

Defenders
www.defenders.co.uk
01233 813121
Biological pest control for the garden.

The Green Spot
www.greenmethods.com
60394 28925
Organic pest control in the USA.

Johnny's Selected Seeds
www.johnnyseeds.com
20786 13900
Wide range of vegetable seeds plus general garden supplies, including organic pest control.

USEFUL ORGANISATIONS

Royal Horticultural Society
www.rhs.org.uk
08450 621111
Excellent source of advice, many gardens and shows to visit, and also offers a soil analysis service. Well worth joining.

Garden Organic
www.gardenorganic.org.uk
02476 303517
A charity dedicated to organic growing. Excellent source of advice (as well as seeds). Well worth joining.

Slow Food
www.slowfood.com
01584 879599
Promoting the locality, diversity and pleasure of food.

National Society of Allotment Holders and Leisure Gardeners
www.nsalg.org.uk
01536 266576
Protecting, preserving and promoting allotment gardening.

Edible Forest Gardeners' Network
www.edibleforestgardens.com
Online resource for anyone interested in forest gardens

Further reading

There are many excellent books, magazines and newsletters out there
if you're keen to investigate further. I'd recommend the following:

BOOKS:

Pam Corbin, *Preserves: River Cottage Handbook No. 2*, Bloomsbury Publishing,
London, 2008

Martin Crawford, *Creating a Forest Garden: Working with Nature to Grow
Edible Crops*, Green Books, Devon, 2010

Bob Flowerdew, *Bob Flowerdew's Complete Book of Companion Gardening*,
Kyle Cathie, London, 1993

Jane Grigson, *Fruit Book*, Michael Joseph, London, 1982
– *Vegetable Book*, Michael Joseph, London, 1979

Simon Hickmott, *Growing Unusual Vegetables*, Eco-Logic Books, Bath, 2004

Christine McFadden, *Pepper*, Absolute Press, Bath, 2008

Jekka McVicar, *Jekka's Complete Herb Book*, 2nd edn, Kyle Cathie, London, 2009

Michael Pollan, *In Defence of Food*, Allen Lane, London, 2008

Sarah Raven, *The Great Vegetable Plot*, BBC Books, London, 2005

Lee Reich, *Uncommon Fruits for Every Garden*, 3rd edn, Timber Press,
Portland, Oregon, 2008

Eric Toensmeier, *Perennial Vegetables*, Chelsea Green Publishing, Vermont, 2007

OTHER PUBLICATIONS:

Agroforestry News (quarterly)
European subscriptions – www.agroforestry.co.uk/agnews.html
North American subscriptions – www.permacultureactivist.net

Permaculture Activist – www.permacultureactivist.net

Permaculture Magazine – www.permaculture.co.uk

Index

Editorial Director Jane O'Shea
Creative Director Helen Lewis
Project Editor Simon Davis
Designer Nicola Davidson
Photographer Laura Hynd
Recipe Developer Debora Robertson
Food Stylist Jennifer White
Production Director Vincent Smith
Production Controller Aysun Hughes

First published in 2010 by
Quadrille Publishing Limited
Alhambra House
27–31 Charing Cross Road
London WC2H 0LS
www.quadrille.co.uk

Text © 2010 Mark Diacono
Crop photography © Mark Diacono
Food photography © 2010 Laura Hynd
Design and layout © 2010 Quadrille Publishing Ltd

Cataloguing in Publication Data: a catalogue record for this book is available from the British Library.

ISBN 978 184400 846 9

Printed in China

Sowing times and planting information are for advice only. Follow the directions given on seed packets and check with your supplier where necessary.

For Nelly, who makes me happy every day

Acknowledgements

Firstly, a huge 'thank you' to Alison Cathie and everybody at Quadrille, for endless enthusiasm from the first moment of seeing the idea, through to publication and beyond. In particular to Jane O'Shea for her vision and passion, to Simon Davis for patient, generous and fine humoured editing, to Helen Lewis and Nikki Davidson for their wonderful, imaginative eye with the design, and to Aysun Hughes and Vincent Smith for their production wizardry. Thank you all for turning some words and some pictures into this beautiful book. It has been a lot of fun.

Without Debora Robertson's brilliant talent and generous imagination this book would've been very different. It would also have been a whole lot less fun in the making. On the upside I wouldn't have had to listen quite so much to how her football team was doing better than mine. I do hope we get to do this again, but in a better season.

The recipe shoots were days you dream of: fabulous food cooked and styled by the lovely Jenny White which, once photographed by the supremely talented Laura Hynd, meant we got to eat far too well all through the day. Thank you both so much.

I've been enormously lucky to have Caroline Michel and Robert Caskie at PFD as agents – both of whom have been enormously enthusiastic and energetic about what I do and what I write. Thank you, it makes a huge difference. And thanks to Tim Binding at PFD for his vision early on in the process of getting this book to where it is.

To Martin Crawford of the Agroforestry Research Trust, a fantastic source of inspiration early on and still, as well as a good friend – thank you. And to Trent Peterson, who's just about the only person I can handle helping me to keep Otter Farm up together and to take it forwards. Your enthusiasm, humour and energy make the world of difference, even if your musical taste could do with a little work.

And to Candida, Nell and the rest of my family – for not minding too much that I'm usually busier than I ought to be, and that I'm often distracted by the idea of the next project. The odd handful of delicious food and all my love may not be a reasonable exchange, but it's yours.